Enrages Dreamie

(Here is another autobiographical chapter in the life of George Spelvin, American,' as recorded by Westbrook Pegler.)

By WESTBROOK PEGLER

LAST YEAR, self and one bought 10 shares in the famed Trans-Universe Biscuit Corp., then they split three for one. It was eight dollars when we bought it but after we got the new shares the price 2½. I am not so very good at figures, ur 30 shares are now worth [illegible] of $80 for the 10. That win 20 shares all right, bucks.

Well, last week we [illegible] they are holding a me[illegible] stockholders. So Dream[illegible] don't we go to this meet[illegible] how come 30 shares is fiv[illegible] than 10 shares [illegible] age of that [illegible]

lic's sen' ER

so much in the noble sport with we who have its avert our eyes now gives it the k behind an ear ous in the arena. Cuban field hand et at the hands of New York has dignation to un- as the editorials

mmon in pugilism, two men beaten to th, and the victor in ghts, Bud Taylor, of d., who died recently lso killed a second one to fall before ure though married ght under the name ot his real name, but St. Jerome's and [illegible] hurch.

ut enough to quali n in the 'twenties eights were a clou eigh 110 pounds or ss. The next class is f 124 pounds. Taylor a r hit Frankie a bombar ad as he stood in a ben [illegible] face and body

ent." n lets Tru[illegible] had the sa[illegible] blame for [illegible] cials of the the FBI rep[illegible] ll investigatio[illegible] was just one [illegible] h Chamb[illegible] mber's [illegible] tment, [illegible] Bureau [illegible]

Spelvin's a Sal[illegible]

He Mal[illegible] For Getting [illegible]

By WESTBROOK PEGLER

[illegible] because human

Me[illegible] 'H[illegible] Here is [illegible] e Spelv[illegible] CAN [illegible] helping [illegible] bode [illegible] hich [illegible] re mo[illegible] nd h[illegible] bu[illegible] tio[illegible]

Juror [illegible] Set[illegible] In[illegible] 'Ge[illegible]

They Never [illegible]

A Vulgar Word

By WESTBROOK PEGLER

[illegible] TO HOPE that the scholars who select [illegible] for the Pulitzer awards [illegible] will recover the [illegible] ards of this age [illegible] American ideal [illegible] composed by an [illegible] he pen-name of [illegible]

n wrote hundreds complete episodes. s true name and I [illegible] y lapse, for he had rong influence on the principles ny generation. He was second, naps, in this respect to Horatio r, another inspiring prig, al- h, more likely, if we could tote eir circulation, they closed careers in a dead heat. I read Hemingway, Jack [illegible] Tobacco Road, all [illegible]

ing a mocker t about a dyi[illegible] how sick I [illegible] n the teeve[illegible] o I put my elf so I w[illegible] en anoth[illegible] d I said i[illegible] me I he[illegible] nk bal[illegible] ar an[illegible] not d[illegible] good [illegible] es b[illegible] ancy you rewi[illegible] for [illegible] ned'

[illegible] Sees It:

Nixon Near[illegible] ed Hiss Case

WESTBROOK PEGLER

the publication of Richard Nix[illegible] ed "Six Crises," a mistake was [illegible] part of the Alger Hiss case wh[illegible] old Woodstock typewriter on wh[illegible] ents stolen from the State Depa[illegible] typed for subsequent delivery [illegible] Russian spies. Nixon blamed [illegible] memory, always a fallible authori[illegible] and there was so much other e[illegible] dence that this error in a hasti[illegible] written campaign book should n[illegible] upset the verdict of the jury [illegible] history.

There are other defects in Nixon story of the Hiss case, however, tha[illegible] re simply impermissible.

Actually, Nixon almost torpedoe[illegible] he case early in the game and it wa[illegible] ot his ingenuity that rescued the -called pumpkin papers from the Truman's Department of Justice, of Robert Stripling, the chief in- ouse Un-American Activities Com- no right to take the "papers" from York for scrutiny by a New York , and he almost lost them to the stice, which undoubtedly would whole affair to vindicate Tru- flippancy. This probably would committee.

ommittee

wholeheartedly with the commit- a freshman member of Congress es "no one was more aware than e's past record had been vulner-

ith Bert Andrews, the New York shington man who was secretly ittee according to his paper's ews proposed that Nixon offer a ss case be lifted out of the com- nd handed over to a Commis- e had absolutely no legal juris- dly would have smothered the One of those whom Andrews mission was Judge Learned of Appeals, a philosophical ankfurter, Oliver Wendell of a self-qualified cult of their pompous souls on

so far that Andrews had the committee's execu- er Chambers in the nd kept popping into

As Pegler Sees [illegible]

Brutali[illegible] In Estes[illegible]

By WESTBR[illegible]

The shocking brutality culture in railroadi[illegible] abiding employe, has be[illegible] ance of Orville Freeman, rious maze.

Miss Jones was phys[illegible] low emp[illegible] in the [illegible] without [illegible] man's c[illegible] herself [illegible] and hit [illegible] If sh[illegible] blown h[illegible] been ju[illegible] defense, [illegible] not armed.

This snatch occurred in Freeman's own official premises and he was aware of the incident within an hour. But when Congressman Robert Dole, of Kansas, dared to suggest that Freeman take appropriate action, this Minneapolis politician refused to comment

PEGLER

en we a[illegible] ion, that may [illegible] came home after that first ni[illegible] how did it go? I said awful, that clown is guilty as h—ck, and [illegible] fe is a fat old tomato— [illegible] aid but you must not slug the poor fel- [illegible] is fat, some people are glandular [illegible] to be so stupid, if their head [illegible] duty.

Fair Enough

ALSO BY FINIS FARR

FRANK LLOYD WRIGHT: A BIOGRAPHY
BLACK CHAMPION: THE LIFE AND TIMES OF
JACK JOHNSON
MARGARET MITCHELL OF ATLANTA
THE ELEPHANT VALLEY
FDR
CHICAGO: A PERSONAL HISTORY
OF AMERICA'S MOST AMERICAN CITY
O'HARA

Fair Enough

THE LIFE OF WESTBROOK PEGLER

Finis Farr

ARLINGTON HOUSE·PUBLISHERS
NEW ROCHELLE, N. Y.

Manufactured in the United States of America

Library of Congress Cataloging in Publication Data

Farr, Finis.
Fair enough.

Includes bibliographical references.
1. Pegler, Westbrook, 1894-1969. I. Title.
PN4874.P43F3 070.4'092'4 [B] 74-32276
ISBN 0-87000-234-1

CONTENTS

Fair Enough

ACKNOWLEDGMENTS & SOURCES

THIS BOOK IS FOUNDED ON PEGLER'S PUBLISHED WRITINGS AND on his collected papers in the Herbert Hoover Presidential Library at West Branch, Iowa. For kind advice and help I want to thank the director of the library, Mr. Thomas T. Thalken, the assistant director, Mr. Robert S. Wood, and Mr. Dale C. Mayer, archivist of the Pegler material. The letters and documents of this collection, which includes unpublished manuscripts, reveal Westbrook Pegler to the inquirer as completely, I believe, as any figure of modern times has ever been identified by what he left behind. The columns run to millions of words, and Pegler was a voluminous letter writer. During life he was the subject of much casual journalism, all of it ephemeral and in the closing years repeating the stereotype of public scold who hated everybody. I hope this biography shows that to say the least, there was more to it than that. But I recommend an earlier biography, *Westbrook Pegler: Angry Man of the Press*, by Oliver Pilat. The author was a working newspaperman and I found him especially interesting on Heywood Broun and the founding of the American Newspaper Guild. Mr. Pilat strikes a different sum from that which I have offered, but he wrote a good book and, like Murray Kempton, showed the fundamental sympathy between Pegler and all good journalists which endured to the end.

Acknowledgments and Sources

Pegler's career followed the fortunes of American newspapers in general. The coming disasters were evident as early as 1941 in John R. Mott's classic *American Journalism: A History of Newspapers in the United States through 250 Years.* But it was not until the late 1950s that the great afternoon papers, and many of the morning papers, began to go down. For the days of the 1930s and for the 1940s when only accounting departments saw the cracks in the wall, I refreshed my memory in the microfiles of the New York papers, especially the *World-Telegram* and the *Journal-American,* at the newspaper branch of the New York Public Library. I also found help, in the matter of World War One which was Pegler's first field of controversy, in *Mr. Wilson's War,* by John Dos Passos, and *The American Army in France,* by General James G. Harbord. I want to thank Mr. Donald Estes of Tucson for information on that city, and for estimates of the Pegler personality I am endebted to Joseph Bryan 3rd, Noel F. Busch, and Paul Gallico. But no conclusion in this book should be charged to these amiable gentlemen, and any errors of fact or implication or inference belong to me alone. And once again I must thank Neil McCaffrey and his senior editor David Franke, of Arlington House. In patience and generosity these publishers are models for the trade.

F. F.

1

THE QUEST FOR PEGLER

THERE I WAS IN WEST BRANCH, IOWA, AT THE CENTER OF Middle America, on a rainy morning in May 1973. My purpose was to examine the letters and papers of Westbrook Pegler, a journalist, which were on deposit at the library and museum that memorialized Herbert Hoover, a politician, amid cornfields and rolling hills in a countryside of singular beauty and charm. I don't know how to describe the soft morning air and the impression of gray-green mist over the rise and fall of the terrain as my taxicab carried me out to West Branch from Iowa City. I am able to give some idea of the damnable motel, the Holiday Inn, at which I had registered late the previous day, after flying from New York City to Chicago, where I changed airplanes for the last leg of the journey down to Cedar Rapids. It is not my intent to sound like the sad old man in Ring Lardner's "Golden Honeymoon" who particularized every stop on his trip to Florida. My complaint and protest about that motel is a general plea on behalf of civilization against commercial bureaucracy gone mad, a protest such as Pegler himself had voiced on many an occasion in the sixty years of indignant writing that had ended when he died in 1969. Think of me, if you will, as arriving at this Holiday Inn after the flight from Chicago in a limping old airplane, every seat in the tourist section taken, and mostly by people who were smoking cigarettes and talking in voices that tore at my nerves like dull saws—except for those who were not fractious children, whom I pitied, for they could not know that their discomfort would soon end. My physical discomfort ended when I got out in Cedar Rapids, and found a car and driver willing to take me fifteen miles to the Inn, where I had confirmed a reservation, and the management had fourteen dollars which my travel agent had sent them as advance payment on what I planned to make a long stay. So in I went, dropping in front of the desk my heavily loaded carryall from L. L. Bean & Co., of Freeport, Maine, sign to any discerning eye that here was a customer who knew how to travel in a tidy way. Now get this. When I signed the register, the girl on duty said I'd have to identify myself. But I have a reservation and it's paid for. Makes no difference, you gotta be identified. Who says so? The local authorities. I am quite capable of saying local authorities be damned; what is this, Russia? But this was a decent, nice girl, and I knew the real villains were elsewhere. I said how about comparing my signature on your register with the signatures on these traveler's checks, of which I have two thousand dollars' worth. No, that won't do, could you just, sir, give us your car registration. Now it came out, I don't own a car, and I didn't add, have no use for one, knowing that this was heresy of the worst sort, if not blasphemy. Now wouldn't you *think*, friends and readers, that a girl with any sense at all—probably a student from the university, working part time—would have been able to *look* at me, and conclude, here stands a respectable elderly person, sober, paid-up reservation, got two grand in travchex on him, *this* one doesn't need identification. But no.

It flashed through my mind that Ambassador David K. E. Bruce, a man of about my age, had recently received the bum's rush when he tried to rent a car at Kennedy Airport, because he had no credit card and tried to pay cash, from a large supply in his pocket. Girl suspicious of man without credit card. And if *I* look like a reputable person, David Bruce is, on sight, not merely a *pukka sahib*, but a *burra sahib* or Number One Boss. As I thought of Mr. Bruce, it occurred to me that I had a credit card in my pocket, and it carried my photograph on its back. I took it out. See, this is I. And I might have added, like the old woman in the nursery rhyme, *If this be I, and I think it be, I've a little dog at home and he'll know me*. Except that I dislike dogs and wouldn't have one around the place. Cats are all right, but keep your dogs away from me, if you please. . . . At any rate, my photograph on the card satisfied the check-in girl and she gave me my key. I went to my room—of course it was noisy and faced the highway—thinking that I had chickened out and should have raised hell rather than show what amounted to a passport within the borders of my own country. But a man is tired after traveling all day and if you make a career of resisting every outrage in contemporary life, you have no energy left for the work you are supposed to be doing. And the Bible says he that is slow to anger is greater than he that taketh a city. And so the next morning I shook the Holiday Inn, never to return, and rode in a taxicab to the Presidential Motor Inn, a place of refuge that ought to have at least three stars in its crown, in the outskirts of West Branch, only half a mile from the Hoover Library. The desk man was the owner, and when I showed up he didn't propose any identification nonsense, being a sharp-eyed, experienced citizen who instantly sized me up as a live one, and liked the look of those First National City checks, of which I immediately signed two just to show how happy I was at having come to anchor at his inn. The well-planned building lay on the shoulder of a hill four hundred yards back from Interstate Eighty on a secondary road that cut across cornfields toward the south and in the other direction led down into the village and terrain that I instantly recognized from Grant Wood's painting called "Birthplace of Herbert Hoover."

I walked across the viaduct over the Interstate and its chain of snarling Diesels down into a beautifully landscaped park on the valley floor. Along the hillside, a magnificent growth of oak, sycamore, and cottonwood subdued the highway noise to the level of distant surf, in a startling effect a thousand miles from either ocean. The Birthplace was a tiny cottage, almost a doll's house it seemed, and the museum and library, close at hand, had been built on a reasonable, human scale which compared most agreeably with the swollen monstrosities dedicated to J. F. Kennedy and L. B. Johnson. I had long harbored certain reservations about Herbert Hoover, yet had referred to him, in my biography of Franklin Roosevelt, as a man of integrity and in spite of his shortcomings one of our most high-minded presidents. I walked through the museum before presenting myself at the library entrance, and admired Mrs. Hoover's collection of blue and white china, displayed against fine rugs and handsome furniture. The other interesting things in the expertly mounted exhibits were also under inspection by crowds of school children, who had emerged from a succession of yellow buses at the main entrance, and marched into the museum in what struck me as a remarkably orderly way. There was no screaming, no pushing, no running, no dropping of candy wrappers. It was obvious that the children had been prepared by lectures about the importance of their visit; all the same there was an eerie quality in their behavior, at least to anyone from New York City, where the police advise frail and elderly persons to stay indoors during the times that school lets out. But here they were filing two by two through the Birthplace, Quaker Meeting House, and museum in a reverent, solemn manner like that of pilgrims viewing the relics of a saint. All around stood the uniformed museum guards, men in later middle life, of a stern but not unfriendly aspect. On their belts they wore those big guns, such a familiar feature of the current scene that one is hardly aware of them. For all of that, the atmosphere was idyllic, and the people at the library couldn't have been kinder or more efficient in showing me what I had come to see. Their names are in a paragraph of grateful acknowledgment at the front of this book. When they gave me a desk in the research section, not a page of this book had been written, and I surveyed the thirty-six large cartons of Pegler papers with keen anticipation. In writing biographies, the research is quite an agreeable way to spend time: you never know when you may turn over a nugget of gold. I had come here for the final documentation of Pegler's life. I had started my search in Tucson, where Pegler had died at the age of seventy-six on the desert that he loved. I had also made inquiries at some offices in New York, and I made a surprising discovery: Pegler's newspaper writings in the 1930s and 1940s had influenced me more than I realized. I had to admit that he was one of the contemporary writers, along with Faulkner, Dos Passos, O'Hara, Fitzgerald, Farrell, Orwell, and Mencken, who had entered my bloodstream for better or worse in my reading life, and had more to do with the man I now was than any but those few men and women who had come close to me in my actual life. It was a startling thing to admit, and in the case of Pegler's influence, a not altogether welcome truth to face. Pegler had grave charges against him—he had gone far in exaggeration, invective, and malice. I was inclined to forgive him much because he was a good writer, even on the final pages when death was near and he wrote statements of breath-taking ferocity about the Kennedy family, outdoing in their terrible intensity even his inveterate attacks on his favorite targets of earlier years, the Roosevelts.

And so I went to work, walking down the hill in the morning and back again in the evening, with the serene happiness of one who has something definite to do, and time and space in which to do it. It soon became clear that I hadn't known as much about Pegler as I had thought, a healthy realization for any biographer; and many wonderful phrases came alive in memory as I renewed my acquaintance with Pegler's early writing. I saw that more than any of those authors who had influenced me, Pegler had given me the gift of irreverence. He had planted in my mind an immovable belief about the big men of government, industry, the religions, and the military services—a conviction that when they got out of bed, they pulled on their pants one leg at a time. This idea was all the more impressive to me in the light of the president-worship that had grown in the United States since the time of Theodore Roosevelt, who believed in a strong chief executive but did not demand obsequious deference or surround himself with toadies. Although he emitted a great deal of hot air, and had muzzle velocity but little else, T. R. felt that he amounted to something as a person in his own right, and not as the holder of an office so grand and mighty that he had to be protected from ordinary people by a palace guard. But nowadays the feeling of reverence for "this great office" had grown dreadfully powerful in Mid-America, along with a lay religion of solemn patriotism that called forth more public ritual than the various sects of Christianity. Ladies and gentlemen our Nashna Lanthem . . . Ipleadgeallegiancetomyflag . . .

The lay religion had shown its power in Iowa when Nixon drew more votes for reelection than his opponent, who had made it obvious that he would start letting air out of the inflated presidency the minute he got in. Now the people of Iowa were in a state of shock, for Nixon had let them down by the blatancy of his uneasy, devious reaction to the Watergate revelations. Only two days before my arrival in West Branch, Nixon had made his first defense on television, in the speech known as Checkers II, or "The Return of Checkers." He had come over on the screen as a sanctimonious liar, half Chadband and half Uriah Heep, and the Iowa newspapers, led by the *Des Moines Register,* had reported that his performance wasn't good enough, and spoke of impeachment as not beyond the bounds of possibility. How Pegler would have relished it! He had never been comfortable with Nixon, sensing his personal nastiness and lack of class. And Pegler loved to see any large section of the public disenchanted, and made aware that some pretentious quack had come to the moment of exposure. Now in the face of this astounding exposure of evil, the people of the smiling Iowa countryside were discouraged and depressed. Soon to come were even more disturbing spectacles—Nixon dancing a jig with the Russian dictator, a thug if ever I saw one; Nixon's people selling our unreplaceable grain to Russians and lending them our money to pay for it, which brought profits for speculators who were in on the deal, and empty pockets and bellies for the rest of us. Great. And there was to be more, the second Nixonian TV Watergate defense, "Son of Checkers," in which the President gave the impression of a cheap crook trying to lie his way out of a jam. And even more fantastic revelations were to come. But so far as my friends in Iowa were concerned, the damage had been done, the hurt inflicted, by a man they had thought to be one of their own. They had suffered betrayal by Nixon the Commie-fighter, the patriot whose eyes dimmed with tears when he saw Old Glory going by. Mid-America believed it had recognized in Nixon a down-home sort of man, the ordinary kind you trusted and respected—the undertaker at an important funeral, the high-school principal venturing a joke at the football rally, the Prudential Man whose only object, as the national advertising stated, was to serve his neighbors and friends. They had venerated and even loved the memory of Herbert Hoover—and now nobody would ever be able to do that for Richard Nixon. I was tempted to laugh, for I had been on to Nixon since the first Checkers speech and the time I discovered that he would have been an FBI agent if they hadn't turned down his application when he came out of law school, a Southern California townie looking for a job. But for the good people in Mid-America, who had another conception of the man, both his rise and his ruin were occasions of tragedy. It was sobering to live among people for whom an important part of life had come loose from its moorings and disappeared, like a barn ripped from a low-lying field by a Mississippi flood. The more I thought of it, the less funny it became. For I realized that something had happened to me, too: the last traces of my pride in being an American had vanished.

It was appropriate that Pegler's papers should be deposited in the Hoover Library, for these two men resembled each other in important ways. Their common stock of ideas had been formed in the last half of the nineteenth century. Each had been born in poverty, and had worked his way to secure financial position—comfortable affluence for Pegler, and a large fortune, derived from foreign mining operations, in Hoover's case. They believed the old beliefs, and bowed before the old ideals of individual responsibilities and liberties. Much that they believed was not so, and to a considerable extent the classic America they cherished had existed only in myth. However, it was a well-intended myth and perhaps acceptable as a plan for the future, if not a system of historical fact. At any rate, Hoover and Pegler were authentic Model T Americans. And in their later years, they had begun to resemble each other physically. Their tall figures became stocky, they resorted to double-breasted jackets above which their heavy, fleshy heads sat on thick necks and sturdy shoulders. I came across a photograph of Pegler arriving in Tucson near the end of his life, which showed so marked a resemblance that he looked like Hoover's double. The noticing of such things requires the biographer to decide if his discovery is significant; and he must find in himself sufficient moral fortitude to resist temptation to make it seem important, if it is not. Without the making of these decisions, and the emotional fatigue that comes from resisting continual temptation to indulge in emotional fakery, writing biographies would be the easiest thing in the world. Lives divide into dramatic passages with scenes of conflict like those that make a play. And the reader is always aware of the inevitable ending, even though the subject is not, if we think of the subject as a living character whom we can observe from a position outside his or her life, while at the same time entering into that life through the reader's imagination and author's industry in digging up the past. After the last scene, the subject is dead, with an elegiac paragraph or two as literary memorial. But the reader is still alive, which explains the fascination of biographies. The subject is gone, and soon enough the author may go: but you can't read someone's life unless you are still in possession of your own, and the act of reading gives temporary relief from fear of your own extinction.

Thoughts of this sort engaged me on the long Sundays at West Branch when the library was closed and I worked over my notes in my room at the Presidential Motor Inn. When not working, I would read the Sunday editions of the Des Moines, Davenport, and Iowa City newspapers, or look at television on the big color set which was bolted to the wall, for some reason, five feet above the floor. There had been much bad weather, and one Sunday of rain and hail I turned on a Pentecostal revival show with a preacher so horrible, I tell you he made Billy Graham look like John Henry Newman. I was held in fascination by this revolting Jesus-creep when suddenly they went to black on the screen and flashed a process shot: CYCLONE WARNING. I was alarmed, and said to myself, that's all I need, getting blown over Kansas like Judy Garland in *The Wizard of Oz.* The thing had been coming our way but in a few minutes they put up word that it was passing north of us and heading east. My thought was, if that twister crosses the Mississippi River, somebody will have to deal with a column of mud 2,000 feet high. And as everything did in those days of watching for ideas, the tornado connected in my mind with Westbrook Pegler. Like Hoover, I thought, he had been born in a midland state, in the belly of the U.S.A., and as it had with Mark Twain, the Mississippi River flowed past the place where he was born.

2

MINNESOTA ENGLISHMAN

PEGLER'S PARENTS HAD BEEN BORN OUTSIDE THE UNITED STATES, and from this he derived an intense narrow patriotism, typical of many first-generation Americans, especially those who did well in material ways. But Pegler's father, an Englishman coming to America in search of work, always maintained a London flavor in his personality. According to Pegler, his father never lost the trace of Cockney on his tongue. Pegler had a superb ear for speech, as his writing showed, but sometimes his definitions of what he heard were imprecise, as he showed by applying the label of "geechee" to Franklin Roosevelt's manner of talking. In fact the Southern Negro dialect called Geechee omits most consonants, whereas FDR talked like a cultivated Easterner and took pains to hit every consonant on the nose. The journalist Jack Alexander gave an accurate description of Arthur Pegler's spoken English when he called it the "speech of a suffragan bishop." Alexander recorded that Arthur also had a face that would have gone correctly with clerical costume, which added an unusual touch to his lifelong occupation of sensational newspaper writer in Minneapolis, St. Paul, Chicago, and New York.

The mother had been born in Canada of Irish parents, identified by Pegler as "potato-famine people." Arthur James Pegler met Frances

Nicholson in St. Paul when she was working as a department store cash girl—a messenger who carried money to a central till and hurried back with the change. Arthur Pegler was a reporter on the *St. Paul Pioneer Press,* not long out of London, and he had come to the store in search of a Christmas feature. He expected to find material about the man dressed as Santa Claus, the starry-eyed children, the tired shoppers, and so on. This was all there in abundance, but what took the young reporter's eye was a fragile-looking girl in the uniform white-cuffed black dress and little white apron, who was constantly on the run between the front counters and the cashier's post at the back of the main floor. Westbrook's reminiscences had it that at this time his mother was "blue-eyed and serious and her small nose was of a cast which writers of that day described as retroussé, meaning slightly upturned. . . ." The delicate little Miss Frances Nicholson captivated Arthur Pegler and they were married within a year. In mature life Westbrook called up memories that told him his parents' marriage had been far from ideal. He wrote that his mother was a devout Roman Catholic, whereas his father had been "English to his marrow and a bigot with enormous grudges against the Catholics, especially the Irish kind. God only knows why she fell for this Englishman, but they were married, and long after he had forsaken her in her old age, although she was not abandoned in the legal sense, he was buried from the altar of the Cathedral in Tucson."

In those days a young newspaper reporter could have cut a romantic figure before any girl, but middle-class parents would discourage such a man from presenting himself as a suitor. It was widely held that reporters were hard drinkers, and there was some truth in this general belief. Even more to the point was the low economic status of the daily newsman. In the Twin Cities of Minneapolis and St. Paul, experienced journalists drew salaries as low as twenty-five dollars a week, with fifty the upper limit for those who had achieved the rank of star. One must bear in mind that the dollar of the 1890s had at least eight times the purchasing power of the anemic thing that passes as a dollar at this time of writing in the early 1970s. Newspapermen in the big cities also had material perquisites, such as free tickets to theaters, circuses, and sporting events, and discounts at restaurants and stores. And there were opportunities for seasoned reporters to earn fees on the side from the infant science of press agentry, or public relations. The ethical dubiety of this practice, with or without the publisher's complaisance, added a certain shabbiness to the trade of city-desk reporter, which was redeemed to some extent by the picturesque aspect of the business as presented, for example, in "Gallagher," the famous newspaper story by Richard Harding Davis.

In the 1880s a tribe of Englishmen had fanned out across the United States, some in search of adventure, and others motivated by the pure spirit of greed. It had been widely reported in England that gold nuggets could be picked from the ground in the Wild West, a region located according to some authorities not far from Hoboken, New Jersey. Some of the English immigrants had left home one jump ahead of the police because of writing checks on nonexistent accounts, or cracking the safes of provincial banks. Late Victorian British jails were such dreadful places that any crook who could make it would gladly take his chances with wild Indians on the American desert rather than face entombment in such correctional institutions as Dartmoor Prison, which had been built in 1806. There also were detachments of drunkards and homosexuals who had left because of scandal, sometimes collecting regular financial allowances that gave them the name of remittance men. Also to be seen among the English immigrants were men whose inherited British feeling for horses and cattle led them to develop holdings in the American ranchlands, where their management equalled that of the natives in prudence and skill. One of these English ranchers took part in the range wars of 1881, and employed the professional assassin known as Billy the Kid, who became a legend after a lawman shot him down.

Another class of human importations from Great Britain consisted of the grooms, valets, and butlers who came over to help rich American families establish an elegant manner of life as a setting for the new wealth generated by the Civil War. In this war the commercial men of the North had been noticeably absent from the field of battle, and their plundering of the victorious government provided foundations for the fortunes of the Gilded Age. Many of the grooms and horse trainers imported by these plutocrats were insolent rascals who sensed their employers' insecurities and imposed on them in every possible way, taking commissions from feed merchants, substituting inferior horses for first-rate animals, stealing valuable dogs, and trading information about the families in which they worked, for purposes of theft and blackmail. The butlers and housekeepers were a less dangerous breed, though they sometimes brought faked recommendations, and invariably took commission on household supplies. The popular author Harry Leon Wilson later portrayed an honest English butler of this period, imported to the Wild West, in *Ruggles of Red Gap*. The movie version of this widely read story climaxed in a scene of revolting sentimentality in which the gelatinous actor Charles Lawton recited the Gettysburg Address. Ruggles has become an American! Fancy that. Arthur James Pegler, by contrast, kept the British flavor of his personality throughout a long life, most probably using it as a shield against the harshness of circumstance that abraded his spirit through years of big-city journalism, without the extra talent or the penetrating shrewdness to make it pay him more than a moderate wage. It would remain for his son to attack the publishers with such powerful talent that Westbrook remained for years the dominant public figure, in turn, at the two leading national newspaper chains and their feature syndicates. Westbrook went against the men in the counting-rooms with the force of money in the cash registers, and he made the managers crawl and beg. But in the end they defeated him. They always do.

The British system of social ratings had placed Arthur James Pegler in the middle of the middle class on his birth in 1862. Arthur's father was inspector of schools for the Bethnal Green division under the London Board of Education, and the boy had an uncle who had risen to the rank of detective inspector at Scotland Yard. Young Arthur received a good basic education, and according to family plans, was to have been apprenticed to a wine merchant in the city. The trade was respectable and could be lucrative as well. Arthur could have looked forward to maturity as a dignified, black-coated partner in the firm, taking sherry with favored clients in the back room, and passing expert judgment on Tokay and Madeira. One examines these details to show that Arthur Pegler's departure for the States was in no way discreditable to him. The situation was that this young shop assistant belonged in the tradition of British adventurers. He saw his destiny in 1882, while reading *The Field,* then as now a fascinating magazine of country life, when an advertisement caught his attention and set up in his mind a panorama of the American West. The advertisement described a sort of British agricultural college in Le Mars, Iowa, where a colony of English people were developing farmland under the direction of Captain the Honorable Ronald Moreton. This was what Arthur Pegler had been looking for, and a few weeks later he stepped from a crowded immigrant train at Le Mars and inquired the way to Captain Moreton's headquarters. Arthur was wearing a suit of the latest London cut, and patent leather shoes. A bowler hat was on his head, and he swung a heavy leather kit bag into the farm wagon to which he was directed. It turned out that Arthur's agricultural studies were limited entirely to practical exercises, so much so that he soon caught on to the fact that he was nothing more than a poorly paid farm laborer. He packed his bag and moved on.

For the next five years, Arthur worked at various places in Iowa and Nebraska, at last finding employment as handyman to a farmer near Sioux City, Iowa. This man was an exceedingly unsatisfactory employer, since he was always drunk. In reviewing this part of his father's career, Westbrook said the man "invariably arose with the farmer's hangover, which is a terrible thing because it begins at dawn." One morning Arthur decided the old drunk had become intolerably abusive. He put on his bowler, and carried the kit bag into Sioux City, which was then a bustling market town of 21,000 population. Down to his last cent on a rainy afternoon, and wearing his last good suit, with carefully patched trousers, Arthur persuaded the editor of the *Sioux City Times* to take him on as a cub reporter. From the start, the work suited Arthur Pegler a great deal more than farming.

The line of employment for provincial newsmen has always been from smaller to larger towns, and so it was with Arthur Pegler. After learning the rudiments of his trade in Sioux City, he moved on to the Twin Cities of St. Paul and Minneapolis. Together they comprised a metropolitan area of half a million people, and supported twelve newspapers. With that number of papers coming out every day, it was comparatively easy for a competent reporter to land a job, while at the same time he would find it impossible to get a decent salary. Arthur Pegler broke in on the *St. Paul Globe*, a paper which shared leading rank with the *Dispatch* and the *Pioneer Press*. Years later he told his son he did not feel at home on the *Globe*, and he went to the *St. Paul Daily News* when he heard of an opening there. The job was that of district man in West St. Paul, which meant that Arthur spent his time sending in routine police news and seldom appeared in the editorial offices. He acquired a reputation as a bright, dependable man, and the city editor of the *Globe* called him in for a talk. As a result Arthur came back, starting at twenty-five a week, and stayed for three years as feature man, sports editor, music critic, and general writer of anything from an editorial to an obituary.

There was plenty to write about, for in those days St. Paul was an open town, through the courtesy of Police Chief John Clark and his chief of detectives, Johnny O'Connor. These officers tolerated the presence of confidence men, porchclimbers, pickpockets, and safe-blowers, whom they did not molest, on condition that the crooks would practice their various trades in other cities and use St. Paul as a peaceful refuge, to the benefit of all concerned. Any crook who broke this rule would be savagely beaten by O'Connor's men and hustled out of town. Criminals and thugs of a lower class were not covered by this agreement, and they contributed to statistics listing crimes of violence, including murder. Before the term "investigative reporter" came into use, Arthur Pegler dug up evidence that sent two thugs to the gallows for killing an associate. After the double execution, word was out that Arthur might be in danger of reprisal from the lowest level of the underworld. The *Globe* editors took these rumors seriously enough to place Arthur under the protection of a dreaded police officer, Two-Gun Tom Horan of the strongarm squad. Horan let it be known that he would put a bullet in the head of any man who threatened Arthur Pegler. This caused the toughs and footpads of St. Paul to avoid all contact with Arthur, and turn up alleys at the approach of Two-Gun Tom.

In any adversary situation short of a gun battle, Arthur Pegler was capable of defending himself without a bodyguard. This he demonstrated early in his career when he went into a St. Paul restaurant and drew the attention of four rival reporters seated at another table. One of these men began to make insulting remarks, intentionally loud enough for Pegler to hear. Arthur got up, walked over to the newsmen's table, and asked if anyone there had been talking about him. The wiseguy was still in his chair when Arthur hit him a solid punch in the mouth, which took the fight out of him. Nobody at the table cared to take matters further, and Arthur returned to his seat with dignity. After that, whenever he heard remarks about English clothes or accent, they were made in a friendly tone.

Arthur Pegler was such a competent and self-confident young man that he must have seemed to be something on the order of a storybook hero to Frances Nicholson at her cash counter. Her brothers were strong men too, but they lacked education. Westbrook's notes on his childhood identify these five uncles: "Jim disappeared in the Klondike; Tom was a copper miner in Bisbee, Pete an artistic draftsman who became a signprinter here and there and wound up with a saloon in Los Angeles just in time to perish by Prohibition. Jack built whalebacks [freight steamships] in Buffalo, and Joe was a wrangler in the St. Paul yards until he went out to Shelby, Montana, where he was grass-hoppered to death in the 1920s." Though none too lucky in life, these Nicholsons were a self-respecting clan, and there can be no doubt that while they were conscious of Arthur's superior standing as a newspaper man, they believed their Frances fully good enough to be his bride. The marriage took place in 1889.

Francis Westbrook Pegler, the subject of this biography, was born to these parents on August 2, 1894. He later acquired the name of James in place of Francis, bequeathing the feminine form of that first name to a sister who was born in 1897. James Westbrook turned into Westbrook J. Pegler, and the initial disappeared in the middle 1920s, when Pegler realized that a friend was right in pointing out that Westbrook was like "the name on a Pullman car" and deserved to stand alone in its glory. Westbrook's lifelong nickname among old friends was Bud, traditional younger sibling's nickname, acquired in relationship to his brother Jack, who was two years older.

By the time Westbrook was able to notice his surroundings, his father had become sports editor of the *Minneapolis Journal*, and the family was established in an unpretentious house at 33rd Street and Pleasant Avenue. He remembered some things about this place all his life, and recalled them in old age, writing in his notes how "Mr. Erickson the milkman carefully poured the milk into shiny pans about two inches deep. After the pans had set a while my mother would skim the cream and slide it into a small pitcher. In winter, Mr. Erickson cruised along in a box on runners." Westbrook also recalled from the days in this house the wonder of a magic lantern, projecting colored pictures on the wall, and the smell of its "little alcohol lamp." The most prized possession of his early childhood was a big multicolored ball, which he took care to keep with him when the family moved in 1899 to an apartment on Eighth Avenue in Minneapolis. These were the most attractive quarters the Peglers had occupied up to that time. They had barely settled down when a case of diphtheria was reported in a neighbor's flat, and the building went under quarantine. At this point, Westbrook complained of feeling bad, and then, as his father put it, "fell over as though he'd been shot." As a newsman, Arthur had one of the few telephones in town, and he used it to call a doctor. Arthur reported that the boy's breathing could be heard throughout the apartment, and the doctor said he'd come at once and bring a nurse. After taking one look at the patient, as Arthur recalled the scene, Dr. Weston said, "Your boy's got an hour to live unless we can relieve him. Antitoxin. Shall we shoot? May kill him anyway." "What d'ye mean kill him. The kid only just got sick." Dr. Weston replied, "This thing is sudden death. Knocks 'em off like flies." Arthur Pegler said, "Do what you can." Nurse Cora Heberd of the City Health Department prepared a large hypodermic and handed it to the doctor. They "poked the syringe under his thin shoulder blades and for the next fifteen minutes watched the boy fight for life." Then the doctor cried, "By

God, it worked! He's coming back!" The first thing Westbrook asked for was his many-colored ball.

Not long after Westbrook's recovery the family moved to a house in the suburban community of Excelsior, twelve miles from Minneapolis on the shores of Lake Minnetonka. Westbrook recalled it as a "clapboard town" whose population came to seven hundred people after the summer visitors departed each September. Here the boy passed his happiest childhood hours. He recorded the existence of a tree house in a stout oak, from which he and his brother inspected the neighborhood activities. In winter months the boys sometimes went out on the frozen lake to fish through holes in the ice, enjoying the shelter of fishing shacks that were heated by coal oil stoves. Near the Peglers' back fence stood the town jail, an object of interest to Bud and Jack. Pegler noted that the jail "had two cells, one for each gender, but I do not remember that any woman was ever locked up. But there was no running water, and I often climbed a little board to which I had nailed a few cleats and succored thirsty, hung-over prisoners with a small bottle of water tied by the neck. I used to have instinctive pity for hungovers. Most times I would have to go back to our kitchen to refill the bottle. If we had the hulk of a roast my mother would make a sandwich and I would pass it through the bars. She was very compassionate."

In 1902, when Westbrook was eight years old, his father gave him a Hopkins & Allen lever action single-shot .22 rifle, with which he hunted muskrat and other small game in the Minnetonka marshes. The rifle also came in handy on a job that eight-year-old Westbrook took on for the contractor building the interurban railroad from Minneapolis to Excelsior. At a salary of ten cents a day, the boy carried water for the tracklayers, and accepted additional duty, rifle at the ready, as rat exterminator in the cook shack. One lifetime recollection of keen pleasure remained: "I also helped the cook paint the frosting on the coffee cake which measured three feet by two. This frosting was largely sugar but it also contained chopped peanuts. We used a paper hanger's brush and slapped it on thick. It was delicious."

Westbrook's coaches in marksmanship were the neighboring Duffy brothers, whose cellar was "festooned with shingles with hides stretched over them and curing in the winter months." Their father was a section foreman on the Minneapolis & St. Louis Railway and Pegler remembered him as "the first man I ever saw who had a prerogative of rank. When they were going out or coming in after work, the other members of the crew pumped the hand-car but he just stood there, and hit that handle a slap as it started its down-beat."

The Pegler brothers planned to go into the trapping, curing, and marketing of muskrat skins on a commercial basis, but nothing came of it, for the hides were few and their mother refused to allow drying operations in the cellar. What spending money Westbrook had came from a paper route, which included a restaurant called the Excelsior Casino, where the boy saw his first Negro. This man was a cook who worked in white apron and cap at an open grill. He would prepare and serve on order a hot Western Sandwich—a delicately cooked omelette with diced ham and green peppers on toast. In maturity Pegler recalled this sandwich: "Price, ten cents, and worth it." Westbrook found that it was not easy to distribute the *Journal, Tribune,* and *Times* to a clientele of summer people plus enough year-round subscribers to keep him ploughing through snowdrifts in the winter months with a bag of papers on his back. He was bright in school, and his teacher Miss Ella Stratton told an interviewer when she had become an old lady that she had no trouble in calling "Westbrook" to mind. The teacher said, "He was a very active little boy, very active. He was good at elocution, and could rattle off the poems of James Whitcomb Riley by the yard."

It is possible that the .22 rifle originated as part of what Westbrook later called the "journalistic semi-graft" connected with Arthur Pegler's position of sporting editor. The *Journal* sport section carried a large amount of outdoor copy about hunting, fishing, and camping, only a column or two a day of football and baseball, and almost nothing on professional boxing, which was illegal in most parts of the United States. From the time he was able to make an estimate of what his father's work involved, and the position it gave him in the world, Pegler said he was "fascinated by the horrors of journalism." It appears that Westbrook was proud of his father, but felt there was something unsatisfactory and even shabby in the nature of Arthur's work and the way the family lived. Arthur was tired, and had to try too hard. He wrote in his unpublished memoirs that he took it as a privilege to have been a charter member of the American Newspaper Guild, which was founded in 1933 and obtained better pay and working conditions for men and women in the newsrooms, although it shared blame with the printers and owners for putting some good papers out of business, the list of victims including the *Brooklyn Eagle* and the *World-Telegram* and *Journal-American* in Manhattan. Westbrook also joined the Guild at its outset. He was then a star and in no need of union bargainers; he later quarreled with the Guild, as he did with so many institutions and people. It is reasonable to suppose that at the time he lent his prestige to the infant Guild, Westbrook had in mind the way his father had to struggle making ends meet in Minneapolis.

Through it all, in spite of his difficulties, Arthur was always well dressed. He achieved this by writing advertising copy for the Libby Brothers tailoring firm, taking his pay in excellent custom-made suits. But keeping up appearances and supporting a family of four almost killed Arthur Pegler. He finally made an arrangement, which would not be tolerated today, to supplement his *Minneapolis Journal* income with four hours of work every night on his original paper, the *Globe*, over in St. Paul. This meant that after a day's work Arthur climbed aboard the electric interurban car from Minneapolis at five o'clock, six afternoons a week, to go to his second job. On top of everything, Arthur took on the work of editing a weekly throwaway bulletin of sports and amusements, and one morning he tried to rise from bed and fell back unconscious. He had contracted pneumonia, and after they nursed him through this, it became evident that Arthur was emotionally and physically drained to the point where work was impossible. The doctors called his condition acute nervous breakdown. This incapacity continued for three months, during which Westbrook noticed that the family received no more free streetcar passes. Frances Pegler said they could get along without riding the cars, but what were they to do for food and shelter?

3

THE PROMISE OF CHICAGO

IN THE WINTER OF 1902, ARTHUR PEGLER TOLD HIS WIFE THEY WOULD have to face the fact that he could not get what they needed in the Twin Cities, and the only chance for family survival lay in the possibility of landing a newspaper job in Chicago. Word had come that William Randolph Hearst was determined to dominate that city with the evening *American* and his newly launched morning *Examiner,* which was to challenge the entrenched *Tribune,* a property of the powerful McCormick and Patterson families. Hearst was willing to pay experienced reporters $75 a week, and he would go to $100 for exceptionally able men. Hearst pay scales had the effect of increasing wages at all Chicago papers, so that even a moderate Chicago salary would come to more than the highest available in Minneapolis and St. Paul. Arthur went to Chicago without a letter of introduction, or any plan other than to apply for work in person. His assets were good clothes and a confident bearing, supported by natural abilities and years of experience. But there was no way of making certain in advance whether Arthur Pegler had enough to offer in the big city; for all he knew, he might be starting on the road toward house-to-house peddling, or night-clerking in cheap hotels, or tossing flapjacks in a lunchroom window, perhaps winding up with a hobo's bindle on his shoulder, undernourished and booze-sick, with death at the end in a freight yard under the wheels of a boxcar. This was the way many a respectable family man had to go in those days between the panic of 1893 and the next one, which was then building up under the economic horizon to move out like a cyclone and cripple the country in 1907. Westbrook never forgot this time in his life when his father left them on an uncertain mission. He recalled that "Poverty is a cruel influence in the home and there had been noisy bitterness between my parents just before my father left. It was a dark and sad day when he lit out for Chicago, with my mother and the children left in that drafty house." The Minnesota winter was not kind to them; serious want came so terrifyingly close that Westbrook later remembered "with a vague pain in my diaphragm a sort of pang as my brother and I sawed up two kitchen chairs and a bamboo bookcase for the kitchen range as the chill closed in."

Away in Chicago, Arthur Pegler found that he had indeed come to "the livest newspaper town in America." In addition to the two Hearst papers and the *Tribune*, there were job possibilities at the *Herald, Chronicle, Times, Inter-Ocean, Journal, Post,* and *Daily News*. The *News* was beginning to shape up into the great paper it is today. But its owner, the pious, hymn-singing Victor Lawson, was much opposed to the Hearstian notion of paying good newshands well. It was said that the granting of a two dollar raise gave Lawson physical pain. Arthur Pegler did not approach this parsimonious man, but left his baggage in a rented room on the North Side and went directly to the offices of the *American*. He got there about eleven o'clock on a Saturday morning and found the place in an uproar. What Arthur didn't know was that on Saturdays the staff of the morning *Examiner* came over to help their colleagues on the evening paper get out next day's *Sunday American*. In the city room when Arthur walked in were eleven editors, twenty reporters, nine special writers, sixteen telegraph operators, ten sportside writers, thirteen office boys and twelve copyreaders. Most of these workers were yelling into telephones or contending with each other in trying to be heard over the clamor, and to gain the attention of the man at the center of the maelstrom—Moses Koenigsberg, the editor-in-chief. In Minneapolis, news executives of this rank inhabited quiet private offices. But here was Koenigsberg in shirtsleeves at a desk in the middle of the city room, like the captain on the bridge of a ship in a storm. A large, imposing man, he was brandishing a proofsheet at his news editor and screaming for a "headline written in English" when he noticed Arthur Pegler standing beside his desk. The editor asked, "What do *you* want?" Arthur said something about looking for work, and that seemed to set Koenigsberg off. He cried, "Work! Work! Then why don't you hang up your hat and coat? Don't argue! No time to talk! Hang 'em up! Hang 'em up! Hang 'em up!"

Arthur Pegler realized, to his amazement, that these maniacal editors proposed to send him on a trial assignment then and there. Except on Sundays, the *American* came out ten times a day, and they tore up the front page every hour, giving the most prominent display to new stories, or frantically concocting new angles for the running stories, always placing emphasis on sex and crime. It was necessary for each edition to have a new banner headline across the top of the front page in the huge lettering known as stud-horse type for its resemblance to the block print on posters advertising champion stallions. Some editors also referred to these block letters as Second Coming type, since it was the size they would order if called upon to scribble a banner line announcing the Savior's appearance in London, Chicago, or New York. Pictures were very important, and sensational papers took special interest in portrait photographs of suicides, murder victims, accused criminals, and principals in divorce or breach of promise suits. At the time Arthur applied for work, a center of attention in Chicago was the Hahnheimer story, which involved a beautiful South Side heiress and her fiance, a man named Sigmund Waldeman, who had been indicted for embezzling half a million dollars. Readers had taken Miss Hahnheimer's beauty on faith, because she avoided photographers and had repulsed all efforts of newsmen to get into her Drexel Avenue mansion, where they might have been able to steal her photograph. "Story and picture!" was the last thing a reporter heard as he set out on an assignment, and that was what Managing Editor Foster Coates now said to Arthur after telling him to see what he could accomplish in the way of an interview with the Hahnheimer girl. Two hours later, Arthur came back with a flat parcel which he laid on Coates's desk. It was a handsome studio photograph of the heiress, who was indeed a beautiful woman. Coates began yelling for the art department as newsmen gathered around his desk to marvel at the photograph. They told each other this Arthur Pegler must have broken in the back way, or managed to get past the front door in some sort of disguise, to snatch the picture and conceal it under his coat. Or had he bribed a servant? "No, nothing like any of that at all," said Arthur in his precise British voice. "I merely went to the house and rang the bell. Miss Hahnheimer came to the door. I asked her for a picture, and she gave it to me."

Arthur Pegler's rented room was in an apartment on the Middle North Side at 1529 Kenmore Avenue, a neighborhood whose drabness was partially redeemed by Lincoln Park and Lake Michigan, a few blocks to the east. Arthur found a vacant flat in the same building, and sent for his family when he drew his first pay check on the *American*. Landing this job had been a bracing and stimulating experience for Arthur, who knew he had caught on with an organization from which large rewards might be earned by those who could stand the pace, and were lucky enough to catch Mr. Hearst's eye at times of success, and to remain invisible when things turned out badly. Hearst could be generous, and sometimes kept veteran employees on the payroll after they had burnt their energies out. But he was capable of firing editors and reporters without warning, an infliction of disaster in those days when severance pay was unheard of. At the time Arthur Pegler broke in, the Hearst chain had grown from its beginnings in 1887 to twelve newspapers, anchored on each side of the continent in San Francisco and New York.

William Randolph Hearst was 39 years old. The son of an oldtime California mining millionaire, he had received the *San Francisco Examiner* as a family gift, and was by now proclaimed a genius of popular journalism, although the newspapers through which he expressed his personality were on the whole almost childishly absurd, and carried a vicious streak of irresponsible sensationalism. So at least it will appear to anyone in the 1970s who cares to roll the microfilm through the lighted viewing machines, and tire his eyesight on page after page of wild typography, exaggerated writing, and blatant fakery.* But in his way, Hearst was a Populist, though perhaps never sincere about that or anything else, and on occasion he exposed rascals in office and acted as champion for the ordinary man. Adding up Hearst's career in historical perspective, or hindsight, we are justified in concluding that the only genuine power he possessed was that which he wielded over his employees. There can be no doubt that they trembled with fear at his frown. Arthur saw an example of this during his first week on the *American*. He was waiting for the day's assignment, when a thin, dark-suited man came into the city room, to be greeted with an instantaneous hush. This was S. S. Carvalho, one of Hearst's aides, and when he appeared the big boss was sure to be nearby. A second man now walked in. With his reporter's eye Arthur saw him as broad-shouldered, stepping quietly like a large gray cat. He was wearing "a sort of pepper-and-salt tweed suit and a black billycock [Homburg] hat. He had queer-looking whitish-grey eyes like those of a dead cod." Such was William Randolph Hearst, making an unannounced

*There was a great deal of what can only be called deliberately bad writing in the Hearst papers. But it must be entered to Hearst's credit that he also published work by Ambrose Bierce, Rudyard Kipling, H. G. Wells—and Westbrook Pegler.

visit of inspection at one of his properties. Hearst and Carvalho went into Koenigsberg's private office, and the business of the city room was resumed, but in a noticeably subdued manner. Next day, some familiar faces were gone. Nobody said anything to Arthur, and he continued to give daily demonstration of his competence in gathering and writing news. Westbrook's notes on this period record that Arthur had no trouble in establishing himself as "a fast and glib newspaper writer." Glibness was a valuable commodity in that office, and Arthur knew he had plenty of it; nevertheless, he had felt somehow demeaned by the icy arrogance that Hearst and Carvalho displayed in their entrance to the city room. The publisher took himself with immense seriousness, and there was something mean and cruel in him, and he seemed to need flattery, as a fish needs water in order to live.

When the time came to join her husband, Frances Pegler sent for men to crate and ship whatever furniture had not been burned in the kitchen, and the Gabler upright piano, which she prized as a symbol that they were "nice people." I could find no record of how Mrs. Pegler felt on leaving Minneapolis, but my guess is that she was happy to think of the opportunities that awaited her husband and children in the great city of Mid-America, which was then enjoying a period of high reputation after the success of the World's Columbian Exposition of 1893. Where New York was foreign and far away, Chicago seemed to promise anything that ambitious young Middle Western people might wish to attain, without requiring them to leave their heartland where they had put down roots. The Pegler family arranged transportation to the big city by purchasing their tickets at a scalper's shop, and since this method of financing travel is now totally unknown, it requires explanation. In those days, the scalpers or cut-rate ticket brokers could be found near the railroad stations in every large town. Their stock consisted of return halves from round trips, and the general passage tickets that railroads issued in large amounts as a sort of scrip in payment for advertising space, and to certain employees. A ticket would be pasted up from various elements and might measure five or six feet long. Westbrook remembered "the green or pink streamers that used to flutter in the windows outside the scalper's shops." Four of these streamers, after many punchings of the gateman's clippers, put them aboard the train for Chicago; Westbrook and Jack made friends with "the candy butcher who kept his wicker hamper of gum-drops, licorice whips and Crackerjack in the baggage car." After getting what sleep they could, sitting up all night in the day coach, they saw the industrial structures of Chicago's back yard swinging up out of land that was flat as the lake, and then they were in the station.

Chapter 3

Here was Westbrook's first big city, which would put its mark on him, as it did on so many talented men and women from its hinterlands. And now that the final score is in, we can say that Westbrook was playing in luck because this city was Chicago.

The apartment at 1529 Kenmore Avenue, just around the corner from Irving Park Boulevard, was roomy enough, but roaches flourished in the kitchen and in addition to these insects, they found the flat crawling with bed bugs, and Westbrook later recorded in unpublished memoirs that his "invalid mother spent many a weary day swabbing the bed-springs with kerosene." The neighborhood was completely deficient in distinction or social tone. This gave dramatic impact to the contrast with the grandeur of Lake Shore Drive, a short walk east. That boulevard of fashion had been built fifteen years before on filled-in marshland, to the immense profit of Potter Palmer, who had bought up land before the Drive went through. Fields and Pullman and Palmer himself had formerly inhabited the South Side, but now a Gold Coast of finance and society had formed north and south of Palmer's castellated mansion, which fronted the lake at Schiller Street. Mrs. Potter Palmer reigned here as Chicago's greatest lady, whose doings were matters of interest throughout the town. At the time, the magnates of all big American cities seemed to take it as a public duty to display their wealth, and the lakefront on Chicago's North Side was a leading showcase. It is evident that as Westbrook grew into boyhood, he became aware of the splendor that the barons of Chicago put before their fellow-citizens' eyes, for when he was not looking at the actual show, he was reading about it in the papers. Generations of writers have noted the littoral nature of Chicago civilization, with its most impressive buildings strung out for miles along the shore. Walk inland west, and soon enough you get—Kenmore Avenue. This aspect of Chicago later brought to Pegler's mind a British architect's remark, in another connection, about Queen Anne fronts and Mary Ann backs. So the boy was living in a world where he often saw people who were far above him in the money department and in the advantages they enjoyed. And yet he did not admit any superiority in those people, for he liked to think of himself as Irish (he was half Irish), and never to forget that he was the son of a talented man who followed a trade that allowed him, on occasion, to speak in tones of equality to the rich and great.

A by-product of Westbrook Pegler's fame in maturity was the constant pressing of interviewers for lists of what he liked, and what he did not like. In the latter classification he gave the works of Charles Dickens a prominent place. It was not surprising that the contentious

Pegler should go against the judgment of the entire human race, or at least that portion of humanity that is able to read the English language. More interesting was the question of what caused him to take this view, and I think the answer is connected with his feeling about that first apartment in Chicago. Pegler wrote in his partially completed memoirs that "My mother's taste in literature ran to Charles Dickens and she spent much of the short winter evenings reading aloud to my brother Jack and me by the light of dreadful jittery Welsbach burners which jiggled and shook themselves to pieces if anyone bumped a table. They cost thirty-five cents and this was a drain on income. The dingy flat on Kenmore Avenue was not wired for juice."

Westbrook and his brother Jack attended the Horace Greeley District Public School. He recorded that "like most Chicago grade schools of that era it was red brick and stone and it must have been put up not long after the big fire of 1870 because its floors and the treads of the stairs were grooved by the feet of thousands of kids. The boys and girls were a very decent lot. I should think Chicago ought to pull down that oldtimer because it seemed a very inflammable heap and it certainly has served its time, by now. . . . In some New York schools the kids are actual little gunmen and knife fighters who terrorize teachers and other kids. In my day in Chicago I guess they may not have qualified us for good prep schools but our people didn't go to good prep schools anyway. We went to public high schools and with most of us that was the end of all that for there were only a few hundred thousand college students in the whole United States."

Within a few years the Pegler family had "moved up in the world," as Westbrook recalled it, leaving Kenmore Avenue for a sunny apartment near Montrose Boulevard, north of their first Chicago home. Westbrook always worked. He got up in the dark to deliver morning newspapers, an ordeal during the winter, as all who have lived through a Chicago February can certify. For a while the boy had an afternoon route as well, which cut down on any time he might have used in promoting mischief. He also put in time running errands for a drugstore on Wilson Avenue, one of the endless east-west arteries of the North Side. As it approached the lake, Wilson Avenue became the main street of what amounted to a separate little city, with banks, shops, theaters, hotels, and large apartment buildings. In those days, the Wilson Avenue enclave much resembled the upper West Side of New York City before the First World War. There were a number of these subcommunities throughout Chicago, and one could live in them year after year without going into the central Loop.

Chapter 3

Westbrook Pegler once remarked, "As we look back on history, we discover in some perspective that history telescopes itself like railroad cars in a wreck." He was expressing his adult realization of the terrific impact of time, which had passed slowly enough for Pegler as a boy in the years of his early residence in Chicago. Looking back, he saw the ten-year-old boy of 1904 as someone in a mist from which there almost immediately emerged the husky young man of 1912 who left formal education behind him to use his father's influence for an entrance into the newspaper world. The telescoped years of Pegler's childhood still have something to tell us about the writer who started his development during this period. It is important to note that Pegler remembered his greatest boyhood ambition as the wish to be a cartoonist. And that, in a way, was what he turned out to be, using the medium of words rather than the drawing pencil. Nobody rebukes a cartoonist for distorting the appearance of a public figure, or exaggerating a trait of personality. Think, for example, of how the newspaper artists portrayed two Roosevelts: Theodore with huge teeth and scrub-brush moustache, Franklin with equine jaw and attenuated cigarette holder. That was all part of the game, and subjects delightedly hung the original drawings on their study walls. When Pegler was seventeen and working at his first newspaper job, he showed a portfolio of his cartoons to T. A. (Tad) Dorgan, the famous Hearst comic artist who diverted the nation with "Tad's Indoor Sports." Dorgan looked through the sheaf of drawings and said, "What else can you do, kid?" Later in life, when he commanded a national audience greater than Tad's, Pegler gave many public figures the exaggerated cartoon treatment by the use of identifying epithets, such as "Old Moosejaw" for Franklin Roosevelt. But there were readers who resented it, feeling that what is written must be gentler and more respectful than what is shown in a cartoon.

Westbrook had begun serious efforts to draw at Lane Technical High School in 1909. After completing the eighth grade of elementary school, he had entered Lane Tech at the urging of Arthur Pegler, who said his son was lucky to be attending one of the most efficient educational institutions in the country. Arthur's father had been an inspector of schools, so he ought to know. The money panic of 1907 having subsided, industrial Chicago had need of young men who could go into the shops as apprentices, operating complicated machines from the first day they came on the floor. But this was not for Westbrook, whose manual skill could never be developed beyond what was needed to operate a typewriter. He saw Lane not as a place of opportunity, but as a school that resembled a factory, with its workshops, foundries, and forges. Aside from the chance to use drawing materials, Westbrook found so little to engage his interest that he dropped out after a year and went looking for work in the stockyards district of the South Side. There was plenty of work down there for a strong boy: the foreman assigned Westbrook the task of carrying tubs of pigs' feet from the slaughtering room into a chill-room where the temperature stood at zero. The monotony of the laborious trips would be relieved by occasional orders to carry large containers of miscellaneous animal parts up to the lard production department and dump them into a seething cauldron, two stories deep. One morning, as he approached this dreadful vat, Westbrook's feet slipped from under him on the bloody floor, and he started a wild dance toward the boiling grease. A Polish workman made a flying tackle and saved him from being melted down. Soon after that, Westbrook resigned the stockyards job.

Arthur Pegler believed that hard work was a good thing for his sons, but he thought Westbrook might put in his time at something less dangerous than the risk of being rendered into lard. By this time, in 1910, Arthur was an established star at the *American,* well known to all newspapermen in Chicago and downstate. Arthur Pegler's recommendation to Ed Conkle, manager at the Chicago office of the United Press, was all Westbrook needed to land a job. It was noted that the boy had developed a clear voice and crisp enunciation from listening to his father; to make use of this asset Conkle put Westbrook on the pony wire desk, where his duty was to read UP dispatches over the telephone to client papers in such small Illinois cities as Joliet, Rockford, Moline, and Galesburg, with Indiana towns like La Porte, Michigan City, Gary, and Aurora also on the list. They paid Westbrook $16 a week for reading a pony wire and doubling as office boy. This was good pay for adolescent labor by the standards of the time, but the greatest benefit Westbrook derived from his daily readings had to do with the formation of his mature writing style. The men of the United Press, struggling to compete with the considerably richer Associated Press, had to be economical in everything, including words. Westbrook noticed this at once, and filed it in his head as a professional solution for the problem of moving news from point of collection to point of publication: "We did not skeletonize, we did not omit the article and certain pronouns as we might have. The object was to evaporate words and deliver a report which would be couched in competent English when it came out in the paper." The provincials taking down Pegler's dictation over the telephone understood that they were getting skilled condensation which needed no further treatment on their typewriters, unless they wished to add frills of their own. Therefore it was a shock to Westbrook when an old German editor in an Indiana town cut him off one afternoon before he had delivered the full "wire" by grunting, "Goodbye now. Ve got enough news." The job fascinated Westbrook and he was proud of his ability to speak clearly on the telephone; but at this time the family came to a decision—that is, Arthur Pegler decided that Westbrook should make one more try at formal education. There would be no more efforts to profit by what Lane Tech had to offer. Instead, Westbrook would be sent to see what some training in the humanities could do for him, at Loyola Academy, up beyond the Montrose Avenue apartment, close to the northern boundary of Chicago.

Loyola Academy was part of an institution that priests of the Jesuit order had founded under the name of St. Ignatius College in 1870, renaming it Loyola University in 1909. Arthur Pegler did not become a Roman Catholic until the last years of his life, but he and Westbrook knew that the soldier and saint known as Ignatius of Loyola had founded the Society of Jesus in the sixteenth century and that these Jesuits had done great things as missionary explorers in the vast northwestern reaches of the New World where Chicago had grown up from a lonely trading post on the river. It was true that most of the rulers of commercial Chicago were Protestants, and that because of families like the McCormicks and the Pattersons the city was a Presbyterian Rome. But the first clergyman ever to appear in that part of the wilderness had been Father Jacques Marquette, the Jesuit who crossed the Chicago River with Louis Jolliet in 1673. The Roman church gained a certain dignity in Chicago from this historic background, even though the communicants were mostly foreign born, poor, and residing in endless shabby neighborhoods on the West Side. Without trying to make evaluations which can't be proved, we are entitled to assume that Westbrook, now in his earliest stage of development as an artist, was sensitive to the psychic atmosphere in which he found himself. It was a good thing, surely, to identify one's self with a school that owed its tradition and name to a brave great man, even though its religion was not the religion of the city's dominating class. My belief in this matter is that quite early on, Westbrook developed a feeling of defiance, the kind that says, "You think you're better than I, but I am really better than you." This emotional attitude must have been the cause of Westbrook's later proclaiming himself to be an Irishman, and there is unquestionably something romantic in the idea of being Irish. Pegler based the claim on his mother's parentage. His English father most probably saw possibilities of intellectual development in the teaching at Loyola Academy, because of the Jesuits' reputation for superior mental powers. According to popular mythology, they were masters of a special method of argument that made them unconquerable in debate on any point whatsoever.

Westbrook found the actual experience of attending Loyola a disappointment. The Jesuit instructors seemed to lack human sympathies, and their authoritarian attitude warred on something deep in Westbrook's personality. He left school in the middle of his second year, with the verdict that he had "endured eighteen months of it" and that was all he could take. The courses of study had failed to turn on lights in Westbrook's mind; and on the physical side, he himself had failed in his efforts to make the football team. He had hoped to win a position in the line as a hard-charging tackle, but even the third-stringers would not have him. This may have been the low point in Westbrook Pegler's life.

There is credible evidence in his memoirs of this period that in his mood of general rebellion, Westbrook talked of socialism with considerably less hostility than he showed toward that political system in his mature years as a national columnist. We should remember that William Randolph Hearst as champion of the people sometimes editorialized in a Populist vein against the trusts and money barons. As recently as 1893, Chicago had set the stage for an immortal Populist battle cry, the Cross of Gold oration by William Jennings Bryan. And now a few years later many Populist and Socialist publications circulated in Chicago, most noticeably among the skilled German workmen who lived on the North Side. Moreover, Chicago was the central organizing ground for the International Workers of the World, known as the Wobblies, who preached pacifism and the doctrine of One Big Union to the hoboes and migrant harvesters who went across the country on freight trains made up in the South Side yards. At this point Westbrook Pegler might well have taken a turn to the intellectual left, and arrived at maturity a Socialist, like his friend and enemy Heywood Broun. But Loyola had one teacher, Father Siedenberg, who seems to have regarded Westbrook as a brand to be snatched from the burning. When Pegler in his years of success was able to syndicate his column to the entire country, he received letters from many Catholic priests who told him they approved of his writings. Answering one such correspondent in 1949, Pegler wrote that Father Siedenberg would frequently summon him from dull routine classes and "conduct a peripatetic course in socialism during walks by the lake, and discourse on its errors as we plodded along. I think he realized that time and other circumstances would preclude my getting to college, and decided that the education which I would receive from his commentaries would be more beneficial than an inch of progress in Algebra and Greek. He was a wonderful man to me."

Chapter 3

Although it appears that Father Siedenberg persuaded Westbrook not to become a Chicago radical, the teacher was not so successful in keeping his disciple at school. Westbrook went back to the United Press early in 1912, and once again he found that many of his duties were those of an office boy. But he had a press badge and used it to cross police lines when Conkle sent him out to cover a fire. And in this year of 1912, Westbrook attended his first national political convention, when the Republicans convened at Chicago to nominate William Howard Taft for a second term in the White House. The candidate's gross corpulence fascinated Westbrook, who was beginning to develop his eye for the grotesque. Taft weighed over 300 pounds, the result of uncontrolled gluttony; he outweighed Grover Cleveland, who had been up to that time the fattest and physically the most repulsive President in American history. Another grotesque human being who came under inspection by Westbrook at this time was Theodore Roosevelt, the former President, who talked in a squeaky voice and waved his short arms when committing partisan oratory. Nevertheless he was an effective speaker, as Westbrook learned when Roosevelt delivered his "Armageddon" speech and set several thousand people moaning and gibbering in political ecstasy. With this effort, "T. R." destroyed Taft's chances of election, and started on the way toward his own nomination at the head of a third party. This opened the White House doors to the Democratic candidate, Woodrow Wilson of New Jersey, with incalculable consequences for the world, for this nation, and for Westbrook Pegler.

The young man learned much at the convention: he saw how an urgent desire for the presidency had made T. R. retract his statement that he would not run again, which he had made in 1908 on leaving the White House after his elected term. Roosevelt had spent seven years in office after succeeding William McKinley, who died of an assassin's bullet in 1901. Having served the equivalent of two terms, Roosevelt chose Taft as his Republican successor. During Taft's first term, Roosevelt slaughtered a number of large animals in Africa and traveled through Europe, representing the United States at the funeral of King Edward VII in London. The former American President brought up the rear. But T. R. caught the attention of the crowd because he stood out as the only man in line not wearing a gorgeous uniform and a hat with rooster feathers. Roosevelt wore plain evening dress and a plug hat, although he could have appeared in the dress uniform of a U. S. Cavalry colonel by virtue of his service in Cuba with the volunteer Rough Riders in the Spanish-American war twelve years before. Westbrook did not miss the extraordinarily comical effect of the personages—all the world's male royalty in fact—dressed in costumes that made one recall *The Prisoner of Zenda.* Admitting this to have been a solemn occasion, for after all, it *was* a funeral, Westbrook couldn't help laughing at news photographs of the dignitaries in line: the German Kaiser had achieved a particularly ludicrous effect with shiny boots high enough to wade a trout stream, gauntlets halfway to his elbows, sword, spiked hat with a pony's tail attached, and a chestful of medals. With his exaggerated villain's moustache turned up at the ends, Wilhelm II looked like a station-house comic in a West Madison Street burlesque show. Theodore Roosevelt had marched from a procession of that kind into the political Chicago of 1912, and it all seemed preposterous to Westbrook. He thought the delegates at the convention little better than low political serfs, directed by windbags. Westbrook's lack of respect extended also to many of the journalistic stars assembled in Chicago by the big-city papers and the press associations, and it caused him to be involved in an embarrassing incident.

The trouble came from a question of professional status, which was very important to Westbrook. His press badge proved that he was a reporter, but he occupied the low rank of a leg man who expended shoe-leather gathering the raw material of news stories to be written by other men. Nevertheless Westbrook cherished his position on the bottom rung of the editorial ladder. He recalled that he was standing in the wooden press bleachers on the floor of the convention hall when "a big man with a brow like the belly of a medicine ball, ripped off a few sheets of copy and, without looking up, handed them to me, saying, 'Boy, copy.' I was a boy, but no longer a copy-boy. I was a leg man, and I tossed it back at him, saying, 'Run it down yourself, I am a reporter.' The Hearst super nearly died and said, 'Run that copy downstairs, or I will kill you. That is Brisbane.'"

Arthur Brisbane was the best known editor and writer on the Hearst chain, and he had become rich because the publisher thought him a genius, and ran his commentary on the front page of every Hearst morning paper under the heading, *TODAY, by Arthur Brisbane.* The products of the great brain were the most stupefying truisms imaginable, written in the one-sentence paragraphs that Hearst himself liked to use when he thought he had some profound message to convey. Arthur was a son of the Utopian social reformer Albert Brisbane; he had come to Hearst in 1897 from Joseph Pulitzer's *New York World.* After his death in 1936, the *Dictionary of American Biography* was to place the following wreath on his grave: "Brisbane provided Hearst with the sensational appeal to mass tastes, the jingoistic propaganda, the surface learning and adjustable conscience that the ambitious publisher wanted in his editors." Speaking of the incident at Chicago, Westbrook said he waived his dignity and delivered Brisbane's copy to the telegraphers as requested. And years afterward he mentioned it to Brisbane in Miami, but got the impression that Brisbane was not amused, and that he regarded Pegler's reminiscence as an unnecessary interruption to a monologue on the virtues of hard work. At the occasion of Brisbane's death, Pegler read the conventional tributes to the supposedly great editor, and said, "There is a prominent ingredient of baloney in much of this copy. The big shots of the world must keep a file of these expressions, like blank dog-licenses and building permits. They are so perfunctory and bloodless and mean." Brisbane's blind spot, according to Pegler, had been lack of humor. He had worked hard to produce an enormous quantity of rubbish; he also had acquired the reputation of being greedy, and none too scrupulous in his methods, for he had used the Hearst papers to promote real estate schemes in which he had interest. They were a remarkable crew, these celebrities of print and politics who came under the scrutiny of Westbrook's dawning maturity—the gluttonous Taft, Roosevelt mostly noise and bluff, and the pompous Arthur Brisbane, who was overrated and overpaid almost beyond comprehension.

The United Press office also spread a gallery of human types before the failed cartoonist's eye of Westbrook Pegler. He discovered that while syndication of features paid the artists and writers well, syndicated news returned the lowest wages in journalism to the desk hands. And here the Associated Press did better than Westbrook's employers. The United Press Associations (later called simply the United Press) had been organized by Edward Wyllis Scripps, a towering figure of the time, who took $50,000,000 out of news publishing before he died in 1926. Born in 1854 in downstate Illinois, Scripps entered partnership with Milton A. McCrae in 1889 and founded the Scripps-McCrae newspapers. In 1907 he set up the United Press Associations as the first news service to operate in connection with a chain of daily papers. In 1908 he put a young man named Roy W. Howard in charge, with orders to sell the service to all comers in addition to the house papers. The historian of American journalism, Frank Luther Mott, has recorded that "The UP report had a liveliness and human-interest value which were sometimes lacking in that of its chief competitor. By 1914, over 200 papers received its full daily service and more than 300 subscribed to an abbreviated service." As to E. W. Scripps, Mr. Mott says "he was not a hard worker nor a man of good habits. When he was forty-six years old, in 1900, he increased his habitual drinking to a gallon of whiskey a day; he was half blind, his limbs were shrunken and partially numb, and his hand was almost too shaky to write." Scripps swore off liquor and tobacco, and "recovered most of his health" though he remained extremely jumpy, because of his ruined nervous system, until he died at the age of seventy-two. In 1922 E. W. Scripps had turned over the newspapers to his son Robert, who put Roy Howard in charge of the entire operation, forming the great Scripps-Howard chain. This organization was to be of primary importance in Westbrook's professional life, and along with the *Chicago Tribune* and the Hearst group, one of his three principal employers.

The national United Press headquarters in Chicago—HXUP in the telegraphic code—occupied the fourth floor of a tumbledown building on West Madison Street. The official saloon was the Steuben, where one could buy two shots of whiskey for a quarter of a dollar. Westbrook sometimes stopped there after work to witness the invariable entrance of Ed Conkle, "presiding elder of the Western synod of the United Press." The minute any bartender saw the managing editor's black sombrero above the swinging entrance doors, he would reach for the Pittsburgh Rye. By the time Conkle got to the bar, his double shot would be waiting; he would lay down his quarter, gulp the liquor, set fire to a stogie, and nod, "Good evening, gentlemen," to any staff members present. He would then march out into Madison Street and go home. In these days there was much talk of commercialized vice in Chicago. Many committees studied the matter—there was a great deal to be studied—and sensational newspaper stories resulted. Ed Conkle used to say, "Keep that vice stuff coming. People like to read about what they like to do." Conkle was the son of a Methodist minister.

The workshop in which Pegler and his more experienced colleagues prepared each day's supply of news was one large, partitionless room, with a gate and railing near the elevator doors. When asked to describe the prevailing atmosphere in one word, Westbrook called it seedy. A sense of possible and even imminent failure hung over the copyreaders and rewrite men who worked at the cigarette-scarred desks. The feel of their desperation came through to Westbrook from the time he first took up his "holy office of cryer" on the pony line. A water cooler stood near the telephone booth, and every day an ice man came and put in a chunk of ice. Soon after joining the staff, Westbrook noticed a peculiarity in a fellow worker. He wrote in notes for his reminiscences, "I came upon our rewrite man, a sickly fellow named Oliver Wendell Jones with a hacking cough, as he returned from lunch and hid his pint of bourbon in the ice compartment. He knew from my eyes that I had seen him in the act and we both knew that if Old

Man Conkle smelled his breath he would follow it to the cooler and fire the poor guy, with the sure implication that I had squealed on him as I vow to this very moment I never did. Nevertheless, the man was let go in a few days and if, in his wretchedness he did think as he had a right to, I can only say that I had nothing to do with the case."

If challenged to name one unquestionable genius among Chicago writers, a guide might point out George Ade, the man from Indiana who had come up to town in 1890 after graduating from Purdue University, hoping to get a newspaper job. He applied first at the *News,* where an executive told him, "If you can prove you're not a college man, you might be able to get into the advertising department and make forty dollars a week." George Ade gladly accepted twelve dollars a week to start as a cub reporter. By the time Westbrook went to the convention in 1912, Ade was an internationally successful playwright and the author of "Fables in Slang," the famous stories read by the entire country in syndication and then collected in books, which had a way of coming to the point and revealing some common human failing in clear light. First the public, then the critics of the literary magazines and universities, recognized the simplicity and naturalness of Ade's writing; in fact, he used little genuine slang, but wrote in idiomatic American English as it sounded to his accurate ear. Although Westbrook at his age and level of development had no way of knowing George Ade in person, it cannot be doubted that the "Fables" had their influence on him. Like George Ade he was to make a style from the absence of ornament and an ear for the rhythm of plain speech.

Another Chicago newspaper writer of originality was Finley Peter Dunne, creator of Mr. Dooley, an Irish saloonkeeper who discoursed to his customer Hennessy, a brutally ignorant and prejudiced day laborer. Mr. Dooley respected no one, and was devastating when he discussed politicians and the ways they used government to plunder and degrade ordinary men who had no power to oppose them. The saloonkeeper also heaped scorn on poor Hennessy; one has little trouble in tracing these two ideas of disrespect for the high, and contempt for the low, in Westbrook Pegler's mature work.

The reporter's byline is still a thing of value, even today in the 1970s, when the *New York Times,* for example, attaches a writer's name to every item on the front page, and to nearly all the inside items. Sixty years before, bylines were not often seen, and the achievement of signed work was an important point in any newspaperman's career. Being fully aware of this, Westbrook managed to get his name on the national syndicate wire at an early date, when he compiled the sports scores and persuaded Ed Conkle to send them out as a standard daily item—"WATCHING THE SCOREBOARD, BY BUD PEGLER." His use of the nickname Bud was in the still accepted style which gives us so many Jims, Petes, Bills, Reds, and Dons on sport pages. It was part of the breezy, bantering manner supposedly appropriate to men who carried, by association, some of the swagger of professional athletes. It can also be noted in the electronic journalism of the present day, among the sports announcers who usually display a certain assumed brassiness in voice and approach. One is especially aware of it in radio news programs, when the institutional enunciation of the newscaster gives way to the less formal tone and rhythm of the sports expert. Westbrook abandoned the nickname to become W. J. and then J. W. Pegler. By the middle 1920s, he discarded that movable J., and for the rest of his life signed all work as Westbrook Pegler. It was a good name to sign to writing, for it had a positive cadence in its four syllables, the *b* and *p* plosives were alliterative, the rhyming *e* vowels were pleasing to the ear, and the *r* sounds gave an impression of briskness. The name looked right, and invited a plain, blunt nickname in the shortening of Pegler to Peg. Many acquaintances of later life used this nickname, while the old and intimate friends stayed with Bud. It also might be recorded as a minor note in social history that around the time Pegler settled his name, the age of famous two-name writers was arriving. Authors' stylings of their signatures along the lines of Henry Wadsworth Longfellow, Harry Leon Wilson, Jesse Lynch Williams, William Dean Howells, and the like, were giving way to the general plain fashion of Ernest Hemingway, Thomas Wolfe, William Faulkner, James Boyd, Philip Barry, and Eugene O'Neill. In this matter it appears that Westbrook Pegler was showing that working sense of fashion, the perception of what is going on that is indispensable to a popular writer. And it need not mean that he is a bad writer: Pegler's nonfavorite, Charles Dickens, knew what the people knew, and he knew what they did not know; and he knew what they liked, and what they did not like. And this was always true with Westbrook Pegler.

His Dickensian eye for the grotesque took in a sociological aspect of employment in the Chicago office of the United Press when he noted that the organization did not encourage younger employees to get married. Taking on this domestic responsibility "usually meant a baby carriage and possibly a mother-in-law who would nag her daughter to make him take her back to Evansville, or the mother-in-law would slip on the soap and break her hip. Single fellows were mobile and less expensive." Whatever their wages, the more competent men in the

UP shop turned out an astonishing amount of work. Westbrook gazed in awe, for example, at Karl Bickel, later a noted foreign correspondent and news executive, who moved so fast that he seemed to be in orbit and was recalled by Pegler as "the first Sputnik," whizzing, buzzing, and flapping while he worked. "Bickel would read the front pages and see what the Associated Press was featuring, gnaw a hot dog, gulp coffee, type, and talk on the telephone all at once." Sometimes Bickel would interrupt himself to ask, "What did I say?" The frantic activities earned Karl Bickel $45 a week. The UP gave no assurance of support during illness, no vacations, and no severance pay.

The tramp copyreaders and rewrite men, who went from city to city as migratory journalists, had a similar breed of tramp telegraphers for colleagues. These wandering craftsmen of the key were skilled at reading Morse code by ear as it poured in like the cry of a flight of gigantic crickets. Each operator kept his "bug" hammering against an empty Prince Albert tobacco can. No one ever explained why, but only a Prince Albert tin could deliver the desired resonance. Pegler made friends with a telegrapher named Jack McCloskey, who had worked all over the world, and now spent his leisure time in the grill room at the Briggs House, where he liked to chase a shot of Pebbleford Rye with a nickel beer. McCloskey recalled the night of Lord Tennyson's death in London in 1892 and described for Pegler how a great and respectfully quiet crowd had gathered in Trafalgar Square for bulletins on the poet laureate's condition, when a gang of clothcapped peddlers suddenly darted out of an alley and began hawking half-penny black-bordered copies of "Crossing the Bar." Official word that Tennyson had died followed in a few minutes.

Looking back over his life, Westbrook Pegler said more than once that the horrors of journalism always fascinated him. Those horrors included a four-floor ride to and from the workroom in a stuffy elevator run by "a pallid little stockyards Mick called Chicken Duffy." The Chicken would go and get a "short" (one-half) pint for a copyreader named Ben Allen "when he was needing." Allen had the morning tremors of the confirmed alcoholic, in addition to a nervous disorder—"some jumpy disease, don't ask me what."

Pegler's recollections of this period show that he liked the idea of getting out the news: something deep inside him responded to it. And he told himself that he admired the scoundrels of the trade, the drunkards, the fakers, even though he had the best of opportunities to recognize and digest the fact that the foundation of serious newsgathering lay in hours of dull routine work on one's legs, or crouched over the telephone with the pencil ripping across the pad—or doodling, as so often happened, when the call turned out to be a blank. But there did exist a kind of independent, swinging style in many of the people in the newspaper trade at that time, especially around Chicago. In a few years Ben Hecht and Charles MacArthur were to captivate the country with a melodrama, *The Front Page,* in which reporters at the Criminal Courts Building were drawn from life. The playwrights showed newspapermen and a managing editor who were little better than ruffians; but bad as they were, they came over the footlights as knightly crusaders in comparison to the sheriff of Cook County and the mayor of Chicago. Pegler's early conception of the newspaper trade must have been something like this: *It's a rough business carried on by hardened, basically unconventional people, who justify their personal and professional excesses by accepting the responsibility of public watchdogs against the government and its employees.* Pegler said that "glancing backward and around a couple of sharp corners in my life," he recalled a newspaperman with whom he had spent some time in his days at the United Press, who could be listed under the heading of bad company. This man was Jack Malloy, who had risen in Chicago journalism to the position of city editor on the *Daybook,* a newspaper that carried no advertising and failed to establish itself financially. After this failure, the idea of a newspaper without advertising lay dormant until it got another trial, in the later 1930s, when the Chicago millionaire Marshall Field, grandson of the department store magnate, published a lively sheet called *PM* in New York City. But interesting though it was, *PM* did not last after the Second World War. The *Daybook* also provided good reading, and Westbrook felt it worthwhile to "loaf around" with Malloy after office hours. He observed that the elder man was a fighting drunk who almost invariably got into a brawl at some point during the evening, and would try to force a quarrel if nobody challenged him. Because of Malloy's standing as a city editor, bouncers would ease him out, instead of hammering on his skull with blackjacks, the fate of most belligerents in Chicago nightspots of the time. Some years later, a heart attack hit Jack Malloy in a place called Chez Paree, and he died stretched out on a roulette table.

Such was the picturesque side of newspapering as the entire concept entered Westbrook's bloodstream; and if he needed other newsmen than Malloy, Conkle, and Bickel as models, there was always his father, self-proclaimed champion of them all. There was no doubt that Arthur Pegler could write a vivid line and turn a telling phrase, as he showed in his description of Hearst's padded footsteps entering the city room on that unexpected visit. And he uttered the memorable remark that a Hearst paper resembled "a whore running down the street and screaming that her throat was cut." Pegler sometimes spoke of his father's writing in respectful tones, as when he credited him with "gifts of nuance and emphasis" along with fluency. All reporters of Arthur's school prided themselves on fluency, their ability to write a coherent news story to any length at any time and place; but they frequently came down too hard in the emphasis department. And they could be careless in their handling of facts, and would sometimes manufacture news to ginger up a story that was turning dull. Arthur was guilty of such tricks on more than one occasion, as when he exploded two cannon crackers in a small downstate city to keep a bomb scare going. And in spite of his alleged skills of "nuance"—by which Westbrook apparently meant a sensitivity to shades of difference—Arthur was, on the whole, a cliché expert like Frank Sullivan's celebrated Mr. Arbuthnot. Westbrook had to admit this flaw when he edited copy for Arthur's unfinished memoirs, a gesture intended to show the 95-year-old veteran that somebody still took an interest in what he had to say. But this could not stop Westbrook's pencil from automatically changing "knights of the squared circle" to "prizefighters," "winter of our discontent" to "winter," and "national grid power" to "football team." But it would be a mistake to belittle Arthur Pegler. He appears to have been a man who was loyal to those who paid him, and like Browning's Andrea del Sarto, had labored somewhat in his time and not been paid profusely. The unavoidable fact that Westbrook exceeded his father in brains and talent may have caused as great a sense of guilt as we believe to be called forth when children fail to measure up to a parent's standards. Sociologists tell us that most Americans want their children to have more than they had. This may be true, but I doubt that parents really like it when children outclass them in natural brain power, as opposed to education that the parents provided.

In any event, Westbrook admired the way Arthur acted as a gospel ghost, in 1909, when he took on a writing assignment for the famous traveling evangelist from England, the Rev. Gypsy Smith. This experienced Devil-fighter had a voice that easily filled a large hall in the days before mikes and loudspeakers, and he played a long Chicago stand of two shows a day, plus weekly services for men only. At these meetings he spoke frankly about the dangers of visiting prostitutes in the Levee, an open vice district on the South Side. Many a yokel fainted with fright when Smith described the ravages of venereal disease, and had to be carried out twitching and moaning. The Gypsy led a parade of church people into the Levee, following a band that played "Onward, Christian Soldiers" (by Sir Arthur Sullivan and the Rev. Dr. Sabine Baring-Gould). He knelt at the principal street crossing and prayed for both resident and transient sinners in the district. But no one came out of the bad houses at his call, and the procession marched away, returning to the Loop with the band still playing. An evangelist of such zeal needed a press agent, and Arthur Pegler was well qualified for the position. It was like the jobs on the side back in Minneapolis. Arthur's most notable feat at keeping Gypsy Smith in the papers was the writing of a daily sermon which supposedly came from Smith's own study. A typical production by Arthur Pegler, speaking in Smith's name, was "ON SOWING WILD OATS." Arthur had the preacher start by saying "This is a word about wild oats for those who are sowing them in Chicago. Sowing wild oats is the most popular branch of the Devil's agriculture. . . . When you see the son of a rich man with crush hat awry, crumpled shirt bosom and inflamed countenance, his hands full of his father's money, buying damnable decoctions in drinking places for other foolish young men and women, you know that the young fellow is sowing his oats. . . . Reaping wild oats is the hardest harvest the world has to face. The reapers bend to their work and the sweat pours down their faces, but the stalks of wild oats are tough and hard to sever. . . ." In another sermon, Arthur spoke with the Gypsy's voice to encourage chastity among young women: "The open gate of the stranger's motor is often one of the one thousand side doors to Hell. . . . Young women who work, I beseech you count the cost. . . . Back, back I say—to the churches you are leaving empty, and the godly gatherings where formerly you were the light and life of religious effort. . . . On your knees, Sister, ere it be too late. . . ." This was a star performance in the role of a cynical newspaperman, hammering a typewriter with his coat off, the cigarette held in the corner of his mouth to keep the smoke out of his eyes.

Arthur Pegler as preacher had cadence and bite—"the reapers bend to their work" and "back, back I say" were especially good. He seemed to enjoy displaying virtuosity at tasks which he could not have taken seriously. And he gave Westbrook another striking example of inspired hackwork in 1913, when a Chicago theatrical company presented a play in three acts called *Little Lost Sister,* by Arthur James Pegler. The playwright based his drama on a series of articles he had written about an antivice crusader named Virginia Brooks, who had been compared to Joan of Arc for her militant leadership of reformers in Cook County. History shows that Ed Conkle was right when he urged his men to keep that vice stuff coming, for public opinion in Chicago and the country as a whole had come to the point of demanding that recognized districts containing brothels under semiofficial regulation must go. The parade of Gypsy Smith's followers was not the only procession of demonstrators to enter the Levee: the reform movement approached its climax in 1912, when Virginia Brooks led more than forty thousand marchers into the South Side entertainment districts in an unmistakable threat of action that drew emphasis from the troop of mounted police that rode at the head of the line. An historian noted that "This procession had an immediate effect on many who saw it: a number of the pimps, whores, and gamblers who watched it pass went to their lodgings, packed their suitcases, and quietly left town." Miss Brooks occupied such a prominent place in the antivice movement that her friends thought she might be in danger from the forces of organized crime. It appears to be more likely, however, that the danger lay in the other direction, for Virginia Brooks had first come to the delighted attention of Arthur Pegler when she announced in her hometown of Hammond, an Indiana suburb of Chicago, that she had marked down eight vice lords to be tarred and feathered. She said this was to be done by a committee of fifty virtuous women, armed with shotguns and revolvers. No manuscript of *Little Lost Sister* has been preserved, and Arthur Pegler never spoke of it as something to be taken seriously. Nevertheless, the show played four weeks at an uptown theater in the middle North Side not far from his first home in the city.

A recognition of the shabbiness of ghost writing for a tent-show evangelist and setting off cannon crackers to manufacture news did not disillusion Westbrook Pegler to the extent of making him look for a start in some other business. His feelings were like those of a man in love with a woman of obvious shortcomings who still possesses overpowering charm. Westbrook could put up with low pay and dingy surroundings, along with the "horrors" he spoke of, in return for the privilege of being a newspaper man. But there was another aspect of West Madison Street that Westbrook refused to accept, and that was the presence of poor immigrant garment workers in the same loft building with the United Press. They were almost all Eastern European Jews, and before the days of a powerful union, such people were cruelly exploited by strawbosses and small manufacturers, mostly their own compatriots. Their plight was severe, but it inspired disgust rather than pity in Westbrook Pegler, objecting as he did to "undersized needlemen, immigrants, consumptives, who carried scabies, which I caught. Thus I was not a stranger to this devouring itch when it bared its fangs at me in the First Division area of France in the fall of 1917." He had hated the idea of parasitical insects from the time the Pegler family encountered them on Kenmore Avenue. He was now about to leave the humiliations and discomforts of those early days far behind, in the progress of a remarkable career. But the dislike and distrust of Jews was to grow as a part of Westbrook's personality until it distorted his vision and poisoned his heart. On the way to this regrettable conclusion, he had so far freed himself from prejudice by 1933 as to write a famous column of compassionate understanding for the troubles of Jewish children in Nazi Germany. Hitler, to be sure, was a natural target for Pegler. But in the end, Pegler was haunted out of rational reaction by the memory of the terribly unattractive needlemen, who had not called forth the sympathy he was able to show for German children; and in addition, there had been war between Pegler and many American Jews of brains and talent, who came to personify some kind of menace in his mind.

Such unfortunate contention was scarcely to be thought of in 1913, with Westbrook in his twentieth year and at almost his full height of an inch above six feet. He had learned to make a good appearance from his father, and wore his clothes with an elegant air, even in his first days of newspaper work when both suit and overcoat might have been supplied by the haberdasher known as Ten Dollar Tom Murphy. What about girls? Westbrook's generation had not dispensed with reticence, and he has furnished few clues in his writing as to his dealings with young women when he was a young man. He did record in his notes for the period when he knew Jack Malloy: "I had a girl at that time and she lived in a tough neighborhood over on Ashland Avenue, but she had grown up in the block where she still lived and I had a safe conduct as long as I was in her company after an evening at a Greek joint called the Athenia on North Clark Street." Although his parents were immigrants, Westbrook did not as a rule think highly of people who had been born outside the United States. One can but wonder how he appeared to the girl from Ashland Avenue and what he said to her during those evenings at the Athenia. I assume that whatever Westbrook said, it had nothing to do with getting married. He was aware, as he recorded, that the United Press discouraged "single fellows" from acquiring wives. The significance of this policy to the history of American journalism is that whatever his personal reasons may have been, Westbrook retained the mobility of a young bachelor, which his employers found useful. And so at the end of 1913 he started across the country on a series of assignments for the Scripps-Howard Newspapers, parent organization of the United Press.

Chapter 3

His first stop was Des Moines, Iowa, where he worked as a reporter for the local Scripps-Howard paper. Westbrook's acquaintance with what he called bowl-and-pitcher hotels began at this time. Perhaps the officials at Scripps-Howard headquarters believed that part of their mobile young men's pay could be collected in experience on the job. Of this there was a great plenty, and Westbrook profited by it to such an extent that the managers sent him to New York to work as "a leg man on the city side" of the United Press. Westbrook first saw New York City in its lovely period at the close of the American Renaissance in metropolitan architecture, giving him an impression of the possibilities of a civilized community, something that penetrated his mind and lasted all his life, to stand in contrast to the realities that came under his observation in New York and elsewhere in America after the end of the Second World War. Two years before Pegler caught his first glimpse of the towers in downtown New York, the English poet Rupert Brooke had the same experience, and his reaction is worth recalling. Taking a distant view of Manhattan, he noted "that higher clump of the great buildings, the Singer, the Woolworth, and the rest. Their strength, almost severity, of line and the lightness of their color give you a kind of classical feeling, and yet not of Europe. It had the air, this block of masonry, of edifices built to satisfy some faith, for more than immediate ends. . . . They could not have been dreamed and made without some nobility . . . the skyscrapers are no longer merely the means and local convenience for men to pursue their purposes, but acquire that characteristic of the great buildings of the world, an existence and meaning of their own."

And so we come to the problem of picturing the spiritual and emotional atmosphere of the time Pegler left home, never to return, to take on the challenges of life as a newspaper man. What was his world like, and how did it influence our young man? To begin with, the world for Pegler amounted to nothing beyond the boundaries of the United States. Within those frontiers, a lay religion of patriotism flourished in a continuing euphoria of national self-praise. A few years before, the editorial page of the *Chicago Inter-Ocean* had carried a typical cry of self-congratulation: "We Americans have some things to regret, but how infinitely more we have to praise and rejoice in! We go forward by looking up, not looking down. Let us look up and go forward. Let the Eagle scream!" The paper echoed a statement by Senator Albert J. Beveridge of Indiana, that "God has marked the American people as his chosen nation to finally lead in the regeneration of the world." And a popular Brooklyn preacher, the Rev. Dr. Newell Dwight Hillis, said that all was well in this country, and getting better: "Laws are becoming more just, rulers humane; music is becoming sweeter, and books wiser. . . . Art, industry, invention, literature, learning and government—all these are captives marching in Christ's triumphal procession up the hill of fame. . . ."

That sort of rhetoric stood in the main line of descent from the orations of Daniel Webster—"Liberty *and* Union, now and forever, one and inseparable"—the windjammer who had harangued the nation for two decades beginning in 1830.* Webster's principal speeches were recited and studied in all public schools, so that Westbrook felt the powerful religion of nation-worship in the depths of his developing mind.

Overblown patriotism in Pegler's youth must have allied itself, as he formed his concept of the world about him, with the spiritual certainties that Father Siedenberg commanded in the walks along the lakeshore. All his life, Pegler showed fondness for clergymen, provided they were Catholic and conservative. In this he resembled J. Pierpont Morgan, whose favored prelates were Episcopalians of the most conservative kind. Morgan appeared to believe that his reverend friends could pray him into Heaven, and they tried to do so, but no reports of success or failure have reached us at this time. The extent of Pegler's piety in his mature years is hard to assess; it is likely that what pleased him about the priests with whom he corresponded was their anti-radical politics in this world, rather than any advantages they might have offered in the world to come.

Westbrook had seen modern American political history begin to take shape at the Republican convention of 1912. It is interesting to note that another young man who looked on at that gathering of delegates was Harry Hopkins, just out of an Iowa college and heading for New York to start his career as a social worker. The spectacle of politicians shouting platitudes dismayed both Hopkins and Pegler; each young man asked himself how things in this country could be put right.

*The political rantings of Daniel Webster had style, and still make entertaining reading. I treasure the peroration of the address on Adams and Jefferson: "If we cherish the virtues and principles of our fathers, Heaven will assist us to carry on the work of human liberty and human happiness. Auspicious omens cheer us. Great examples are before us. Our own firmament now shines brightly upon our path. WASHINGTON is in the clear upper sky. These other stars have now joined the American constellation; they circle round their center, and the heavens beam with new light. Beneath this illumination let us walk the course of life, and at its close devoutly commend our beloved country, the common parent of us all, to the Divine Benignity."

Chapter 3

Hopkins thought the government itself might be reformed into an instrument of direct service to the people, whereas Pegler decided that the government was the enemy of the people. Neither Hopkins nor Pegler could see anything resembling principled convictions in the party platform, and they found nothing to admire in what H. L. Mencken called "the belch and bellow of oratory." Prospects seemed poor indeed for the survival of civilization in a country where men could utter such stuff and expect the public to take it seriously.

Out of that convention in 1912 came the Taft nomination on the Republican ticket, and Theodore Roosevelt's third party campaign, as we have seen, with the result that Woodrow Wilson entered the White House, bringing along his singular collection of personal vanities and erroneous ideas. Wilson was nationally known as president of Princeton, where he had received credit for great improvements in higher education. John Dos Passos wrote that Wilson's accession to the university presidency in 1902 had been a splendid affair: "Ex-President Grover Cleveland and Governor Murphy of New Jersey led the academic procession. Friends remarked on Woodrow Wilson's slim erect keenfaced appearance under the mortarboard. Henry van Dyke the poet preacher, Booker T. Washington, Hadley of Yale, Lowell of Harvard, Butler of Columbia added their varicolored hoods to the train. The participants were astonished by the size of J. Pierpont Morgan's nose. There was Mark Twain whitemaned in his inevitable linen suit, and William Dean Howells. Plughatted Colonel Harvey and Walter Hines Page followed in the rear as the faithful publishers of the professor's books. The new president's inaugural speech was received with acclaim. Only Grover Cleveland is said to have muttered under his moustache: 'Sounds good. I wonder what it means.' "

Established in academic office, Wilson had persuaded the trustees to approve a budget for hiring fifty young instructors, called preceptors, to teach undergraduates in groups of five or six, discussing the assigned reading and writing in an informal atmosphere. This "preceptorial" plan worked so well that even the students approved, and added to their traditional "Faculty Song" a verse that began "Here's to those preceptor guys/Fifty stiffs to make us wise . . ." Although it differed but slightly from the tutorial system at Oxford and Cambridge, the preceptorial plan so enhanced Wilson's reputation that he became one of the nation's oracles, like Lowell at Harvard and Harper at the University of Chicago.

Had he stayed in this field, for which he was quite well fitted, Wilson would have achieved a respectable and useful career, and instead of dying a bitter and broken man, would have died happy in Bermuda or in the town of Princeton, a tranquil retreat for scholars and their rich admirers during his lifetime. But Wilson was one of those people who have to do everything the hard way, and he became ugly if anyone crossed him. He had a mean streak. Woodrow Wilson's inability to establish any sort of workable compromise with opponents brought on a war at Princeton, and it was a war that Wilson lost. At the head of the opposing forces stood Andrew F. West, dean of the Graduate College, who fought Wilson over the question of where to locate the new graduate buildings for which some of the wealthier alumni had put up money. Wilson said the Graduate College must be on the main campus, but West thought he had found a better site about a mile away, on the crest of a hill above the golf course. As this controversy went on, Wilson became nasty, and bitterly denounced close associates and old friends when they failed to agree with him. It looked as though Wilson was going to get his way in the dispute until a rich man died in 1910, left several million dollars to the Graduate College, and directed in his will that Dean West should have the handling of the money. This Wyman Bequest represented a smashing defeat for Woodrow Wilson, and the results may be seen to this day where the buildings designed by Ralph Adams Cram stand on their hill, and the main quadrangle encloses a statue of Andrew Fleming West. Wilson wrote to a friend, "I have got nothing out of the transaction but complete defeat and mortification." He would, of course, leave Princeton and its ungrateful professors and trustees; his resignation was accepted in October 1910.

For some time Wilson had been listening to Democratic politicians in New Jersey, who had groomed him for the governorship, and the voters elected him to that office one month after his departure from Nassau Hall. By 1912 Wilson had built himself up to the Democratic national nomination and the presidency of the nation, which he captured, as history records, because of the Republican disasters that fascinated Harry Hopkins and Westbrook Pegler in Chicago.

There were people in this country who did not share the optimism that broke out after Wilson entered the White House, an ostentatiously high-minded chief executive offering something for everyone under the general title of the New Freedom. Wilson did not explain what was wrong with the old freedom, nor did he offer any clues as to where it might have gone. Some of the Chicagoans of Pegler's youth had long been skeptical about this doctrine of American perfection. The ranks of critics and doubters contained such unselfish helpers of the unfortunate as Jane Addams, the pioneer social worker who devoted her life to the poor, the uneducated, and the foreign born who came to her headquarters at Hull House on the West Side. Pegler has left no record that he had even heard of Jane Addams and her friends, or made any attempt to analyze their ideas. Westbrook would instinctively distrust Woodrow Wilson, and in this, perhaps for the wrong reasons, he would be right. A more sophisticated critic than Pegler was the British ambassador Cecil Spring-Rice, who took Wilson's measure at Washington in January 1914. At that time the British with good reason feared the German Kaiser, and they were making careful estimates of the United States, for they had a feeling that there was an east wind blowing, as the aging Sherlock Holmes warned Dr. Watson, such a wind as never blew on England yet. Spring-Rice wrote back to headquarters that "the President has maintained and rather increased his influence in Congress and the country, but he is as mysterious as ever. When he summons the newspaper men he talks to them at length and in excellent language, but when they leave his presence they say to each other, What on earth did he say? When he sees the members of Congress he reads them a lecture and tells them what he thinks is good for them to know, which appears to them to be very little. He asks the advice of no one."

Wilson needed no advice on public relations, for he had made himself a standard front-page character like the Pope, who got respectful treatment and plenty of ink no matter what he was up to. The country knew about Wilson's fight with Dean West, and by the time of his nomination on the Democratic national ticket, it was also common knowledge that he had cast off the politicians of the New Jersey state machine who had given him his start. Naturally enough they were common grafters, thieves, and State House loafers, but without them Wilson would still have been throwing tantrums in the Trustees' Room at Princeton. He exiled these men from his presence and made it clear that he had reached an ethical plane to which low political operators could not aspire.

Wilson granted intimacy to one man, a rich Texan named Edward Mandell House, the Bebe Rebozo of his reign. House bore the title of colonel, the rank of any Southern white man who had not served prison time on a morals charge. These two men took to each other the first time they met, when Wilson still occupied the State House at Trenton. Each tried to con the other, but House got the worst of it later, when Wilson kicked him out after the Versailles Peace Treaty went sour. The danger for Pegler and all Americans in the relationship between House and Wilson lay in the fact that the President had made his friend a powerful public official in everything but responsibility to the people. Expressed in a mathematical equation, the Wilson-House relationship would show that power exercised by House equalled the square of the power originally granted by the people to Wilson according to the Constitution, since House was under no legal restriction. But the *control* remained with Wilson, for having made House without reference to the people, he could at any time privately destroy him. One cannot think that this made for a healthy friendship, but they were not ordinary men. And when Wilson appointed House his side-door prime minister, he founded the tradition that the American president needs a confidential agent at his side, in possession of awesome secrets that ordinary people are forbidden to question. This led to that frosty coat-and-carpet aide from New England in Eisenhower's office, and to the arrogant nonentities who surrounded Richard Milhous Nixon in the days preceding his fall.

The reporters were aware of Wilson's shortcomings. But an ironclad convention in journalism at that time protected him from the likes of Westbrook Pegler, and it may be that some of the scorn which developed in Pegler's mind while Wilson ruled the country descended later on the head of Franklin Roosevelt. In any event, Pegler's instinct about Wilson was correct—the President was sanctimonious, bullheaded, and odd. Wilson showed an especially unattractive weakness in his slavish devotion to his father, an old Scotch preacher down in Virginia, to whom he wrote letters that cause queasy sensations in anyone who cares to examine them. Ambassador William Bullitt submitted the letters and other documents on Wilson to Dr. Sigmund Freud, and when the great Viennese psychiatrist had studied this material, he pursed his lips, steepled his fingers, and looked very wise indeed. Bullitt and Freud then wrote a book in which the doctor gave professional opinion that Wilson had an emotional crush on his father which was unwholesome, to say the least, and that he added up under expert appraisal to the psychic equivalent of something that runs out from under a stone—far from the personality one would wish to see at the head of a powerful nation. That sounds about right, but a certain amount of skepticism must apply to Freud himself, who had been by his own account a cocaine addict and a believer in numerology, and was the author of allegedly universal psychological laws which are not demonstrable as such. Nevertheless, Freud had drawn a convincing picture of Wilson, who made a fine example of the horrible type of man who so often seeks the U. S. presidency, a position to which no first-class man or woman would aspire in modern times.

H. L. Mencken has pointed out what a dismal job the presidency has become with its endless dealing in sham heroics and dreary subterfuge. But Wilson ate it up. He thought himself appointed to straighten out the entire world, and in 1914 started his global mission south of the Rio Grande where a warlord named Victoriano Huerta had shot his way into the leadership of Mexico. John Dos Passos says that with Wilson, "forcing out Huerta had become an obsession," and the policy can hardly be stated more concisely. There was trouble at Tampico in early April of that year when Mexican officers detained a U. S. Navy paymaster and his crew, who had been proceeding under Our Flag. An American battle fleet was standing offshore, and its admiral demanded that Huerta break the offending officers down to seaman second, and fire a twenty-one gun salute to the Stars and Stripes. Huerta offered to arbitrate, but Wilson said he would consider no such thing. He said the Mexicans must salute Old Glory by April 19, or—never mind what, just salute that flag and look sharp about it. Huerta refused and word came that a German ship carrying a consignment of arms was heading for Vera Cruz. There was war talk in the Senate, especially among the tobacco-chewing stage Southerners with longtailed coats and string ties who dominated that chamber. But Wilson figured it wouldn't be right to seize the cargo of a friendly ship on the high seas. Instead he gave orders to wait until the weapons were unloaded in Vera Cruz and *then* take possession of them. They sent in 4,000 bluejacket sailors and U.S. Marines; a battle took place and 126 Mexicans lost their lives. Maybe they deserved it for showing disrespect to Our Flag, and for many Americans, greasers didn't count anyway. But wait—nineteen of our boys got killed and seventy-one took wounds from Mexican bullets. Woodrow Wilson did not have the faintest glimmering conception of what this was like—shooting at other people and having them shoot back. He reacted like a Mafia don, talking about compelling "recognition of the dignity of the United States. . . . I have no enthusiasm for war but I have enthusiasm for the dignity of the United States. . . ." They always talk that way.

In May there was a big funeral at the Brooklyn Navy Yard for some of the Americans killed in this invasion of Mexico. Wilson was there and moving under a head of emotional steam. He made the main speech, offering the suggestion that it would have been disgraceful to die in a war of aggression, but "to die in a war of service was glorious."

He said he had never been under fire but he figured it was "just as hard" for him to do his duty in the face of hostile criticism as it was for troops to face death in combat. He seemed to feel entitled to take some sort of bow for personal courage while remarking that "the cheers of the moment are not what a man ought to think about but the verdict of his conscience and the conscience of mankind." As Mencken had observed, the American people were the most gullible and submissive of all people in the world. The crowd of 10,000 listeners demonstrated this melancholy fact when they failed to rush the platform and chase Wilson down Sands Street to the Brooklyn Bridge. Wilson dined that night at Colonel House's apartment on Murray Hill. The host recorded in his diary that after dinner the President favored the company with a little entertainment, by reading aloud from the works of Wordsworth and Matthew Arnold. What a pity we did not have tape recording in those days.

The assassination of an Austrian archduke on June 28 in 1914 gave European governments the excuse they had been looking for to get into a fight. By August 4 they were all going at it, and to Americans who shared Westbrook Pegler's cast of mind it was a struggle among foreigners who were not to be taken seriously. But the influential commercial, publishing, and university people on the Eastern seaboard had a feeling of solidarity with the British, for it long had been obvious that the established rich families in our cities tried to take their social tone from England. This admiration for the British had not affected Pegler, who had no connections in Eastern college circles or in any group that might be called select. But anyone could see that the English were brave and deserving of respect. Ghastly casualties among their volunteers were to inflict a terrible wound on England in the first two years of the war. Their generals sent an appalling number of the best young men to death—young men who cheerfully left their schools, universities, offices, factories, and shops. The whole thing was insane.

Meanwhile, the fortunes of journalism sent Westbrook by way of a short stay in Denver to St. Louis, where he took the position of bureau manager for the United Press. At this time a house-organ photograph of the young news executive revealed a bony, freckled face with a skeptical look about the eyes. A stylish collar and tie also showed in the picture. The UP copy on Wilson's activities that Pegler moved through the St. Louis bureau showed that the President was determined to keep this country out of war and thus demonstrate to the world the advantages of peace. Wilson thought he could stop the fight by preaching in the form of official papers, but he knew it was useless to try any sermons on Francisco (Pancho) Villa, the warlord who ran things in the northern Mexican State of Chihuahua. Trouble broke out when Villa invaded U.S. territory, attacked an Army post, and burned the town of Columbus, New Mexico. He pulled out after an hour of hard fighting, killing eight soldiers and eight civilians. Although there were sixty Mexican dead, the audacity of this raid on U.S. soil made it impossible to claim victory for our side. There now was no question about it: we would have to go after Pancho Villa and shoot him against a wall. The U.S. soldier entrusted with this mission was to play an important part in the unfolding career of Westbrook Pegler.

This man was Brigadier General John Joseph Pershing, who was fifty-six years old at the time he took charge of the punitive expedition into Mexico. Pershing was the son of a Missouri railroad foreman, and he got into West Point at the age of twenty-two, which was old for an entering cadet. He was known at the academy more for good riding and fine military bearing than for prowess at the books, but graduated a cadet captain, and soon experienced active service killing Indians out west. Pershing saw action at Santiago in the Spanish-American war of 1898, and came out with a good reputation for steadiness under fire and the nickname "Black Jack." After hard years of obscurity, he made a late marriage, at forty-five, to the daughter of an influential legislator who held the chairmanship of the Senate Military Affairs Committee. In 1904 Theodore Roosevelt advanced Pershing over the heads of eight hundred officers and gave him the buck general's single star. Dos Passos said "Pershing had always been a silent grimfaced man." His look of iron control was deepened and his neatly trimmed hair grew grayer from the day in August 1915 when a fire in quarters at the San Francisco military base known as the Presidio killed Pershing's wife and three small daughters. After that there seemed to be nothing left in Black Jack Pershing's life but Army duty. One would suppose that this hardbitten Cromwellian figure would ride Villa down in short order. With that in mind, Pershing and his horse soldiers penetrated 250 miles of Chihuahua desert, but the hostile population refused all help and Villa remained at large. When his people harried the flanks of Pershing's army, they would hit and run in classic guerrilla style, and Villa had an additional striking force in a brigade of *renegados*—some of them Negro and white U.S. deserters—to whom no deed of cruelty was inconceivable. Fear of such brigands reinforced the people's natural hatred of the gringos in making Chihuahua a scene of failure for Black Jack Pershing and 10,000 men. They got out of there after eleven months of it, in February 1917. Villa remained in business for six years until the *pistoleros* of a rival faction shot him dead. But General Pershing and the Washington brass did not write off the American pursuit of Villa as wasted time. They told each other they had learned valuable lessons about tactics and supply, and they believed we had need of such lessons, for they felt sure that our armies would soon be fighting in Europe. And by this time Westbrook was over there ahead of them, as a London correspondent for the United Press.

Pegler had impressed Roy Howard as an able young man whose mobility was part of his value. Having put down no roots, with possessions filling one suitcase, Westbrook could leave for any destination at an hour's notice. Howard had not hesitated to transfer Pegler without warning from St. Louis to a vacancy in Dallas, and then in June 1916 to the London bureau. Westbrook started there on the nightside, working from nine P.M. to seven the next morning for a salary of $27 a week. Every night he would hammer out 3,000 words in the abbreviated style known as "cablese," and dispatch this budget of European news to the New York office before returning to a furnished room in Bloomsbury. This refined neighborhood was under colonization by a set of literary people that included Virginia Woolf, Lytton Strachey, and Katherine Mansfield. It is a curiosity of literature that Pegler should be living in the same district with Lytton Strachey, a writer to whom he had a certain resemblance. The inner motivation of the British highbrow and the American lowbrow was the same: irreverence toward figures of authority. At this time Strachey was preparing his *Eminent Victorians,* in which he laughed at bishops, headmasters, and generals, selecting the ludicrous and absurd detail with deadly accuracy. He would later write his book about the Queen who had given her name to an age of Western civilization, pointing up the absurdities of great Victoria, and laughing at her high-minded Prince Consort with his many schemes for general improvement. Pegler and Strachey saw the silk hats and sashes, the property swords, the medals, the rooster feathers and gold braid. And each writer promised himself, "Those people shan't put themselves above me."

In the afternoons and on his weekly night off Pegler got acquainted with London. He found at least one girl, later recording that he passed some time in "flaring his nostrils at a young American dancer in a music hall act." With that he leaves to our imaginations two Americans in wartime England. Westbrook was aware of "the terrible casualty lists of boy officers," some of them younger than he. Old men sat back and sent young men to die. A Welsh politician named David Lloyd George was Prime Minister, and Pegler knew that this Lloyd George was skirt-crazy, to put it in polite language. That interesting fact could not be included in the nightly load of cables. But those were exciting times, to say the least, and all the more so for Westbrook after our country entered the war on April 6, 1917, and the UP raised his pay to $45 a week and sent him to Queenstown to cover the operations of the U.S. Navy.

Shortly after the American declaration and Pegler's assignment to Queenstown, old Marshal Joffre arrived in Washington to tell Wilson and Black Jack Pershing that we must get fighting soldiers into France without delay. The sawed-off, sixty-five-year-old Joffre made a comical sight alongside the handsome ironfaced Pershing. "Papa" Joffre had a belly rounded out from years of hearty peasant feeding, and a moustache like something worn by a second banana on the Mack Sennett lot. He wore leather puttees resembling those of a rich lady's chauffeur, in which his legs seemed to connect with the *middle* of his feet, leaving as much heel projecting to the rear as toes in front, like the feet in funny pictures of Negroes drawn by the popular artist A. B. Frost. Though no fashion plate, this Joffre was a life taker, and he got what he came for. On May 18 Congress passed a Conscription Act which set up press gangs, called draft boards, to take men into armed forces without consulting their wishes in the matter. Wilson coined the phrase "selective service" for this business, which failed to conceal the fact that you couldn't have a big war if every Tom, Dick, and Harry were allowed to decide for himself whether or not he wanted to risk being killed. Of course Wilson and the other big shots would not go: they were too old, and if not that, too important, like Franklin D. Roosevelt, assistant secretary of the Navy, and Captain Ike Eisenhower, whose brain was needed for deskwork at home. Those were great days for generals, contractors, and manufacturers, and for workmen in the war industries, who for the first time began taking home good money from routine factory jobs.

Behind the industrial organization of the United States our conscript army started to form up, with good humor and unselfishness for the most part among its lower ranks. In advance of the drafted millions, General Pershing came to France in June 1917, and it is no disrespect to Pershing's memory to say that his soldierly bearing was worth a division of troops to Allied morale. This was providential, for we had some generals who were competent enough but fat, pie-faced, or distressingly ordinary in appearance. Our Secretary of War—in those pre-Orwellian days not called Secretary of Defense—was Newton Diehl Baker, a capable citizen but no more impressive on the hoof than the average Midwestern banker or businessman. Woodrow Wilson's face had distinction, but there was harshness in it unrelieved by human sympathy. Pershing's expression was not friendly—but where Wilson looked vindictive and cruel, the general gave an impression of being competent and stern. Those were the qualities we called for in the head of our armies overseas. And we were lucky to have Pershing, for he proved to be a fairly good man in a bad trade. A giant for strength of character compared to some we've had, Pershing made his contribution to grand strategy by refusing to put American units into the French and British armies out from under his command. He had been told about the suicidal infantry tactics of the British Field Marshal Haig, and the waste of 200,000 lives by General Nivelle of France, who had managed to sell his government the strategy of attacking points that could not be captured, and defending salients that had no military value. The British correspondent Philip Gibbs wrote of the leaders on both sides that "war had put them under a black spell." But he did not write this until the fighting stopped and the censorship ended. Then he wrote in a book called *Now It Can Be Told* about the immeasurable sufferings of the maimed and mangled and blinded and wrecked, all sacrificed to "the enormous impregnable stupidity of our High Command." Pegler's observations as an American journalist with his country at war made him agree with Gibbs and any other writers who criticized the brass; and his experiences with military authority influenced Pegler's writing throughout the rest of his career.

The first of Pegler's battles with the brass occurred shortly after he took up his duties in Queenstown, where the fortunes of war brought him into contact with William Sowden Sims, the American admiral. Sims was an able man, one of our authorities on gunnery, but like most of his sort, crazy about the British. In 1908 he made a speech at the Guildhall and threw his cap into the crowd while leading a cheer for the Lord Mayor and City of London. Pegler got into trouble with Sims on June 16, 1917, after filing a story that a U.S. destroyer had claimed the probable destruction of an enemy submarine. When he read this in the paper, Sims came running out of his office yelling that no such action had taken place. Westbrook displayed a copy of his story bearing the stamp of approval from the official censor. Admiral Sims reached for the flimsy, and Pegler held it away from him. Sims could hardly believe his ears when he heard Westbrook say, "You can see it but you are not going to touch it because that copy is going back to Roy Howard and we will see if he is going to let any admiral accuse the United Press of faking. Yes, you are accusing us of faking a story, and we'll see who wins." It is safe to assume that Sims resented having Pegler treat him like a police captain on the South Side of Chicago. And he behaved like one by ordering Westbrook placed under something called "open arrest." Although this meant nothing, the UP bosses thought it best to take Pegler off the naval beat and send him to cover the ground war in France. It was a professional gain for Westbrook, the prime assignment for American correspondents because of Pershing's arrival on the scene. Pegler never forgot William S. Sims. From time to time thereafter he would take a shot at the admiral, and he wrote in 1934 that "Sims had a bad rep from the China Station," adding that Navy Secretary Josephus Daniels had told President Wilson that Sims was "the greatest fool who ever represented this country in a foreign land."

Be that as it may, any experienced observer would have predicted that sooner or later Pegler would exasperate Pershing as he had irritated Sims. But Westbrook began his assignment to ground warfare like any other American correspondent looking for action to report. Soon enough he was under fire around Verdun and Rheims, and in Nancy when a heavy bombardment came in. When asked how he felt about such experiences, Pegler would reply, "Of course I was scared." Pegler considerably increased his danger of coming under fire of official disapproval when he joined the correspondents attached to U.S. First Division Headquarters at Gondrecourt. One of the officers with whom he had contact was Lieutenant Swing, adjutant of the 8th Field Artillery, who wrote to Pegler after the war that he "didn't know who was the biggest headache—you, the Marines, or Robert McCormick." In uniform as a major, Robert McCormick was still the publisher of the *Chicago Tribune*, which made him special, although he was mostly concerned with seeing action as a combat officer. Pegler had Roy Howard behind him, and sometimes may have given the impression that he thought he *was* Roy Howard. But his lapses of conduct were due to his youth and lack of experience in civilized adult life. Pegler's private memoirs describe how he tried to impress Miss

Hannah Steele, a beautiful Red Cross lady, in December 1917. Westbrook recalled that he "lured her into the dining room of the big hotel in Chaumont where one of us overestimated his capacity for Martini cocktails. About sundown I handed her into my Cadillac touring car which was regulation for correspondents, and ordered my driver to take us across a little river down in the valley. He did so and it became necessary for him and Hannah Steele to take out the back seat of the car and lay it flat on a field of snow where a sentry discovered us." After Miss Steele talked the guard out of arresting Pegler they managed to revive him with snow and get him back to his quarters.

It is unlikely that Pegler would have suffered expulsion if the provost marshal had learned of his lying down in a field to rest from the effects of too much gin. Only a few weeks before, this officer had commended Westbrook for a story about the burial of some American troops killed in action. It was a delayed dispatch which came out of American Field Headquarters on November 7, under the byline of J. W. Pegler, UP Staff Correspondent. He had written the piece in standard elegiac newspaper diction, conveying a sense of restrained patriotic sadness. A French general participated in the ceremonies, and students of Pegler will note that he treated this Frenchman with respect and not as a comic figure. Nor did he show any indignation that ordinary Americans should have come all this way to fill the graves. Pegler was writing under the urgencies of censorship. And this conventional death notice, so pleasing to the authorities, showed that Westbrook could function like his father when he had to, and turn out a facile piece of newspaper prose.

Not long afterward, Pegler got in to see Pershing. Just what Westbrook expected to learn is not clear, but his biographer Oliver Pilat says he asked Pershing for a statement about conditions at the front, and that the general growled, "Get out of here." Once again Pegler had approached high military authority as he would a Chicago police captain. There *is* a resemblance, but the military men have an advantage over reporters that police officials do not enjoy in the matter of censorship and granting permission to work. In spite of this rebuff, Pegler continued for a time to harbor a grudging admiration for Black Jack Pershing.

Even when his personal admiration had faded away, Pegler did not make the mistake of trying to deny that Pershing played his part well. After his rebuff in the office, Westbrook said he found the general "no more friendly than a gila," referring to a large and dangerous lizard of the American Southwest. But Pegler saw virtue in Black Jack's public image as "the most beautiful, handsome figure of an American soldier ever seen. There is nothing in the book that says he has to be a handshaker." Granting that, Pegler noticed things about Pershing which he couldn't include in the UP file—significant acts of pettiness like those of a prima donna unjustly abusing the stagehands. Westbrook never saw Pershing smile or show any courtesy to an ordinary soldier except when the newsreel cameras were grinding. And Pegler knew that a general's rank entitled him to the services of "dog robbers," enlisted men working as valets for high officers. The dog robbers saw to it that Pershing always turned out in immaculate breeches and tunic, with a mirror-like polish on his boots. This standard of neatness could not be attained by junior officers and enlisted men who sometimes had to sleep in mud. But the general refused to make allowance for conditions in the field, and Pegler saw a shameful scene when Black Jack came upon a company of the First Division eating noontime chow beside a road near Neufchateau. A few of the men had decorated their helmets with some kind of weedy wildflower that grew nearby. The sight enraged Pershing and he roared at the men, ordering the entire company including the young captain to stand at attention for fifteen minutes. Pegler noted that "the First Division had terrible losses, so many of these boys and their captain may have died in battle within the next year. If they died forgiving Pershing, they let me down."

Men like Black Jack Pershing have psychic radar for the detection of those who do not respect them. The thought of Pegler made the general uncomfortable and he sent word to Roy Howard in New York, complaining of Westbrook's "immaturity." Whether or not Pegler knew of this, he had complaints of his own and set them down in a letter to Howard, in which he criticized Pershing and his staff and the way they administered press censorship. Westbrook told Howard that the brass often used censorship to hide incompetence under the cover of national security. This was true. He also criticized the supply system, which the papers had ballyhooed as a miracle of distribution due to American know-how. Westbrook thought otherwise and raged about men living in leaky barns, wearing porous shoes, and suffering from inadequate supply of clothing and other necessities. All true. But Howard did not have to answer, for he never got the letter, which was intercepted and returned to Pershing's office where it caused an explosion of wrath. Pershing ordered his press officers to withdraw Pegler's accreditation as a correspondent. This made Pegler useless to the UP so far as land warfare was concerned, and he had already worn out his welcome with those whose approval he would need to report on the U.S. Navy. Pegler returned to London and worked for two months at the UP office. Then in June 1918 he enlisted in the Navy, where he drew office duty as a yeoman or clerk, and passed four uneventful months in the shore establishment at Liverpool. The Navy released Westbrook shortly after the armistice of November 11, 1918, and he returned to New York City. It was a time when most Americans looked into their country's future, not so much with hope as with the conviction that unlimited prosperity lay ahead. We had made the world safe for democracy, and here at home the sacred patterns and colors of Old Glory flapped in a favoring breeze from coast to coast.

4

AFTER THEY'VE SEEN PAREE

PEGLER HAD NOT DONE WELL OUT OF THE WAR. HIS SITUATION was less fortunate than that of other young Americans, who had come home as heroes with their prospects enhanced by the admiration and gratitude of their fellow countrymen. The heroes deserved their advantage and Pegler did not begrudge it to them. But he could not help observing that the material benefits of the war had come to dealers in military supplies who piled up fortunes in the greatest seller's market this country had ever seen. The wealth that followed the Civil War might be compared to the prosperity of 1919 and ten years that were to follow, except that the Civil War had inflicted heavy damage on the Southern states. As it entered the 1920s our country had no such material hurts, and the spiritual damage appeared to be only that which came from the presence of 204,000 wounded men, and the absence of 116,000 dead. For the most part, the wounded stayed out of sight, and dead men are easily forgotten except by families and friends. Although he had run risks during his months as a war correspondent, Pegler stood outside the brotherhood of combat veterans and the wounds he brought home from war were internal, the results of psychological injuries that he had received from Pershing and Sims. These hurts did not entitle him to a stripe on his sleeve.

Chapter 4

With high hopes for postwar careers, the able and talented young men among the survivors turned to the big cities. In their thousands they posed the question of the popular song whose writers asked, "How yah gonna keep 'em down on the farm, after they've seen Paree?" Pegler felt the impulse toward metropolitan competition, and told himself that New York City with its twelve daily papers would seem to offer plenty of choice for qualified newsmen, except that experienced journalists from all over the country were standing in line for every job as soon as it became available. Many had come into town to live on savings until something opened up; others kept in touch by way of letters from friends who had caught on and could send word of pending staff changes that might make room for newcomers in the New York press. For the city had an attraction for ambitious young people that it has not held in more recent days: at the dawn of the 1920s New York seemed to be filled with light. Here was a city of smiling aspect for young talented people, who felt a lessening of tension as they walked from their incoming trains through the clean metropolitan grandeur of the Pennsylvania and Grand Central Stations out into the air of a civilized town that seemed to have expected their arrival.

Arthur J. Pegler had been in New York since 1917, mostly on the afternoon *Journal* and morning *American*. He had ventured into moving picture publicity with dubious results, and was out of work at the time Westbrook got back, and unable to help him. Westbrook felt that his own best chance was with Roy Howard, and he went to the publisher with a definite proposition. Although he recorded that his appearance was "threadbare," Westbrook told Howard that he would be willing to take on the duties of sports editor in the New York office of the United Press for a salary of sixty dollars a week. Howard replied, "Bud, pull up a chair." And so, Pegler recorded, there he was, facing a rickety Remington. He also faced a disappointment that hit like a punch in the belly when Managing Editor Fred Ferguson told him it would not be possible to give Pegler the title of sports editor. At the end of the week, Westbrook's check was ten dollars light, a familiar stratagem in the hiring of newshands at that time. Pegler complained to Howard, "I'll do assignments, rewrites, and features, and sweep out the office, but my father's out of work and I've got to have that sixty." Howard ordered an adjustment, and Westbrook settled to the work the UP demanded of him. There was much unpaid overtime, and the grueling "night trick" often came up on Pegler's schedule. Then late one afternoon, as Westbrook was starting a night shift, an escape route opened when a telephone call came in from Floyd Gibbons, the famous war correspondent of the *Chicago Tribune,* who had known Pegler in London and France. Gibbons came right to the point: There was a good job available for Pegler at the *Tribune* Paris bureau if he would act immediately. Westbrook wrote in his notes that he would never forget how "Fred Ferguson put out his hand to wish me luck and then put on my green visor and crouched under that goose-neck lamp to put in my whole night trick after a whole day's work. But after all, I had no contract with UP, and they had reneged on the job of sports editor. So I went down into the subway under Brooklyn Bridge and in fifteen minutes was in Floyd's room at the Vanderbilt." Gibbons was living in style, and Westbrook found no change in this striking personage, with his battered face, gravelly voice, and black patch over the socket which had lost its eye in France. He greeted Pegler like the father of the prodigal in the parable and began opening bottles. But when the question of employment arose, Gibbons said, "About that job in Paris. This is a little embarrassing. They just gave it to somebody else." Westbrook got Ferguson on the telephone and told him what had happened The editor said, "All right, Peg. Come in in the morning and start over."

After that things went better at the office, as Pegler began to master his work and relish the aspect of the streets and alleys around Park Row. The National Prohibition Act took effect on January 17, 1920, and the neighborhood saloons turned into speakeasies where reporters, copyreaders, and rewrite men could eat and drink at any hour of the day or night. A favorite resort was Hallahan's where "they kept the windows boarded up as a stall for the tax people and the Prohibition department to make it look like abandoned premises, and they usually had a dozen redhots spitting like tomcats on a gas plate that burned up the oxygen. Then there was Perry's, where they made a wonderful Martini for fifteen cents, and when I say a Martini was wonderful you know it must have been good because there is the orneriest, meanest, no-dam-goodest mess of rancor ever concocted and it causes more fights and more people get their glasses broken and arrested and divorced on account of Martinis than for any other reason."

Most of the high grade professional newspaper work of New York centered in this Park Row neighborhood, where the *Tribune* occupied a rookery near the statue of Benjamin Franklin, patron of printers, that stood in an open space known as Printing House Square. The *Sun* had quarters in a graceful Federalist building two blocks west on Broadway, and the famous Pulitzer dailies, the *World* and the *Evening World,* gave their name to a golden-domed building that towered above City Hall Park. This building also housed the eastern headquarters of the United Press. And on its twelve floors were many cubbyhole offices of ambitious syndicate promoters hoping to build up stables of feature writers and artists, and lists of client newspapers buying their work. For that kind of business the World Building was an extremely good address. Coming and going one would see the executives and star reporters of the *World* newspapers and the *Sunday World Magazine,* along with such impressive performers as the syndicated cartoonist H. T. Webster, satirist of suburban bridge tables, "Life's Darkest Moment," and Mr. Caspar Milquetoast the Timid Soul. Webster worked in a sunny room high up under the dome and was a handsome, vital, friendly man, radiating an air of well-deserved success, who answered all who spoke to him whether or not he knew who they were. Heywood Broun had come to the *World* from the *Tribune,* and had started a daily column of his own opinions called "It Seems to Me." He usually wrote his copy uptown and sent it in by messenger, but would appear from time to time in World Building elevators on his way to confer with Managing Editor Herbert Bayard Swope. Already a well-known figure in New York, Broun was a large untidy man with courteous manners and a remarkable way of talking: although born in Brooklyn of educated parents, and a product of Harvard, he gave the impression with his slow, drawling speech that he came from Mississippi. Another mainstay of the *World* was Franklin P. Adams, who conducted a column called "The Conning Tower" in which he published all sorts of prose and verse sent in by "contribs" whose only payment was the satisfaction of being recognized by "F.P.A." The conductor of the column also included his own work, and a diary of what he had seen and read each week, written in the manner of Samuel Pepys. F.P.A. wielded influence in theatrical and publishing circles, for the column was respected by intelligent people all over the country. The arbiter in person was a small stoopshouldered homely man who made no impression on first sight. But those who knew him could testify that Adams was not only one of the brightest men in New York, but a generous helper of newcomers. He gave Westbrook a high mark to shoot at in the matter of brightening a newspaper page.

During these days Pegler displayed no interest in political ideas. How much then did he invest in the lay religion of patriotism and its worship of the Grand Old Flag? One would assume that it did not greatly move him and that his basic reaction to the concept of governmental authority as a sacred thing must have been the same as his reaction to Sims and Pershing—an indignant and embittered denial of anyone's right to push him around and try to take away his bread and butter. Let us bear in mind that Sims and Pershing struck at Pegler by means of complaints to his employers, like customers at the supermarket trying to make trouble when angered by a fresh kid punching checkout. The aura of power around high officials can sometimes have a tendency to soften the journalists dealing with them. It worked exactly the other way with Pegler. He was aware of the U.S. government's anti-Red campaign of 1920, during which the attorney general arrested more than 4,000 persons on a single night, charging them in vague terms with disloyalty to the country. Although Woodrow Wilson approved, the anti-Red campaign got out of hand, to put it mildly. Even Colonel (formerly Major) Robert McCormick denounced it. Some evidence of violent radical conspiracy might have been established by the Wall Street bomb explosion, but the authorities never found out who set off the wagonload of explosives that rocked the financial district like an earthquake on September 16, 1920. Pegler came on that scene of wreckage after the blast and made a note of it, recording that as he walked past the Sub-Treasury curb, "Three dead women lay in our path, their skirts pulled up to conceal their faces. A company of Infantry came stomping up Broad Street from Governor's Island. They had their bayonets on and they were bawling at the people and shoving with their gun butts. I recognized the patch of the First Infantry Division, the Big Red One. I had gone into the line in France with the first little units of the Big Red One. But now I hated their guts. Shoving Americans around that way! Bawling and threatening us. These weren't the soldiers I had known in France. They were replacements."

There were some American radicals who charged that the Wall Street bombing was a government job, undertaken to discredit all left wingers, in the subsequent style of the Reichstag Fire. While that seemed unlikely, at least a theoretical approval of the radical approach to politics could be found among many young writers in New York. And Pegler was not entirely out of place among these theorists; while he displayed no ideological coloring of any kind, he was most certainly "agin the government," as Mark Twain was, in his dislike of authority and his suspicions about any motive that might lead people to puff themselves up, seek power, and try to order other people around. But his main interest lay in promoting the welfare and advancement of Westbrook Pegler.

Lacking the prestige of a home paper in New York City, Pegler did what he could with UP clients across the country. Along these lines, in the summer of 1920, Westbrook used the syndicate release to promote himself both as an expert on yachting and an alert general newsman.

Chapter 4

The chance came during the races for America's Cup, when Pegler happened to draw a seat on the press boat next to an experienced yachting reporter, and peering over his colleague's shoulder, saw a complaint that yachts in competition for the Cup had become so over-refined in shape that they had to stay tied up on an ideal racing day because a twenty-five-knot breeze was too much for them. Pegler's version of this story went all over the country on the UP wire, and he stated the case so vigorously that the item made front page in most cities with the J. W. Pegler by-line on top. The germ of his future work may be discovered here, for this was a Pegler story in pure elemental form: something was wrong, and needed correction. At the next races for the Cup, in 1930, the yachts were of sturdier design.

Sir Thomas Lipton was the sportsman who financed the British challengers for the Cup, using part of the fortune he had acquired in selling tea. He asked Pegler to attend an afternoon party on board his yacht, which was no sailing vessel but a private ocean liner with a butler and footmen serving in the paneled lounge. Lipton's guest of honor was Lord Dewar, the Scotch whiskey man, and Pegler made Dewar's eyes bug out by escorting one of the most beautiful women on earth, the Swedish film star Anna Q. Nilsson. Westbrook could not afford a taxicab from Manhattan to Gravesend Bay, so they rode the subway down to the Bay 50th Street Station. Pegler did not attempt to describe Miss Nilsson's beauty, but recorded that his own appearance furnished an effective foil for the actress, since he was "skinny as a pencil, with freckles and buck teeth." He owed the invitation to his friend Gene Fowler, a star feature man for the Hearstpapers and later the biographer of John Barrymore and James J. Walker.

In that summer came the most important development so far in Pegler's personal life. Its beginning lay in a bizarre event, the murder of a man named James Browne Elwell, who was one of those metropolitan characters who cannot be precisely defined other than as a man about town. Elwell was in his fifties and vain of his appearance, which he thought to make youthful by wearing false teeth and a wig. The teeth were out and the wig off when police found Elwell shot to death in the study of his home on a street in the upper West Side, a circumstance establishing the theory, since there were no signs of forced entry, that he must have known the person who killed him. The murdered man had been an expert at the bridge table, often playing for high stakes against notable sports and gamblers of the town. He also knew many show girls, actresses, and high-class prostitutes. Although the police never caught Elwell's killer, the story was fascinating and

King Features Syndicate

Pegler in school sweater poses beside friend's car in 1911

William Randolph Hearst, 1916

Culver Pictures, Inc.

Culver Pictures, In

Roy W. Howard, Pegler's publisher and friend

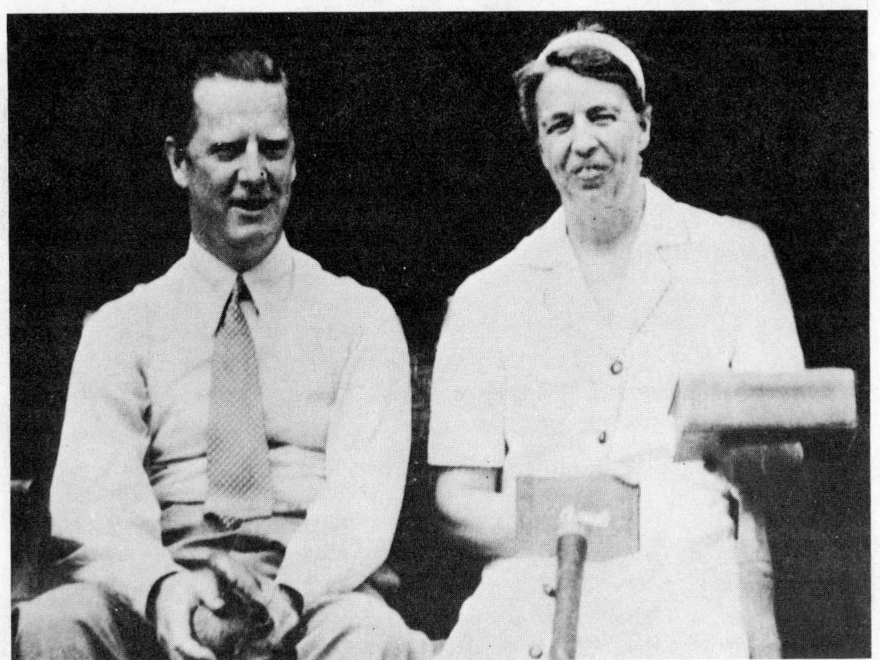

Herbert Hoover Presidential Library

Eleanor Roosevelt and friend at a 1938 picnic

At the poker table, left to right, James Reynolds, Heywood Broun, Connie Broun, Quentin Reynolds. Two unidentified players sit with their backs to the camera

Culver Pictures, Inc.

A well-tailored Pegler at the height of his career with Scripps-Howard in 1939

King Features Syndica

Heywood Broun differs with Inspector Harry Lobdell at the *Brooklyn Eagle* strike

Culver Pictures, Inc.

King Features Syndicate

Pegler in a rare public appearance, 1940

Herbert Hoover Presidential Library

With the president of Knox College, where Pegler was awarded a Doctor of Laws in 1943

Herbert Hoover Presidential Library

In 1948, Peg had yet to kick his smoking habit

The Peglers with Clark Gable at Casa Cholla

Herbert Hoover Presidential Library

King Features Syndicate

Pegler settles in for a hot afternoon's work at Casa Cholla

King Features Syndicate

A relaxed moment

Herbert Hoover Presidential Library

In his library at Casa Cholla

Herbert Hoover Presidential Libra

Peg and Julie lunch with the Banshees after the Reynolds trial

Herbert Hoover Presidential Library

Arthur James Pegler, Peg's father, at the famous steam-heated typewriter

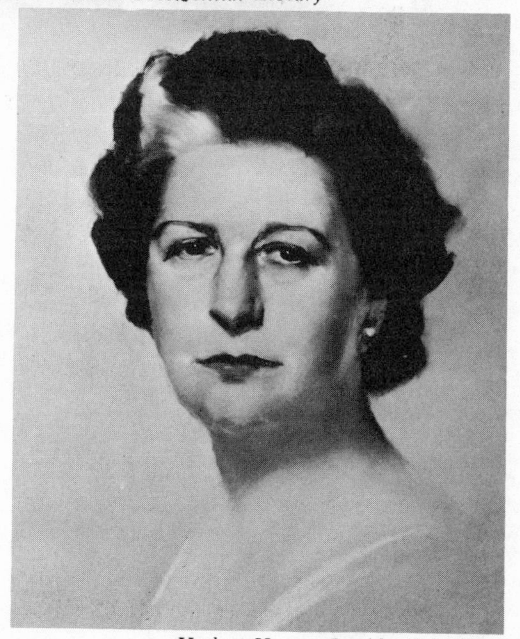

Julia Harpman Pegler

Herbert Hoover Presidential Library

King Features Syndicate

This portrait headed Pegler's column during his last years with Hearst

for some time the papers gave it space. Pegler drew the assignment in his role of general feature man and went up to Elwell's house early on the morning of June 11. Among the reporters on the sidewalk waiting for detectives and high police officials to emerge from the "murder scene," he saw a good-looking girl with sparkling brown eyes and an air of knowing what she was about. This was Julia Harpman, who represented the tabloid *New York Daily News.** The available evidence seems to show that Pegler fell in love on the spot. At least, he was sufficiently impressed to introduce himself and make the start of a comradely relationship. Julia was twenty-four, an educated girl of gentle background from Memphis, where her father and uncle, Sigmund and Solomon Harpman, were tobacco brokers and her mother society editor of the *Commercial Appeal.*

In February 1921 Julia, or Julie as she was generally called, went to the hospital after a taxicab accident, and Westbrook was assiduous in sending flowers, telephoning, and visiting. Not long after Julie's recovery, Pegler invited his father to meet the young lady at lunch. It seems that there was awkwardness here: Westbrook got the impression that his father had stopped for cocktails before joining them. Arthur recalled that perhaps he "chinned a bit too cheerily when he met Miss Julia Harpman." He thought he saw a look of anxiety on his son's face. We can understand that the nervousness arose from the fact that these were the two most important people in the world for Westbrook. Arthur approved of Julie, but he had unspoken reservations about the paper she worked for. His private feeling was that "the *News* was the most awful spectacle ever erupted by a printing press." Even though Arthur kept this opinion to himself, his son thought the lunch party a near disaster. Westbrook's agonizing over the effect his father might make on Julie indicated that he was now seriously in love.

In 1921 Westbrook began sending out a daily sports summary under his by-line to all clients of a UP subsidiary called United News, a feature syndicate which served morning papers. His biographer Oliver Pilat has called 1921 "the greatest year in Pegler's life" because of his success with this compilation of sports news for morning papers in the important cities, and it was without doubt the year in which Pegler emerged from the ranks of routine deskmen and journalistic second stringers.

---

*Captain Joseph Medill Patterson had started the *Daily News* on June 26, 1919. A cousin of Colonel McCormick, the Captain belonged to the family that controlled the *Chicago Tribune.* By 1974 the *News* had outlived all the general dailies in New York except the *Times* and *Post.*

Chapter 4

The appearance of the Pegler by-line on a regular basis had the power of repetition, day after day, plus the extra authority of appearing in papers that came out in the morning. It may not be possible to explain why, but the morning newspapers, on the whole, had more dignity and authority than those which appeared in the afternoon. It was also to be noticed that morning papers issued a preliminary or "bulldog" edition around ten or eleven P.M., dated the following day. The bulldog seemed to wrap everything up and give readers an odd but exhilarating sense of looking into the future; city people who worked or stayed up late were especially fond of these early editions, and liked to go out and buy them on the safe night streets of the time, or pick them up after the theater to read while eating late suppers in hotel grill rooms, or in the spotless Childs and Thompson lunch rooms where excellent omelettes, waffles, or chili con carne could be enjoyed on order.

As he filed his daily sports roundup for these discriminating readers, Westbrook remembered how he had promoted his Bud Pegler by-line from Chicago when he was little more than a glorified office boy. Now in New York he was acting on one of the basic tenets of the day, "It pays to advertise." And he was following the ancillary law of advertising which is that promotion of the brand name is a waste of time unless the product is something that people want to buy. And like an alert merchandising manager Westbrook put an extra element into his product from time to time; for example he had established by 1922 an additional feature, a bonus of brief paragraphs which he called "Six Short Pegs from Pegler." The managers of United News soon got a letter praising the "Pegs" from one of their most important clients, Clark Howell of the *Atlanta Constitution*, the leading Southern newspaper. The publisher said his sports editor had told him this material was too good to be used merely as filler. And Howell went on to say that "in our estimation, there is no more attractive sports writer in America—possibly excepting my good friend Grantland Rice—than Pegler." This testimonial from a paying customer showed that Westbrook was riding high so far as his work was concerned. And in Pegler's private life all was going well, for Julie accepted his proposal of marriage, and the wedding took place on August 29, 1922, at the Church of the Blessed Sacrament a few blocks from the Elwell house where they had met two years before.

Westbrook's theory of marriage held that if it did not transform the male partner, at least the experience of living in wedlock made him a better man. He recorded that he felt he had been "wandering in a rough and lonely wilderness," until with marriage he "blundered into a new world of elegance and grace." In this happy frame of mind he began the ten years' passage in his professional life which was to take him into the first rank of those few newspaper writers who could claim to be molders of opinion. He had already become an accepted newspaper entertainer, and his writing was the sort that writers applaud. What the professionals admired in his work was its simplicity and directness: Pegler making a point seemed to go in directly over the horns, as Ernest Hemingway advised in the killing of a bull. Westbrook liked verbs and nouns, and always inspected his copy to hunt down stray adjectives and adverbs. And he had in his service an ear for speech that touched the inner ear of the reader with the rhythms of ordinary conversation. This he could do with taste and skill like that of Ring Lardner and George Ade; in 1923 a trade magazine, *The Writer's Monthly,* commented in a survey of the literary scene that Pegler was "doing fine work" and had become a first-rate humorist. At about the same time, according to Pilat, Edna St. Vincent Millay was lecturing in Hutchinson, Kansas, and happened to read Pegler for the first time in a local paper. The poetess found Westbrook's writing such a delight that she telephoned the editor and said, "That man Pegler should be in New York." The editor thanked Miss Millay for her interest and explained that Westbrook had already set up shop in New York, reaching the provinces by syndication.

The year 1924, in which Pegler attracted Edna Millay's favorable attention, appeared to be an advantageous time to engage in newspaper work. Indeed, the papers of this country had taken center stage so far as public acceptance was concerned; commercial radio broadcasting, which had started on KDKA-Pittsburgh in 1920, could scarcely be called an industry and nobody harbored any notion that such a thing as television would ever supplant the printed word. Yet the men in accounting departments were becoming aware of faint but noticeable signs that something bad might happen to newspapers. It was a matter of production expenses: the price of manufacture kept creeping upward, like a "silent" cancer in a man who thinks himself quite healthy. In 1915, there had been 2,250 daily papers and 12,500 weeklies for a total of 14,750 publications in business. But after the war in 1920 a census of the trade counted 2,435 papers gone forever. Some of the vanished papers may have had little importance, but Westbrook and his friends witnessed a merger in New York City in 1924 that left one morning paper in place of two when Frank A. Munsey sold the famous *New York Herald* to the *Tribune.* Some of those who felt a chill of apprehension at this deal took heart from the fact the respected

Reid publishing family would be in control of the new *Herald Tribune*. But any way you looked at it, there was one less large general paper in New York.

Westbrook met with further encouragement in 1924 when he ventured into popular fiction. On October 20 the weekly magazine *Liberty* sent his agent a $400 check for "The Palooka," a story about prizefighting, and when it appeared in January 1925, "The Palooka" read like the work of an experienced hand. It should be noted that a palooka was a second- or third-rate pugilist, a predictable loser that managers called on to fatten the records of fighters heading for the top. Pegler's palooka is Steve Roskosh, who has stopped too many punches and ought to retire for his own good, but is still training for a fight by running around the "reservoy." Steve quarrels with his girl Olga and sends her away: "Go on, then; lam outa here. Be absent." He has become fascinated by a bar hostess named Bianca, whom he follows "like a small boy wandering after a marching band." Weakened making the weight, Steve suffers a brutal ordeal in the ring, although he slows his Irish opponent with a punch to the chin that has him "stepping with the uncertain stride of a performing bear walking on a ball." At the end, a fight critic remarks, "When they fall backward, you can reach for the old overcoat, because then you can be sure they're out."

Pegler wrote no more short stories. United News was now paying him $125 a week, and as he did with all employers, Westbrook gave good measure in return. It may be that he felt he could not find the extra time and energy to write magazine fiction. And he knew he had achieved with newspaper copy a success that deserved careful handling: he was beginning to hear of other possible employers, among them the *Chicago Tribune*. The *Trib* had its own feature syndicate, and in the early fall of 1925, Robert McCormick told his people to get Pegler on the team. "Find out what he wants," said the Colonel. Pegler asked for twice his present salary, which would bring him to $250 a week. McCormick said to put it through and on the first of November 1925, *Editor and Publisher* carried an advertisement stating that Westbrook Pegler, formerly of the United News, was now eastern sports editor of the *Chicago Tribune*, whose syndicate would distribute his weekly letter, "The Sporting Goods." The advertisement also spoke of his personal brand of humor and his "sardonic touch." And so at the age of thirty-one Pegler was a star. But no matter how much they make, the stars of journalism are people who live by their wits. This is not a soothing and restful method of meeting life's demands.

It was obvious that Julie had smoothed the edges of Westbrook's personality, and friends observed that he was becoming socially assured. Some time later, Westbrook said that 1924 was the year in which he lost his awe of exclusive clubs, realizing that such things had little importance. In 1925 he joined the Port Chester Country Club and found it convenient and agreeable. Julie had continued her newspaper work, but in 1926 she decided to devote herself exclusively to being a wife. The assignment with which Julie ended her career was to cover the achievement of another woman, and Julie watched from a boat while Gertrude Ederle swam from Cap Gris Nez to Dover in 14 hours 39 minutes. Then Julie wrote her last story. If she had regrets about leaving her job, Pegler never heard them. Soon after the Ederle trip, Julie and Westbrook moved to Larchmont, a suburb on Long Island Sound, where they rented a large comfortable house within easy distance of the Port Chester Club.

In the following year, Pegler's old friend Roy Howard established a New York base for his newspaper chain by taking over Frank Munsey's *Evening Telegram* for $4,000,000. Howard was a small man of commanding presence who had his shirts made up in solid shades of red, green, and orange, with neckties cut from the same goods. Everything he put on in the morning was made to order, and wherever it was possible he displayed the monogram RWH for Roy Wilson Howard. Leaving his syndicate and news workers to dingy quarters downtown, Howard rented space for his corporate offices in the handsome new Grand Central Tower overlooking Park Avenue. He decorated his personal suite in Chinese red, a color he picked up from the *Chinoiserie* of that building's elevators. When the decorating was done, Howard summoned his shirtmakers, who matched this red in madras and silk for the publisher's haberdashery. Nobody who knew Howard took him for a fool because of his affectations—he was one of the country's important men. He always spoke well of Pegler, pointing out that "Bud" got his start with Scripps-Howard and the United Press.

Like all who read Pegler, Howard noted that the weekly roundup had a new name in March 1927 when "The Sporting Goods" gave way to "The Say-So of Holleran Yell." Thus Pegler presented himself as a professional scold in admitting that he hollered and yelled, from which one might infer that nothing came of it. In September of that year the *Tribune* syndicate house organ said that Westbrook was "a crusty cuss, and very comical." Pegler now decided to call his weekly general article "Speaking Out on Sports." If you spoke out, while you might be crusty and comical, you addressed the reader whether or not all persons were pleased when you made your opinions heard. Editors usually shortened the title to "Speaking Out." It was the first thing many people read when they picked up the paper. Westbrook's use of language seemed to appeal to poets so strongly that they would try to help him professionally, and in addition to Edna Millay, Carl Sandburg found the stuff so much to his liking that in April 1929 he wrote to Pegler: "I have told my publisher, Alfred Harcourt, that you may go big in the literary racket some day, having a keen eye, and wide curves."

In 1928 the *Tribune* syndicate obtained a New York outlet for Pegler in the *Morning Telegraph,* a sporting sheet which should not be confused with Howard's *Telegram.* The main purpose of the *Telegraph* was to supply racing information, and the paper is remembered today for ten or twelve daily square yards of fine print that recorded every furlong down to the most obvious swindles of the betting public on the remotest tracks, where jockeys made their business arrangements under tumbledown grandstands before saddling mounts of doubtful pedigree. It all appeared in the *Telegraph* by means of cabalistic abbreviations printed in blindingly tiny type checked by mole-like proofreaders in a tottering structure on Eight Avenue, where the city room furniture was so stained and battered that it made even the editorial chambers of the *Chicago American* look like the National Institute of Arts and Letters. One might have expected Pegler to appear as a feature in the *Tribune's* New York associate, the *Daily News.* And in ordinary circumstances this successful tabloid would have carried Pegler along with such popular *Tribune* comic strips as "Andy Gump," "Little Orphan Annie" and "Gasoline Alley." However, the *News* already had the services of Paul Gallico, who edited the sports section and supplied a penetrating and humorous "main column" of his own writing. The managers of the *News* passed up Pegler because they did not want two such commanding virtuosi in one department. Rather than keep Pegler out of New York, they gave permission for the *Telegraph* sale. The gesture cost little, for the racing paper enjoyed only a modest circulation at 25 cents a copy, while the *News* had already passed the million mark.

Pegler's editors at the *Tribune* syndicate occasionally sent him on a general assignment, in the same way that Brisbane would take Damon Runyon off the sport beat for an important political or courtroom story. In June 1928 Pegler went to Kansas City for the Republican national convention, and one of his dispatches has historical significance because it shows tension between Pegler's approach to his material and the law of journalism, unquestioned at the time, that there was something funny about Negroes. Pegler led off by saying

"It has been alleged that the Negro Republican statesmen of the South are permitted to vote only once in four years, on the floor of the national conventions, and the reason for this precaution on the part of the Caucasian Democrats of the South now begins to dawn on the outsiders." The convention chairman, dreaming about seidels of bootleg beer, would wake up with a start and begin flailing with his "bungstarter." Then a storm of balloting would rise, for "the brethren are full of a four years' accumulation of pent-up votes, whether there is something to vote about or not. . . . It appears that when the Southern Negro brethren get started voting they carry the thing to excess and unless restrained one way or another are liable to overvote themselves. I understand this is a weakness of Caucasian voters in certain localities, notably in some regions of Chicago and New York City, but it is a practice that cannot be too strongly condemned. . . . Down yonder, Republicans are great natural voters so that when you get really steaming on a proposition they are not only remarkable sprint voters, but great endurance voters as well. You might sum them up as splendid all around, free style voters who would be a valuable asset to any candidate if the opposition didn't draw the color line." In this dispatch Westbrook was feeling his way toward a proposal that Negro Republicans should be excluded from the convention for their own good, and the piece failed because Pegler did not know what ground he stood on. He struck more closely to the center of his personal right note, in the same year, with his first important journalistic crusade, in which he exposed a number of Florida gambling clubs and caused indignation among the thieves, loafers, and politicians of that state. But in 1929 Westbrook was still at his best on sports, as he showed by his remark that fur-clad Yale football partisans "rose as one raccoon." And in the early fall of 1929 Pegler wrote a series of articles that revealed much about the workings of his mind, after visiting the football players of the United States Military Academy at West Point on the Hudson.

At that time people regarded the Army as an honorable career, and no one thought its officers would ever do any harm except to Mexicans and Germans, who had it coming. In this climate of opinion football stars at the Military Academy enjoyed as much admiration as any college athletes in the country. Their arch-rival was the Naval Academy, but they also played against Yale, Princeton, Harvard, Stanford, and other leading universities of the time. There was trouble between the Naval and Military Academies about the recruiting of athletes at West Point, and Pegler decided to look into it. He had special interest in two Army stars named Mortimer E. Sprague and John Murrell, who played college football before coming to the academy; so had the famous running back with the rhythmical name of Christian Keener Cagle. Sparing of praise when he first arrived at the Point, Pegler wrote that the officers in charge "make much of their hard regime but the one at Sing Sing just a few miles down the Hudson is harder and the warden doesn't call his boys supermen." But he observed that Sprague looked like Jess Willard, the gigantic boxer who had defeated Jack Johnson, and "his hands could palm a German pancake." The West Point press officers billeted Pegler in a room with the football captain and two other cadets. When the lights went out on the first night, the young men politely continued talking until Pegler said, "If you think you're doing me a favor you can drop off any time. After a day of dashing about with your dashing officers, I can sleep on the spur of the moment." In a few minutes "the big football captain lay still as a dead man on the upper shelf." Pegler found that the academy had started football "back in the days of hour glass uniforms and buttons as big as new potatoes." He discovered that "proselyted or not, 35 percent of the West Point cadet corps has had education in a variety of colleges, ranging from the big state universities down to little tin-roofed institutions far off the branch lines, whose football teams have to accept dates with the famous teams and take grotesque lickings in order to pick up gate receipts to buy next year's equipment." Westbrook observed that nobody tried to draw Cagle into the horseplay of the mess hall, and wrote that "they would call him a loner in the major leagues." Pegler made no attempt to find out what the cadets were supposed to be learning in their classrooms. The thing that struck him most forcibly was the hearty, mindless, masculine atmosphere of barracks and dining halls. He was not insensitive to courteous treatment, and warned himself against developing a prejudice in favor of the place, writing that "it was easy to become infatuated with a school, a club, even a prizefighter when the camp is thrown open to you and people are lavishly civil for a purpose, whatever the purpose." Readers seeking to analyze what Pegler had told them in his West Point series would conclude that he found the cadets a set of brainless young men who lived by idiotic customs and were not by any means the best human material to be found in this country. But as far as football was concerned, Westbrook held that the academy had as much right to recruit athletes as any other institution.

According to government statistics, the national income for 1929 was eighty-seven billion dollars. Pegler's share at the *Tribune* was twenty-five thousand or twice his starting salary, which as we know was twice what Roy Howard had been paying him. The federal tax on earned income still lay within rational bounds, and the Peglers felt justified in moving from Larchmont to Pound Ridge in a part of Westchester County near the Connecticut line where worked-out farmlands were adaptable for small estates. Julie and Westbrook bought twenty-five acres of scrub woods and rocky hillsides overlooking a private lake, near which they built a stone house of Bavarian style.

In that year it was a common occurrence for prosperous Americans to make the same move as the Peglers, but many of these people soon had to give up the new houses and go to earth in railroad flats and furnished rooms. For 1929 marked the end of a boom in manufacturing and general business which had started after the war when prices of securities began their steep climb on the New York Exchange. Men at the universities were talking about an infinitely expanding universe; the same idea appeared to motivate the securities market. And instead of advising caution, bankers and brokers loaned money with which customers made further purchases of stock, the shares returning a profit for all concerned when sold at the rising prices. What happened to the last purchaser when the price stopped going up? Nobody paused to consider what the answer to that question might be. It was not an interesting question to speculators who had no intention of buying shares to finance industry and collect dividends, and were using stock certificates as nothing more than counters in a gambling game. Some of the speculators obtained gratifying results, but failed to recognize that their profits lay in pieces of paper rather than money in the bank. And on October 24 in 1929 came Black Thursday, when traders lost their nerve and sold more than twelve million shares at falling prices. They dumped prime stocks such as United States Steel, General Electric, and Radio Corporation of America along with less desirable issues before the bell hammered to end the riot on the floor. President Hoover led the economists and bankers who announced that the country was fundamentally sound and a Wall Street panic was no cause for general alarm. But by the end of October it had become obvious that a huge amount in profits no longer existed even on paper, and public confidence went under in a wave of terrifying anxiety that swept across the country. Some asked what had happened to the old American tenets of hard work, thrift, and a conservative return on sound investments. Apparently the First World War had nullified these doctrines. And so a numbing sense of guilt and a fear of retribution were added to the anxiety about the present and doubt as to the future that ran through the country like an epidemic of disease, when the extent of the stock market failure came to be fully recognized in the winter of 1929. People began telling each other that the time for retrenchment had come, that a national business depression was a certainty, and that things would be a great deal worse before they got better.

Historians from that day to this have asked why a mood of defeat seized the American people, when the country held more material assets than at any time in its past. A parallel line of inquiry has tried to determine why losses incurred by a small number of speculators should have so profound an effect on that majority of citizens who never owned a share of stock. Why should average citizens suffer because the prices of shares collapsed? It is not possible to give a simple answer. There is mystery in economics, and magic in the idea of money and its use that cannot be explained. But looking outward from the United States, our rulers saw world trade off balance, and the experts said this would have an effect on business in the United States, and it would be a very bad effect. And when the artificial values of the boom market in stocks vanished into air, people began to hide their real money. The financier Bernard Baruch had done it in 1928. He said, "I like to have cash on hand, especially in bad times." And with the real money hidden away, manufacturers decided they couldn't sell the full lines they'd planned for; they fired workers, and these wageless men no longer had money to buy products, even if anyone manufactured them. Like a snake with a broken spine, the economy bit itself, and sank the venom of inactivity into its own veins. People said there was one man who could save us, and he was the Republican President, Herbert Clark Hoover. There was magic in the presidency like the juju of a primitive tribe; it came in part from the gods Washington and Lincoln, and in part from tribal virtues having no precise definition. We turned in our fear and misery to the high priest and head magician, a man called Hoover who also bore the mystical title Presnenuninestates. He could invoke both material and spiritual powers to put things right.

No evidence has been found that Pegler attacked this doctrine of the omnipotent American president in 1929, but he could not have failed to be aware of it, since the idea was universally held, and promulgated without question by talkative men in speakeasies, garages, and American Legion halls. Herbert Hoover accepted like a natural law the notion that he as President could save the country's economy. He was a decent man, and his aides said he was a good boss to work for. Hoover had been Secretary of Commerce during eight prosperous years before his election to the Presidency in 1928; before that, he had earned the world's respect as administrator of relief to the starving populations of Europe after the First World War. In his beginnings, he had made a fortune as an international mining consultant and engineer. Here was a man, one would have thought, with every needed qualification to lead the country out of the financial wreckage into another period of prosperity. But Herbert Hoover confronted a task beyond the power of one man. For, in spite of the widely advertised prosperity of the 1920s, the figures of the Brookings Institution showed that in 1929 60 percent of American families had incomes of less than $2,000 a year, and 42 percent less than $1,500, while at the bottom of society one fifth of all families in this country existed on less than $1,000 a year. The statisticians concluded that at 1929 prices a yearly family income of at least $2,000 was needed for the basic necessities of life. Therefore one had to infer that 60 percent of American families in that year of peak prosperity were underneath the floor of adequate living. When we reached the end of 1931 hope was dead for millions of people, and it was painfully absent from the eyes of men who came to the door and asked for any kind of work. By early 1932 the fortunate ones who still drew wages were to read that 10,000,000 of their fellow Americans had no jobs. At this rate there would be 11,000,000 out of employment by 1933. This meant that more than one out of every four able workers would have no jobs, and no pay. Using the accepted figure for dependents, 28,000,000 people would have to get along without regular income. The suffering was indescribable, and some feared that a revolution would start among the ragged people turned out of doors by landlords in the cities, and living in the shantytowns called Hoovervilles. That was what Herbert Hoover got for his pains—his one permanent contribution to American language and history as he toiled on in his tireless and conscientious manner.

So far as Pegler was concerned, Hoover could have spared himself his extra efforts. Westbrook's earning power was as much a part of him as his power over words, a gift which continued to delight other writers to such an extent that they would approach their publishers in his behalf. An example of these helpful colleagues was George Pattullo, a regular contributor to the *Saturday Evening Post,* who advised Editor George Horace Lorimer to get some of Pegler's writing into the magazine without delay. Lorimer replied that he considered Pegler to be "a thousand word man" and he made it a rule that *Post* articles should run to at least 2,500 words. Although Lorimer paid good money, Pegler was one of those who could get along without his patronage. Maybe he *was* only a thousand word man, but his essays pleased readers by the million, and in the years of Pattullo's recommendation,

Chapter 4

Pegler drew praise from the Great Cham of popular literature, Professor William Lyon Phelps. By general agreement the most popular teacher at New Haven, "Billy" Phelps had imparted to generations of Yalemen the news that there had been a man called Tennyson, and another man called Browning, and that this Tennyson and this Browning had written poems, and that many of these poems were worth reading and even worth remembering. In addition to the missionary work of his course in "T and B," Phelps reviewed books for a national syndicate, and each year made a fortune for some author and publisher by announcing the best book of the past twelve months. Billy Phelps liked everything about Pegler's newspaper pieces except for the half-column cut which showed an apparently solemn and self-conscious author. The professor wrote a rhyming fan letter: "I like your 'Speaking Out on Sports.' Always read it reg'lar. But are you feeling out of sorts? Is that your real face, Pegler?"

In 1932 Pegler watched with interest while the Democrats passed over Alfred E. Smith as presidential candidate and nominated Franklin D. Roosevelt, the governor of New York. Pegler admired Roosevelt, whom he called a champion because of the way he had compensated for a crippling attack of infantile paralysis. Roosevelt broke with tradition by coming to the convention hall to make the acceptance speech promising a New Deal for everybody. Hoover had earned the world's praise and gratitude for relieving Europeans by means of public funds, but had not been able to accept the conclusion that public money had to give direct relief to destitute Americans. Hoover had kept on saying that each neighborhood should care for its own in the good old American way—a way that existed only in Hoover's private vision of the great country that had afforded him such wonderful opportunities when he started out in life, a poor boy from an Iowa farm. In fact the Hoover fortune came from the development—polite term for exploitation—of mineral deposits throughout the world. And strangely enough, Hoover *did* make federal funds available to cure the depression, but it was through a Reconstruction Finance Corporation that poured money in at the top of the economy by helping manufacturers who could not borrow at the banks. Presumably the bankers knew what they were doing when they refused to make dubious loans; nevertheless, the RFC bestowed millions of taxpayers' dollars on distressed businessmen, and Hoover figured the benefit would trickle down to the ragged men on the soup lines, as indeed some of it eventually did. But by June 1932 Hoover was politically doomed, and had made it inevitable that he would not win reelection through his insensitive handling of a protest march on Washington by an army of jobless war veterans that called itself the Bonus Expeditionary Force.

Twenty-five thousand strong, these men maintained military discipline under the watchwords "No Panhandling—No Booze—No Radical Talk." They had organized to petition for advance payments of bonus money that would fall due in 1945 according to the Adjusted Compensation Act of 1924. This measure had been enacted to make up for their absence from high paying war production jobs; in 1925 each soldier and sailor had received an insurance policy that could be cashed for one thousand dollars twenty years later. When panic and depression came, the veterans fell into desperate need of cash and began to ask Congress for immediate payment on these bonus policies to ease the pinch of destitution. When the administration opposed payments and Congress refused to act, the ex-service men grew resentful. They got no satisfaction at the offices of their congressmen, and Hoover refused to see their leaders. There was something in the Constitution about rights of petition, but this BEF was nothing but a bunch of bums, and Hoover was the Presnenuninestates. On July 17 Congress met to adjourn. On July 22 the government ordered a detachment of BEF men out of abandoned buildings near the Capitol where they had camped. But they did not go. On July 28 police moved in and killed two veterans when fighting broke out. Hoover then called for the Regular Army. Advisors had begged the President not to make the political error of sending American troops against American veterans, but he refused to listen, and treated us to a rare spectacle put on by Pegler's old enemies, the military brass. At the head of the troops rode General Douglas MacArthur, Major George Patton, and Major Ike Eisenhower, all three booted and spurred. Unfortunately, they *looked* wrong: after the First World War, our people had tried to imitate the British officers' field uniform, derived from English riding clothes, but couldn't get the hang of it and the results were awful. The little pointed lapels on the U.S. jackets spoiled the whole effect, and in the news photographs of of MacArthur and Ike going into battle, even the pants looked wrong—like Dutchmen's breeches. In addition, MacArthur had ribbons up to his left shoulder like a Peruvian admiral. Ike wore no ribbons, for during the war he had remained away from the field at discretion. The third commander, Patton, was a half-crazy, ugly customer with a well-earned reputation for boldness under fire, although the luster of his Distinguished Service Medal was not enhanced by the fact that he had pulled wires to get it, as he admitted in his memoirs. Under this leadership Regulars drove veterans from their Hooverville on the Anacostia Flats, pinking the shabby men with bayonets, knocking them down with gun butts, and blinding them with tear gas. One good thing happened when a brick flew from somewhere and knocked Major Patton into the mud.

As the waves of indignation over the treatment of the bonus men subsided in August 1932, Pegler heard from Arthur Brisbane, who was now at the summit of power in the Hearst organization. Brisbane sent a letter from the Ritz Tower in New York, an apartment hotel he had promoted with W. R. Hearst, and suggested that Pegler pay a visit to the ranch, where the Chief would like to have a little talk with him. The ranch was Hearst's luxurious California estate at San Simeon, where he lived with the beautiful actress Marion Davies, entertained movie stars, and called in his executives when he had orders for them. Pegler knew that Brisbane's letter amounted to an offer of a job at more than the *Tribune* syndicate was paying him, but replied in polite language that he was not interested in visiting the ranch and talking to the Chief. The obsequious deference paid to Old Man Hearst set Westbrook's teeth on edge; and he was proud to be among the men and women in the newspaper trade who got along quite well without reference to Hearst or any of his holdings. The truth was that with some exceptions—such as Damon Runyon—few really first-class newspaper talents worked for Hearst. Pegler would not have described himself as a starry-eyed idealist; but into the ethical swamps of the Hearst papers he did not have to descend.

At that time the existence of the Scripps-Howard chain with its United Press wire service and United Feature Syndicate gave encouragement to all who thought it should be possible to maintain a great organization of civilized American newspapers. As far back as 1921, Robert P. Scripps had been acting on his father's principle of putting one-third of the profits into expansion. In recent years the company had operated large and successful papers in Cleveland, Cincinnati, and Detroit, along with nine lesser ones in the West. By founding or buying papers, Roy Howard had put twenty more dailies on his list, now headed by the *New York Telegram*, in Baltimore, Indianapolis, Pittsburgh, Denver, Washington, Buffalo, and other large cities. In 1931 he took over the *New York World* when the Pulitzer family found it impossible to continue the paper. The employees had hopes of raising enough money to keep the *World* going, and they might have succeeded with a little more time, but the surrogate in bankruptcy liked the looks of five million dollars cash that Roy Howard proffered, and brought down his gavel like the crack of doom. Twenty-five years before, Howard had asked for a job on the *World*, but failed to get past the outer door, from which an office boy dismissed him.

He now proceeded to kill the morning *World* and merge the evening edition into the *World-Telegram.* Howard presented "It Seems to Me, by Heywood Broun" in two-column width at the left side of the first page, second section, where each day brought a spread of special articles and examples of investigative reporting. Howard was spending money on this "split page," and the results were day after day of first-class journalism. Editors at the *World-Telegram* called it the smorgasbord page, but they were proud of it, and Pegler noted that the "sportside" was losing its prestige to the split pages. The Hearst dailies in New York at that time were the evening *Journal,* the tabloid *Mirror,* and the morning *American,* the latter featuring a regular front page column of what *Time* magazine referred to as "Brisbanalities." In its field the *American* was losing to the *Times* and the *Herald Tribune.* And what the Chief thought of it all, at the ranch, no one really knew.

The success of Roy Howard and his colleagues had been a remarkable thing in those days of financial depression, but it is a fact of social history that journalists, authors, and entertainers prospered during the lean years that afflicted people in other lines of work. People in the new trade of broadcasting flourished, as did the associates of Henry R. Luce, publisher of the recently launched magazines *Time* and *Fortune.* And Pegler perceived that in his earning power he had a gratifying and reassuring personal gold mine. Moreover, the dollars he earned were loaded with purchasing power far beyond that of U.S. currency in the middle 1970s—perhaps about seven times as much. And he could buy things worth owning with these high-powered dollars; the quality of life, about which we have been hearing complaints, was good in the 1930s—if you had earning power and no anxieties that it might suddenly fall away.

Some worthy projects that had been started in the late Twenties retained their momentum and came to completion after the panic downtown. One was the graceful George Washington Bridge over the Hudson. Dignitaries opened the bridge in October 1931; someone had started it four years before, in good times, and no authority could be found to stop it. In the same way a tower in Chicago (now the Playboy Magazine Building) rose to completion with a Lindbergh Beacon at the top, which began to rotate when President Hoover pressed a button in Washington. Life went on and shocking events sometimes took place, like that of March 1, 1932, when a man named Bruno Hauptmann stole Charles Lindbergh, Jr., from his crib in a lonely house on the Jersey hills, and murdered the baby within half an hour. The long strain of this mystery, which was not solved until the capture of Hauptmann two years later, would dampen even the spirits of the fortunate, the talented, and the employed. But on May 14 of that 1932 spring Pegler observed a turnout that temporarily cheered many a soul—the Beer Parade of New Yorkers demanding that the sale of their favorite drink be legalized without delay. First in line strode Mayor Jimmy Walker, the engaging rascal who ruled New York. He marched nimbly along, twirling his cane and doffing his high silk hat; Cagney could not have done it better in a movie scene. And near the front came heavyweight boxing champion Gene Tunney, riding in a hansom cab. Next year saw the Volstead Act repealed, and Pegler noted the circumstances of his first legal drink in thirteen years. The scene was the Oak Room at the Plaza Hotel; the novelist Katharine Brush was among those present; Pegler ordered Dubonnet and gin.

As historians look back at it now, the winter of 1932-33 held the turning point in the misery that had overtaken this country; after these months the look of things got gradually better. A simple instinct called for putting our national business under new management, and so the presidential election in November 1932 had gone to Roosevelt by 23,000,000 votes to 16,000,000. If for no other reason than the dismissal of Hoover & Co., the fall of 1932 seemed a time for boldness and planning and acceptance of changes. And while many ruined Americans were still doomed to sad and lean years, others saw splendid opportunities arising in the years immediately ahead. Pegler for one felt the excitement and challenge in the air when Roy Howard began talking to him about coming off the sport pages and starting a column of general comment for the *World-Telegram* and the Scripps-Howard papers, plus all others that United Features could sign up. Howard and his salesmen felt they had a sure thing in Pegler and they made him a sweet offer. Pegler was to draw base pay of $30,000 a year, and in addition they would give him one-half of all syndicate money above $60,000. They expected sales to reach $150,000 within a short time, which meant that Pegler's yearly earnings would come to $75,000 in addition to anything he made from books and magazine articles on the side. Through Scripps-Howard alone the audience, the fame, the influence they offered was tremendous, for in addition to the flagship *World-Telegram* in New York, Pegler would start with substantial papers in nearly all the important cities in the country, although Roy Howard admitted he didn't have a foothold in Colonel McCormick's back yard. But here the *Chicago Daily News* had been pleased to step in and take up half of Pegler's basic contract. And so, at the age of thirty-seven, Pegler was one of the most important men in the country. What happened in his brain on any particular day would enter millions of other brains on the following day; and his singularly persuasive way with words made it likely that these ideas would take root and grow in the minds of his fellow men. His first column under the Howard management was to run on December 11, 1933.

5

PEGLER IN THE SILVER DECADE

UNTIL PEGLER ARRIVED, HEYWOOD BROUN HAD BEEN THE brightest star of the *World-Telegram* and the Scripps-Howard papers. "It Seems to Me" was a joy to read because of Broun's quiet humor and the simplicity of his style, which made the whole thing appear easy, as though the gregarious Broun had drawn up a chair and started talking in his agreeable low-pitched drawl. It did seem easy for Broun, who could turn away from the bridge table and type off his column in remarkably quick time like a man writing a letter to a friend. He had the facility in composition of a writer who has been able to complete his work in mind before he touches a pen or hits a typewriter key. Pegler did not have this kind of fluency and it took him all afternoon to get a column finished. But Roy Howard and his editors judged the two writers only by results, and made it evident on Pegler's first day under their management that he was to be considered an equal of Broun, for they trimmed the width of "It Seems to Me" and balanced it on the right side of the smorgasbord page with the new daily feature, "Fair Enough, by Westbrook Pegler." One might take this cutting of space as a comedown for Broun; but letting him continue at two columns and giving the same space to the newcomer would leave only four columns for smorgasbord. Therefore it was mainly a consideration of makeup, rather than editorial demotion that squeezed "It Seems to Me." Still it amounted to cutting the lines of a star actor so that another leading player might perform. But Broun gave no sign of annoyance, and welcomed Pegler to the Scripps-Howard stable.

The two men had known each other for some time and were good friends. Broun was a liberal, sympathetic to organized labor, and an infracaninophile or friend of the underdog. He was in the process of becoming a Socialist and it was a novel thing in the journalism of the day that such a man should have a sounding-board in the midst of the capitalist establishment. His new colleague across the split page was not to be immediately defined in ideological terms. Pegler was coming off the sportside where his eye and ear had produced some marvelous copy, but very little comment on serious problems in the world. Now he was entering on the position of an independent general writer for the press, in fact taking office as a public preacher licensed to preach five or six sermons a week. He was in charge, nobody could give him an assignment or alter his copy, and anything resembling censorship would have to be fought out with Roy Howard alone. On any day, Pegler could write on how he felt getting up that morning, or the gold standard, or Shakespeare and the musical glasses—choice of subject was entirely up to him. All this in the hands of a young man having little formal education, whose experiences, while keenly felt and vividly observed, had been limited to a few months fighting the brass as a war correspondent, and for the rest, the boxing camps, the press stands of the football fields, the speakeasies, the nightclubs, the grill rooms hearty and masculine, the poker parties and social life with other popular writers and their wives. Libraries, picture galleries, and concert halls were not Westbrook Pegler's favorite places of resort.

Roy Howard had plenty of experts on art and literature on call; in Pegler he had something different, although he was unable to announce where the difference lay. But Howard did not find it embarrassing that his new writer defied identification, and he made Pegler appear to be something like the Royal Nonesuch *in Huckleberry Finn* by proclaiming that a combination of H. L. Mencken, Ring Lardner, and Mark Twain was joining his staff. This gave Pegler so much to live up to that he decided to shock his audience with a tremendous sensation on the first day. With that in mind he chose for the subject of his opening piece an occurrence that had disturbed the entire nation a little more than two weeks before, as the result of an unusually callous murder that had been committed in California on November 5.

Two loafers named Thurmond and Holmes had killed a young man named Brooke Hart in the small city of San Jose, eight miles southeast of the southern end of San Francisco Bay, on November 9. The victim had been not far past his twenty-second birthday when they caved in his head with a stone, shot him, weighted his body and threw it in the bay. As such cadavers will, it rose and came to shore. Meanwhile, the police had captured Thurmond in a telephone booth while he was giving Brooke Hart's sister directions for payment of ransom on the man already dead. Thurmond confessed the murder and implicated Holmes. There was talk of lynching in San Jose, and on the night of November 26 the talk led to action when a mob seized Holmes and Thurmond, and hanged them to trees in front of the jailhouse. Six thousand people cheered the lynchers while the police stood off 150 yards from the self-appointed hangmen. Thurmond they hanged semi-conscious from blows received as they dragged him out, but Holmes knew what was happening to the last; he fought like a wildcat, and twice managed to get the rope off his neck. They pulled him up still struggling to the jeers of the crowd.

Descriptions of the scene appeared next morning on the front page of every paper in the country. Throughout the following week what seemed to be a national consensus of disgust and indignation appeared in editorials, man-on-the-street interviews, statements by important people, and letters to the editor. The lynchers, the crowd that stood by, the authorities who let it happen, all came in for rebuke. And California's Governor Sunny Jim Rolph heightened the general outrage when he stated that "This is the best lesson California has ever given the country. We showed the country that California is not going to take kidnapping." A rain of reproof fell on the head of Sunny Jim. He even got into trouble with ex-President Herbert Hoover, who rebuked the governor for his explanation of why he had not sent in the State Guard when lynching talk started. Sunny Jim said he was not going to call out troops against good folks—here you had these young fellows armed with guns and bayonets and not with too much sense and somebody might get hurt. Rolph then added, "But I don't advocate lynch law!" The image of California was in very bad repair.

It was this ghastly occurrence, charged with primitive emotions and morbid interest in public atrocity, that appeared to Pegler as an opportunity to demonstrate journalistic showmanship while making his entrance with "Fair Enough." His idea was to take the position that the lynching at San Jose was an act of civic virtue. By instinct Pegler knew that this would be the view of many a man and woman out along the grey streets of the industrial suburbs, around the flatland filling stations, and among the turtlefaced leathery oldsters racked out under the sun in

Fort Lauderdale and St. Petersburg, land of Ring Lardner's "Golden Honeymoon." Howard understood it at once but advised, "Not on the *first* day, Bud. Take a day or two to let them learn where to find you in the paper." Pegler accepted the advice and led with a piece that asked readers to bear in mind that he had "started a new line of work." He concluded that first column by saying, "I'm scared of this place. I wish I was back where I came from already."

That day the main *World-Telegram* story "outside"—on the front page—had to do with the international gold standard. On the sport page the big story was the death of Bill Roper, an oldtime football coach. Pegler seemed to be saying that he was neither outside nor inside, and that he felt exposed in a journalistic limbo. It was a feint to set his audience up for the punch. Next day Pegler still withheld the shock and rattled on about almost nothing until he reached some significant lines: "For myself, I would say that my hates always occupied my mind much more actively than my friendships. Of friends I will venture to say that I have had a few, but the wish to favor a friend is not so active as the instinct to annoy some person or institution which I detest. I think I would go much further out of my way to inflict such annoyance than to remind a friend, for no particular reason, that I was thinking of him and to advise him that I was sending him a ham. And my friends, I am sure, are less alert to make me feel good than to make their enemies feel otherwise." Pegler here set down a rule of conduct which he would observe in his subsequent career. And he indicated that whatever you might think of him, he was going to be frank and say what he had to say; it is the time-honored excuse of all aggressive bad-tempered people, as well as the motivating force of the writer who has learned that one sure way to interest readers is to denounce something. With a touch of menace in his manner, Pegler had now gathered an audience before his booth among the Scripps-Howard sideshows, and on the following day, Wednesday, December 13, he presented himself as the journalistic wild man from Borneo.

Pegler sailed into it with an appeal to the lowbrows of the country, or what he called "the rabble." He wrote, "As one member of the rabble, I will admit that I said, 'Fine, that is swell,' when the papers came up that recent day, telling of the lynching of the two men who killed the young fellow in California, and that I haven't changed my mind yet for all the storm of right-mindedness which has blown up since. I know how storms of right-mindedness are made. The city editor calls a fellow over and tells him to call up a lot of names on the office right-mindedness list and get about a column of expressions of horror and indignation." Pegler went on to develop the idea that such protests were all very well, but the two kidnappers "are permanently dead. They did it, and they got theirs. . . . I claim authority to speak for the rabble because I am a member of the rabble in good standing." Pegler now turned his attention to Governor Rolph, who would appear to be a spokesman for that group. But with calculated perversity, Westbrook complained that "the purity of the California lynching was fouled up by the endorsement of a politician."

Pegler had succeeded in offending one section of his audience and pleasing another part of it. Those who agreed with him were members of what I like to call the meatball underground, the people you see standing at the start of football games, right hands on their bellies and muttering the words as the band plays Our National Anthem. These were the readers who would believe in Westbrook to the end, although they never understood him, and he never identified with them. Those whom Westbrook shocked with his endorsement of the "two passenger lynching" in San Jose included most of the intelligentsia in New York where his writing had become an object of cult worship among publishers, authors, producers, editors, and all who made or followed intellectual fashions. It was the manner that charmed them, the crispness of Pegler's attack and his capture of visual detail, as when he wrote that serious drinkers avoided silver flasks from Cartier and swallowed their booze direct from "neck and shoulder bottles." But the artist in words handed out a Mickey Finn with the lynching column. "Did you see what he wrote?" a man would ask as he joined a woman at a cocktail bar, indicating the *World-Telegram* on the banquette beside her. "Yes," the woman would say, "how can he *do* it?" The meaning was clear: How can he do it to *us*?

What disturbed these readers was Pegler's plain insensitivity to the horror of the lynching. He had written that Holmes and Thurmond had it coming, and there was no denying the cold-blooded ferocity of their crime. Who were they, indeed, to decide the world had seen enough of an inoffensive young man who had done them no harm? The mindless cruelty of their act made it impossible to defend them; nevertheless, few cared to argue that two evil acts cancelled each other out. In the discussion of the lynching and the murder that preceded it, the papers invariably referred to Holmes and Thurmond as "confessed killers of Brooke Hart." But Heywood Broun wrote that he wasn't altogether happy with the confessions, and would have liked to hear them tested in court. Now it was too late. This raised the question of legal capital punishment and its irrevocable finality. Was it, perhaps, something close to murder by the State? Whatever opinion you might hold on crime and punishment, there was agreement on one thing: in his first week at the new job,

Chapter 5

Westbrook Pegler had stirred up fundamental controversy. He also had planted in a number of liberal minds a suspicion as to his basic motivations that would follow him throughout the thousands of columns and millions of words he was yet to write.

From hard experience Pegler had come to understand the law of physics which states that if you throw a brick, another brick is certain to fly back at you. But he neither forgave nor forgot the attack he drew in the San Jose affair, and could recall it four years later with a vivid picture. At this time Westbrook wrote that his original argument had been merely that "there were two murderers at least who would not be turned loose on the country after ten or fifteen years to do it again." Whereupon an uproar had arisen and "All the coffee-room philosophers and shaggy thinkers of the butchers' paper magazines dusted off their big foreign words, and all the flat-heeled intellects of the female auxiliary came storming down the street heaving bricks of indignation and scorn. The high note of their cry was the sanctity of the law, orderly procedure and the disruptive force of lawless action, although most of them had been drunk often enough on illegal hooch during prohibition. I was a long time combing the mortar and shattered bottle glass out of my hair, and I still wear some of the knobs they raised. . . ."

Thus Pegler depicted himself in an animated cartoon, pursued by yelling enemies and grotesquely bruised. He may have been abnormally sensitive to hostile criticism. But nobody likes it. And in his first months as author of "Fair Enough," Westbrook could find encouragement in the fact that the President in Washington also was feeling his way into a new job. Franklin Roosevelt appeared to be doing so well that Westbrook wrote, "Never have I encountered a subject of this type who lays it on the line as Mr. Roosevelt does. . . . I am afraid I couldn't be trusted around Mr. Roosevelt, because for the first time in my life in this business I might find myself squabbling for a chance to carry the champion's water bucket." His approval included the President's wife and he wrote that with Eleanor Roosevelt as its hostess, the White House saw nobody wasting time or energy on useless formalities and that "Mrs. Roosevelt has been busy on such undignified frivolities as old age pensions, a ban on child labor, and the protection of health of mothers and children."

The off-year election in November 1934 indicated that the country agreed with Pegler as to Roosevelt's performance in the role of champion. The President had come forward in the prime sense of that word, as one who acts in behalf of others, or in defense of a cause. And Mr. Herbert Hoover did him the favor of rising for air in California and announcing that we must have a Republican Congress if we wished our governmental institutions to survive. The exaggeration was worthy of Pegler himself. But the political experts observed that the country had loaded its woes on Hoover's back and driven him into the wilderness; now here was the scapegoat returning to offer an invaluable recommendation for the man who had turned him out. It was satisfactory to Roosevelt, and the people he had championed were happy to show their appreciation by voting 332 Democrats into the House of Representatives over 102 Republicans, along with 69 Democratic senators to 25 of the opposing party. Democratic mayors, state legislators, and governors swarmed over the land: it would have taken 100 garbage scows to hold them in some majestic riverine procession. The papers said it was the greatest Democratic victory of all time.

No matter what Westbrook might write in contradiction of basic liberal tenets, the people living in large cities who considered themselves enlightened felt that the country was heading in the right direction. There was something reassuring in Roosevelt's personality that made people feel optimistic about the future, whether or not they understood the workings of the New Deal. And our President looked even better when you compared him with Benito Mussolini, the bigmouthed former Socialist politican who had inaugurated the Italian Fascist corporate state in 1928, and with Adolf Hitler, who had seized power with his Nazi partisans five years later. The two dictators were sawed-off strutting men who looked even worse than MacArthur and Eisenhower in military suits; put them beside Roosevelt and you compared a gentleman with two common-looking little foreigners. There was more in it than a question of personal style. Roosevelt had a sane mind, but there is no way to frame a definition of sanity that would include Adolf Hitler. Dr. Russell Lee of the Stanford University Medical School has put it that "Hitler could well have been used in the medical school classroom as an example of paranoia." The same authority observed in Benito Mussolini "an enormous egocentricity" and "delusions of grandeur suggestive of paresis," by which he meant the progressive paralysis of the insane. The year 1895 had seen an invasion of Ethiopia in East Central Africa by Italian armies, and that war had ended when a decisive battle at Adowa compelled Italy to recognize Ethiopian independence. Mussolini the superpatriot never stopped complaining about this blot on Italian honor until he was able to launch an invasion of Ethiopia in October 1935. Pegler and his fellow Americans found the spectacle of this military adventure contemptible: here were modern armies with enormous firepower devastating a primitive country, and blowing villages off the map by attacks from the air. One thing was certain, Americans would never do anything like this. Even with modern weapons, it took the Italians seven months to subdue their primitive victims. Much sympathy and no material help went to Haile Selassie, the many-titled Emperor of Ethiopia, also known as Lion of Judah, Lord of Lords, and King of Kings. Pegler made the country chuckle when he referred to the struggle of Selassie and Mussolini as a fight between the King of Kings and the Bum of Bums.

Pegler's achievement of a position from which he could call Mussolini a bum had been a rapid development at the *World-Telegram*. Six months after the appearance of "Fair Enough," salesmen had come into Roy Howard's red-walled office with joyful tidings that they had signed up enough papers throughout the country to cover Pegler's base pay with Scripps-Howard and start making a profit for the syndicate. And Pegler's additional pay from national sales came to the figure they had estimated for him. This gave Westbrook a higher income than that of the President in Washington, and once again, I respectfully ask the reader to bear in mind that Westbrook's $75,000 contained high voltage purchasing power which he could spend on well-made goods and satisfactory services. The tax on earnings by personal effort was severe, but not yet completely out of hand, and the insolence of the Internal Revenue Bureau (today called "Service" in Orwellian style) struck only the defenseless and the uninformed. The salesmen celebrated with stone cold white Martinis at the elegant bar in the Ambassador Hotel, near Howard's office. And a few blocks down Park Avenue, Pegler drank a toast to the future in his town residence, an apartment in the fashionable Park Lane. A number of insiders in the newspaper business learned that Westbrook had made up his commercial guarantee and justified Roy Howard's faith, and they wrote or called to congratulate him. Among these well-wishers was Heywood Broun, the rival star attraction on Howard's smorgasbord page. Broun liked to see any newspaper man make good.

The friendship of Pegler and Broun did not have a foundation of similarity between the two men. They had come from noticeably different backgrounds: Broun's father was a successful printing contractor, now retired, and well liked all over town for his kindly disposition and unfailingly good manners. The older Broun even maintained his poise when Heywood called at his club to announce that he had joined the Socialist Party. On this occasion Mr. Broun said, "Do what you think is right, my boy," and returned to the backgammon table. After his father died, Heywood wrote that "All he ever wanted to know was whether I believed honestly and sincerely in what I had chosen." The mother was a handsome, assured woman of strong conservative beliefs, who disapproved of her son's running for Congress on the Socialist ticket, and his appearances on picket lines. Mrs. Broun said a couple of months in jail would do Heywood no harm. Broun wrote that his mother "would make an excellent agitator herself, but she doesn't want to see anyone else agitate. . . . When the revolution comes it's going to be a tough problem what to do with her. We will either have to shoot her or make her a commissar. In the meantime we still dine together." They also played bridge, and Heywood said "she leads away from aces and neglects to keep jump bids alive. But she is still my mother."

Broun was at home in the world, especially so in New York City as an Easterner in the place where he had grown up, with a Harvard education and a gift of fluent expression that publishers had recognized and rewarded since he first started writing sports on vacation out of college in 1908. At that time Westbrook had been an unresponsive pupil in the grim technical school, with parents whose appearance and manner showed that life was pushing them hard. Without assuming the beard and Dutch-comic accent of a fashionable psychiatrist, I assert that common observation tells us the children of happy and self-assured parents have a fairly good chance of growing up secure in their identities, and not altogether vulnerable to the hostilities of our time. What it amounts to in this instance is that Broun had enjoyed "advantages," Pegler had not, and there was consequently something irritable and suspicious in Pegler's soul, born in harsh childhood, that had not developed in the pleasant surroundings of early youth that formed the personality of Heywood Broun. And it was Broun who made the decision to venture his prestige as a star of journalism in the founding of a union for newspaper editorial workers.

The suggestion that it was time to organize had appeared in Broun's column four months before Pegler joined the *World-Telegram.* It was not a piece that would warm the hearts of Roy Howard or Colonel McCormick, for it quoted a letter from a certain "Reporter Unemployed" which accused the publishers of planning to cheat reporters of the gains due them under the National Recovery Act by "classifying their editorial staffs as 'professional men.' " The average newshand worked an eight-hour day six days a week, and Reporter Unemployed charged that "the publishers, by patting their fathead employees on the head and calling them 'professionals,' hope to maintain this working week scale. And they'll succeed, for the men who make up the editorial staffs of the country are peculiarly susceptible to such soothing classifications as 'professionals,' 'journalists,' 'members of the fourth estate,' 'gentlemen of the press' and other terms which have completely entranced them by falsely dignifying and glorifying them and their work." The writer went on, "the printers are getting an average of some 30 percent more pay than the smart fourth estaters who will continue to work forty-eight hours a week because they consider unionization as lowering their dignity." Broun wrote, "I think Mr. Unemployed's point is well taken. . . . After some four or five years of holding down the easiest job in the world I hate to see other newspapermen working too hard. It makes me self-conscious. It embarrasses me even more to think of newspapermen who are not working at all. Among this number are some of the best. . . . Fortunately, columnists do not get fired very frequently. It has something to do with a certain inertia in most executives. . . . And nothing happens to the columnists. At least, not up till now."

With that column on August 7 in 1933 Broun dedicated himself to organizing a national union of reporters. On December 15, four days after the start of "Fair Enough," delegates representing newsmen in thirty cities came to Washington and organized the American Newspaper Guild, "to preserve the vocational interests of its members and to improve the conditions under which they work by collective bargaining and to raise the standards of journalism." They elected Broun international president. Arthur James Pegler signed up and Westbrook also joined, but gave the Guild no public encouragement. If there is one thing we may be sure Pegler lacked, it was the heart of a union man. He set his own conditions of work and needed no union to raise his pay.

Although his work went well in these years, Pegler suffered from personal griefs and problems of the sort that seem to mobilize as one moves into middle age. It had become clear that Julie was not in good health. She had recovered from a heart attack in 1933, and "would have to be careful" for the rest of her life. And Westbrook's mother died in March 1934. Frances Nicholson Pegler had aged a sad woman, separated from the husband who had come into her life a fascinating suitor in the Twin Cities, far away and long ago. In 1935 a second heart attack struck Julie; Pegler called it "a rough time" but the invaluable wife got better, and continued her watch over Westbrook, soothing his angers and welcoming his friends to the homes in Pound Ridge and Manhattan.

Pegler remained on apparently good terms with Broun, continued to hold his card as a Guildsman, and subscribed $50 to the strike fund when the union went out at the *Newark Ledger* in 1935. Any politically informed person who attended Guild meetings during this period would be aware of disciplined left-wingers who agitated and voted as a unit—the Communist "party fraction." They made trouble for Broun, because their aim was not the betterment of reporters, but control of the union. Nevertheless Broun said, "You have to have Reds in a labor organization." It should be noted that this was in the period of the United Front in which some Socialists and many liberals thought they could work with Communists as allies against Fascism. For reasons not yet fully understood, the most influential American liberals and progressives of that time perceived the wickedness of Hitler and Mussolini in clear detail, while the crimes of Stalin seemed only the movements of shadows behind a Russian mist, and his millions of victims nothing more than ghosts of a romantic revolution. In such an ideological atmosphere it was not surprising that Broun praised Reds as union members, for they came to meetings and helped get things done. A strong Communist sympathizer moved in as head of the Guild's New York local, the most important in the country; and there was strike talk at the *World-Telegram* unit. Broun announced that "Anybody who withdraws his designation of the union as his collective bargaining agent thereby excludes himself from employment at any plant which subsequently adopts a preferential or closed shop with the Guild." Pegler resigned at once; his decision was like that of George M. Cohan in opposition to Actor's Equity—nobody was toing to tell *him* what to do.

One reason for a reporters' union was demonstrated in 1936 when Arthur Pegler retired at the age of seventy-four from the *Daily Mirror,* and the management handed him $750 to see him through old age after thirty years of work for Hearst newspapers. Had the Guild been in existence during those years, Arthur would have gone out with something more substantial in his pockets. As it was, the executives added to their cash payment the prehistoric typewriter Arthur had used throughout his career, shipping the machine to his house in Connecticut without charge. It had been thought that the Arthur Pegler memoirs would be worth money, and he sat for long hours hammering out pages, but could never get the material into publishable shape. Meanwhile Westbrook continued to visit his father and stepmother, Arthur's second wife. He deferred to the old man, addressed him as "Governor" in British style, listened patiently to the opinions Arthur delivered in "a voice like a snare drum," and what was more important, took up the burden of his support. Arthur lived on, an incurably unhappy man who had the crotchets of genius, without the talent.

Pegler's crowded year of 1936 brought work and travel along with anxiety and sorrow; Westbrook had set out in January to cover the winter Olympic games at Garmisch-Partenkirchen in Upper Bavaria. This was an assignment of political as well as sporting interest, since the Nazis were hosts for the occasion, and Adolf Hitler therefore would come under direct criticism by an uncontrolled foreign press. Breaking his journey in England, Pegler could compare himself as he now was with the skinny, freckled youth who had seen London for the first time twenty years before, an underpaid employee in a cable office. The famous columnist in his hotel suite and the young newsman slaving on the night trick were much alike. For Pegler in his vigorous early middle age had kept intact his youthful suspicions about those who claimed authority and listed themselves among the great. It happened that King George V had died at Sandringham on January 20, and on the following day Westbrook wrote a piece about the crowds outside Buckingham Palace waiting for news. Pegler reported that "This queer, contradictory race called the British actually loved the little wasted and exhausted man who died of fatigue more than anything else last night. . . .

"There were people in the gathering as poor as poverty, sniffling and shuffling toward the little bulletin board, and they all spoke whispers and mentioned the dying man as though he were some very dear personal friend. Although he died just before midnight it was 12:40 before a man came out of the palace and hung up a bulletin that the King was dead. At that men in the front row took off their hats and those behind, seeing this done, understood and took their hats off too. . . . They didn't weep and no patriot with a streak of ham in him had thrown a fit, as might have been expected, and, finally, they did not sing 'God Save the King.' They just broke and went away. . . ."

Two days later Westbrook began his criticism of the public ceremonies connected with the king's death. He led from a reliable suit, the English weather: "Nobody knew better than the King that the English climate is a loaded gun pointed at the head of every inmate of the islands, which goes off frequently and mows the victims down in appalling numbers." Westbrook did not go so far as to suggest that King George had purposely died in January in order to bring his patient subjects out into the winter rains. But within a week, Pegler had reached the conclusion that "There will never be a better opportunity than the present to observe the operation of the ballyhoo by which the British royal family is sold to the people of the country." Pegler viewed the proceedings with his cartoonist's eye while his mind went back to the year 1910 in Chicago, when he had hooted at the outlandish costumes worn by the mourners who followed the coffin of Edward VII. Now in 1936 he was delighted to observe that there were "Oriental dignitaries in snake charmer's regalia" trudging along in line, and the entire fantastic spectacle inspired some thoughts on the symbolic purpose of military dress. "The profession of killing," he reflected, "has never enjoyed a greater prestige than at the present hour." There were only a few civilians marching in the procession, "and those few were not doctors, teachers, or working people but diplomats, whose occupation may be said to consist of the arrangement and promotion of wars." But the highest honors went to the warriors, and they wore the most beautiful costumes the tailors of the world could produce.

"It is a popular thing in some quarters to sneer at the killers, deride their honors and finery, and point out that their whole work in life is to destroy life. But that is a mere affectation of people who want to be regarded as different. After all, if it were not for the professional gunmen who would carry civilization to the backward peoples of the earth?"

A few days later Westbrook linked his impressions of the British funeral procession to an American theme. He wrote that "the weakness for chicken feathers and garish colors and high-sounding titles might be more profitably expressed than repressed and thus compelled to express itself in equipment and honors which are unofficial and therefore meaningless. If, for example, General Pershing were an English officer he would be the Earl of Missouri, G.C.G., G.C.M., D.S.O. and a field marshal entitled to a wooden baton studded with four stars. General Bullard as a British officer would also be a marshal and Lord Bullard a Knight of the Bath no less. Mr. James Farley would be Sir James and Mr. Mellon, of Pittsburgh, Sir Andrew at least." And what did it all amount to? The honors of British Empire, Westbrook decided, were nothing more or less than "the greatest ballyhoo machine in the world, with the aristocracy turning the crank."

The visit to England put Pegler in a good frame of mind to inspect the proceedings at Garmisch-Partenkirchen, where he found that "the yodellers howled in the beer parlors by night and the apple-cheeked killers of the Storm Troops went about in civilian clothes pretending to be jovial Bavarian villagers." During the day, at the games, Hitler's bullies appeared in their true colors and Westbrook saw "people herded by long cordons of officers, beefy young Nazis in various kinds of uniforms, whose only duty was to flatter and accommodate the former house painter who became head man of the Third Reich." This failed to make a hit with the German press officials. The dispatch continued, "The Olympics were of secondary importance, if any. This was the Dictator's day, and it's a good thing for the Americans present that this was so, for they have nothing important to learn from the athletes but much to learn about absolute authority in government.

"You must picture this town. Ten thousand swastikas stir faintly in the light winter wind along the streets of Garmisch-Partenkirchen. The flag is the color of blood, with a white circle containing an ancient device in black. The swastika flies from every house and store and some homes are adorned with long ribbons of little pennants strung together from window to window, fifty or a hundred swastikas in a row. . . . At home we've never found it necessary to mobilize an army for a sporting event."

The Nazi press agents in charge of the winter Olympic press room frowned on Pegler and went as far as they dared in the direction of threatening to lift his credentials. Seasoned to such disapproval by his fights with the United States Navy and Army, Pegler let the Germans know that he held them in personal contempt, and feared them not at all. Nevertheless, Pegler did not send off his final judgment on what he had seen until February 28, on his arrival in Prague. This dispatch said that the National Socialist (Nazi) party was Hitler's version of the Ku Klux Klan. Pegler congratulated those Germans who resisted the regime for their great courage, and went on, "it is a strange method, Hitler's. He reduced his people to trembling cowardice, told them how brave they were to submit to a few hoodlums and organized a government combining the methods of the Ku Klux and Al Capone."

Hitler had shocked the world by the cruelty he inflicted on the German Jews. The sadism and meanness of the official persecutors sickened Pegler and caused him to write his famous column about what it must be like to be a Jewish child in Germany and be told that you were a monster begotten of monsters. The sympathy and indignation of this column caused many readers to suspend judgment of Pegler a little later on when impatient excessive rancor began to show in his writing with increasing frequency. We remembered the piece about the Jewish children, and told ourselves a good man wrote that.

Pegler made another visit to London on the way home from the games, and sent a dispatch to his New York office that might have been written by Mark Twain in *Innocents Abroad*. Westbrook had looked at St. James's Palace and found it "a dull building smudged with the soot of Welsh coal, and it looks less like a palace than the back end of a warehouse down by the railroad tracks in Indianapolis."

Pegler was in a benign mood when he got home, ready to give credit where it might be due for any virtue he could discover in his native land. Additional recognition that he addressed a large national audience came when Doubleday, Doran published a collection of his writings, *'T Ain't Right*. The jocosity of the book's title showed that Westbrook clung to the role which had served him during his days with the *Tribune* syndicate, that of a public scold or jester who does not take himself too seriously. But Pegler kept an alert watch for villains, and struck at a big one late in April when he labeled William Randolph Hearst "the leading American Fascist."

A few days later Westbrook attacked another American institution, on a visit to the Kentucky Derby at Louisville. Pegler knew that this annual horse race was overrated from every point of view, although a parroting crew of track reporters had built it up through years of ballyhoo into an event at which a lot of wealthy and publicity-conscious people felt obliged to put themselves on display. Westbrook was in good form at Louisville when he reported that the Kentucky Derby promoters "subject their customers to bad food, poorly prepared and served at exorbitant prices." Bad handling by the staff and generally careless management made attendance at the track an ordeal for everyone but a few rich patrons, and they got a trimming since even the clubhouse fell short of what such a place should be. The suckers formed up in great masses, and money was so loose that "nobody could ever suspect that the people who came down in private cars, shooting craps on the floor with thousands of dollars exposed to view, had passed by the wretched cabins of some of the scrawniest and most miserable sidehill dodgers that the American race has produced." In addition to the big shots of society and corporate management, there were plenty of ordinary whores and thieves in Louisville. "It is a sort of old home week for the underworld. . . . Mr. Capone is away now, and the angels have taken many of his boys up to heaven, but others have taken their place. The Derby attracts that kind of men and also the kind of ladies who prowl about the halls of the hotels and barge in at the doors where they hear the voices of males to inquire prettily, 'Is this Mr. Smith's room? I am looking for Mr. Smith of Quincy.' Usually they are not looking for Mr. Smith at all. . . ."

Another aspect of the Derby promotion that amused Pegler was the effort of its managers to give the thing a touch of class by importing a distinguished foreigner as a guest of honor. And whom do you suppose they managed to get for this position? Sir Bede Clifford, the governor of the Bahamas—a moth-eaten little Englishman holding one of the least important jobs in the British Empire. Pegler had to laugh when he saw the socialites bowing and scraping before this insignificant man. He found it especially entertaining, when Sir Bede came in sight, to observe "Mr. Joe Widener of Philadelphia . . . his nostrils flare, his back hair goes up, he puts out his elbows and scampers like a colt in the presence of people like that. . . ."

Having noted the absence of Al Capone from the Derby, Pegler decided to visit the famous and respected gangster in the federal penitentiary on Alcatraz Island in San Francisco Bay. He planned also to write one or two pieces about life in that prison, a place that the government administered in a way that made Joliet and Sing Sing seem like country clubs. The proposed interview required a pass from authorities in Washington, and when Pegler went to obtain it, he ran into concrete-lined bunkers of bureaucracy. Allow Mr. Pegler to visit Alcatraz? No—not for any purpose. Alcatraz is off limits to Mr. Pegler and everybody else except the inmates and their guards. On June 1, Westbrook reported this rejection to his readers, starting the piece in a moderate tone: "I take Mr. Sanford Bates, head of the federal jails, to be a man with honest motives, although he is a cop, and cops develop a curious mental slant all their own." Pegler then told how Bates had barred the way to Alcatraz, a prison described as the American Devil's Island. Pegler thought that a poor boast, for it admitted that our government maintained "a secret prison in which anything might happen." It suggested "the island of Lipari, in which Mussolini filed away a lot of good, respectable Italians for the offense of speaking out of turn, and the oubliette camps where Adolf Hitler hides some tough, courageous Germans who had the reckless gumption to rise up and declare he wasn't any superman but just a crazy Austrian house painter." It all pointed toward the danger of "the idea of secrecy in an American prison, which some tough guy might be tempted to use for a political dog house a few years hence. Government is getting bossier and more impudent toward the people day by day in the United States, and the attitude of a government official in declaring that nobody has a right to know what goes on in a big government institution is symptomatic of what I mean.

"Some intuition, perhaps, tells me that the emotional or sentimental regard for J. Edgar Hoover, the chief of the G-men, is going to result in a reaction one of these days. Hoover, in his love of personal publicity and his self-approval, closely reminds me of old Ellis Parker, the celebrated hick detective of Mount Holly, N. J., who has just been arrested on a charge of kidnapping and second-degree assault in the political mixup which followed the Lindbergh-Hauptmann case . . . old Parker would trample down everyone in his path to get his face in the picture. . . . Melvin Purvis, the man who got Dillinger, left the Department of Justice soon after this triumph, and the reasons have never been told. But inasmuch as the Department courts publicity, Mr. Hoover ought to give us a 'tell' with particular reference to the suspicion that Purvis fell because he outscored the boss in publicity. . . . Hoover is all showman and apparently quite vain, for he is always appearing in public places to take his bows, and he can't pass a pine table and a water pitcher without jamming one hand in the breast of his coat, clearing his throat and beginning, 'Ladies and gentlemen, we are gathered here today to consider the growing menace of crime, which is a festering vulture on the sacred wellsprings of our great democracy. . . .'"

At this time Hoover was busily presenting himself as a Commie-fighter and protector of America against organized crime. There was something personally repulsive about him and the cult of leader-worship he had already established in the Federal Bureau of Investigation. Hoover liked to picture himself a steel-jawed crook-chaser, tough as they make them and fast on the draw. He was in fact a product of the District's white lower middle class, one degree above trash, a former low-grade government drone who saw his chance to build an empire of toadies in the bureau, which had been a haven for amiable rummies of the federal marshal type. Whether the country has benefited from the growth of the Hoover FBI is a debatable point. The Mafia stood Hoover on his head for thirty years while his men would occasionally surround some rustic gunman, like John Dillinger, and shoot him full of holes. What Hoover did succeed in doing was to establish a national secret police force, which might be a greater menace to our liberties than it now is if there had ever been any first-rate minds connected with the running of it. Fortunately there were none, a fact which Pegler sensed when he dismissed J. Edgar Hoover as "a night-club fly-cop." He added that Hoover's favorite newsman, the Broadway gossip Walter Winchell, was "a gent's room journalist." The head G-man couldn't have liked any of this comment by Pegler, and I would be willing to bet money that he opened a "politically subversive" file on Westbrook and that it remains in the archives to this day.

Many people had begun to disapprove of Pegler by this time, even though he rode sufficiently high to speak contemptuously of J. Edgar Hoover. A writer said that Westbrook's mouth was sometimes surly and his eyes defensive and angry. But those expressions could not have been seen in the August following the unsuccessful attempt to visit Alcatraz, when Westbrook opened a note of congratulation from Damon Runyon. Even though he wrote for Hearst, Runyon understood what made newspaper pieces readable, and what gave them their chances of survival beyond the life of yesterday's Five Star Final. He wrote, "Congratulations on the columns. I don't make a practice of scattering rosebuds, but you're one bloke that's got 'em coming."

That fall Westbrook reported the World Series of baseball, which he could cover without leaving town because the games were played in a

"Subway Series" between the New York teams, champions that year in the two major leagues. Pegler found the spectacle at Yankee Stadium and the Polo Grounds almost benign. The New York fans had not turned into the foul-mouthed hoodlums we know today, and Pegler wrote that he could see no uniforms at the ball parks. Approval warmed his heart when he viewed "a crowd like this, behaving well and having a good time under no more compulsion than the people established for themselves." We were in much better shape, from every point of view, than those Europeans who had to put up with dictators and secret police. He philosophized, "The government bubbles right out of the character and quality of the people." The Yankees won, four games to two.

At this point Westbrook had not yet made up his mind about the Roosevelts. He was planning to vote for FDR in the election of 1936—as he later revealed—but had begun to show disapproval for exploitation of White House connections by members of the President's family. Many of the side pickings in official Washington were regarded as honest graft—Senator Harry Truman had his wife on a government payroll, for example. It was felt that rural, half-educated types like Truman, who could not compete with superior people in the real world were entitled to the gleanings of government, as their time in Washington would be their only chance at putting together a stake to keep them off the county farms when they got old. But the Roosevelts began to run it into the ground, and the first of them to attract unfavorable attention was the President's oldest son James, who traded on the name in booking orders for a Boston insurance office. In fairness to the young man it was admitted that he had to make a living. But it seemed regrettable that he got into sales, where inside influence and name-dropping are part of the game. This is all right for Joe Blow, Dartmouth '34, but please, not for a Roosevelt. That was how we felt at the time, and the business operations of James's brother Elliott had not yet come into public view. The trouble was that the fake grandeur and air of royal authority around the presidency, beginning in Theodore Roosevelt's time and rising to a boil in Franklin's—the yacht, the limousines, the Secret Service gunmen giving the eye to spectators like goons escorting Al Capone to the Chicago Opera—had gone to the presidents' heads, swelling them to monstrous size, and had acted with equally unfortunate results on members of their families. You take a young fellow who really amounts to nothing at all, and give him the royal treatment, as though he were a fur buyer from Cincinnati, simply because his father has won an election, and he will quickly get used to it and consider it his due. He is entranced by the maiter dee rushing forward as though prodded with a cattle starter, hissing like a cobra at the room captains, "Mister Roos', yes sir Mister Roos', for you Mister Roos', a nice a fresh," and the other tables craning, the requests for the autograph, the discreetly cancelled tab, the hack driver who says wait till I tell the wife. It starts out on the cuff, but keeping it up requires real money, and then the young ones are hooked, and on the take they go.

Westbrook rode with the opinion of the country when he decided to give Franklin Roosevelt his vote. Coming up from the low point of early 1933, people now were feeling better about things in general, and millions had retrieved their self-respect by drawing pay checks again in jobs the government created. Works of the great relief administrations can be seen to this day in schools, highways, dams, and bridges; and the magnificent series of state and city guidebooks, written and edited as relief for writers and scholars, were by far the best things of their kind since Baedeker. The emotional credit of universal gratitude was entered to Franklin Roosevelt's account in the primitive style of reasoning that made a president the nation's head medicine man, warding off demons who attacked the general good. In fact Roosevelt deserves credit for selecting two able men to administer the federal relief programs. After being compelled to fire General Hugh Johnson, a bibulous nonfighting soldier of the Ike Eisenhower sort, Roosevelt found his almoners in Harold Ickes and Harry Hopkins. Ickes was a pretentious old fathead, but honest to the backbone. He was so aggressively commonplace in appearance that it would take a Daumier to draw him, but made a good Secretary of the Interior because of integrity and capacity for work. Not at all willingly, Ickes shared relief empires with Harry Hopkins, an odd, skinny, ailing man with a background in social work. Hopkins had a feeling for people down on their luck, and he understood Roosevelt's human sympathies in such matters as providing school shoes, a decent dress for a woman to wear while going to the corner store, stout work clothes and new tools for men starting back to jobs after years on the park bench or the bar stool. Hopkins came to be so close to Roosevelt that he moved into a White House bedroom where he became a none too edifying example of the man with no personal life aside from his cultivation of The Chief. The rest of us have an instinctive wish that these people would work from nine to five and go home. But the big men in their vanity must have slaves, and the toadies would not mean much on their own.

Pegler was aware of all this because of his special sensitivity to human degradation, but it was not possible for him to believe that the majority wanted anyone other than Roosevelt in the White House as the 1936 election came on. In opposition was Alfred M. Landon of Kansas, by no means an unattractive candidate, but doomed to defeat because he was a Republican in high Democratic times. There were Landon supporters, however, who believed he was going to defeat Roosevelt. One of these partisans was H. L. Mencken, the famous editor and critic who could write on serious matters in an uproariously comic style. Mencken briskly denounced FDR as a rogue and charlatan, and predicted a Landon victory, a curious mistake for a man of Mencken's usually clear understanding of what went on. Pegler took notice in October: "We find old Henry Mencken gone Republican and gibbering in unknown tongues." It had dawned on Westbrook that some Republicans were willing to bet on Landon. This was the easiest money ever heard of, but the victims must be tactfully approached. There were herds of Republicans, for example, peacefully grazing in the Yale Club, and Pegler rebuked a friend for "frightening game" when he disturbed these people. "There is plentiful game for all," said Pegler, "and we should treat one another by the rules of sportsmanship." In round numbers the vote added up to 27,000,000 for Roosevelt against 16,000,000 for Landon. Pegler did not record his winnings, but nobody denied that Roosevelt had a commanding majority. Nevertheless, 16,000,000 men and women are not negligible in number: by units, voting was a little less than seven to four. Yet the preposterous Electoral College gave Roosevelt 523 votes against 8 for Landon. You can't tell how politicians' minds work, but it is likely enough that FDR took the Electoral College balloting seriously. This would bring all the closer his fall from Westbrook's short list of approved people; but as it was, Pegler not only gave Franklin Roosevelt his vote and endorsement, but also told the readers of "Fair Enough" that Eleanor Roosevelt was "America's greatest woman."

After his endorsement of Franklin Roosevelt, Westbrook may have felt some misgivings at finding himself in agreement with a large majority of his fellow citizens. Still he continued to hold some of the basic Rooseveltian ideas, and he kept an eye on the discredited bankers and market manipulators to whom the President had given the name of economic royalists. In January 1937 Pegler had news of Al Wiggin, a banished New York financier whose activities had typified the greed and sharp practice of the royalist faction. Westbrook wrote that "if anything should happen to Mr. Wiggin, your correspondent would be deeply distressed not to hear all about it. Now comes an acquaintance from Charleston, S. C., however, who reports that nothing has happened to Mr. Wiggin, which would justify rejoicing by persons whose savings were invested in the stock of his bank at the time that Mr. Wiggin himself was selling short about 60,000 shares for a profit of four and a half million dollars. Mr. Wiggin has built a home for himself in a colony of economic royalists near Charleston known as the Yeamans Hall Club and, not to put a fair face on the news of him, he looks all right and seems to be his old self. He has plenty of money left from the sales of the stock of his bank and the unloading of his B.M.T. when his position gave him the know that the subway was going to pass its dividend, and he has no major vexations except the time the builder proposed to build a wall around his property according to the local custom. Mr. Wiggin objected to the wall, saying the place would look like a jail. . . .

"'What about friends,' your correspondent asked.

"'Oh, I don't know whether they are friends or not,' said the gentleman. 'You can't really tell who is a friend in this world. After all, you must remember that Mr. Wiggin is a very rich man who never did anything unlawful. Whether he did anything wrong is another question, but he wasn't even indicted, much less convicted, and the only comfort I can give you is to refer you to the record of the Senate investigation where you can refresh your memory and decide for yourself whether he ever did anything wrong. And you can recall that they grabbed back the bank pension of $100,000 a year that he awarded himself, if that is any pleasure.'

"'What about the people of Charleston? Aren't they supposed to be very aloof socially?'

"'Well,' said the gentleman, 'there isn't much money around there these days and these economic royalists in their little colony are big spenders. One day they ordered the caterer to get several dozen lobsters for dinner the next night, and he telephoned Bar Harbor and had them flown down in a special plane. All along the coast economic royalists are settling down in mansions and clubs on ground so poor that even the poorest people finally were starved out. That kind of money makes for tolerance.'

"'Is this an exclusive club, this Yeamans Hall?'

"'Well, what would you say?' said the gentleman from South Carolina. 'A Wiggin belongs.'"

After this handling of what amounted to a piece of novelist's material, Westbrook later in that month scouted Washington at the time of Roosevelt's second inauguration, for he was beginning to sense that many of his best targets lay in the District of Columbia. On January 21 he reported the inauguration as something similar to the main event and sideshows of a championship fight: "The heavy sound of male voices through the transoms and the shrill, rising cackle of ladies who have dipped their bills into their third cocktail of the evening indicate that there will be at least some survivors of the Great American Coronation Show.

"The valets are hustling through the corridors with soggy clothes for the pressers and gentlemen are peering out of bedroom doors wearing shorts or bathrobes, which expose their hairy, blue-veined shanks, crying plaintively for their pants.

"Other sounds in the night include the clink of ice in the pitcher as the boy goes down the hall and early, premonitory bleats of 'Sweet Adeline.' It was an ordeal, and some must die of it if there is any truth in what the doctors say about wet feet, exposure and chills, but we got our President, perhaps our last President or the last but one, officially sworn in, nevertheless. . . .

"Possibly those who were elsewhere have some notion of what Mr. Roosevelt said as again he stood to his pulpit on the Fourth of July platform facing the back yard of the national Capitol and sounded off on one thing and another. Those who were present for the turning of a page or the spinning of a reel of history will have no idea, however, until they read the text in the papers.

"The inauguration is an old ceremony by now, and the show has been greatly curtailed this time. In London, on the other hand, they had not buried a king in twenty-five years, but when it came time to lay away George V they got their foreign kings and ambassadors in line, even though they had to pull the bedclothes off some of them and pour them into their lion tamers' suits in the dark before the dawn, and the parade went clicking along strictly to the same time table. . . .

"The mass in the park were almost totally deprived of the show for which they had walked up the long, long hill, because the umbrellas shut off the view. Someone seemed to have an idea that it would be a treat to people exposed to these conditions to observe some thirty-odd governors, lieutenant governors and attorney generals riding slowly by in commonplace automobiles. If that idea was correct, then a good time must have been had, for the governors dragged by haltingly in low gear, waving and blowing kisses and gumming up the works remarkably well even for governors.

"Incidentally, Governor Earle of Pennsylvania, who appears to be the Prince of Wales of the present dynasty, was the only one other than the President to ride in an open car, and he made a handsome progress down the line, hoisting his hat and baring his teeth in a very fair imitation of Number One. Moreover, Mr. Earle had stooges planted along Pennsylvania Avenue who shouted 'Our Next President!' with great spontaneity. This did not appear to take the Governor by surprise, and he may think well of the idea himself.

"There was only one other attraction in the parade of governors, a lady in a gray car in the Illinois section, who rode with her window down and responded smilingly to cries of 'Hi'ya, Toots!' The others rode with the windows shut—which may have been a good thing."

This was prime Pegler—the President talking into "the back yard," the people who couldn't see or hear a thing, the claque saluting Earle of Pennsylvania, the boozing in hotel rooms. Westbrook intentionally echoed a poem by Eugene Field in "the clink of the ice in the pitcher"; and for avoiding the pedantry "attorneys general" he deserves high praise. Altogether a craftsmanlike piece which still reads well and carries a hint of doom in "perhaps our last President or the last but one." When he stayed in this vein Pegler was worth every cent they paid him.

Next day Westbrook took leave of Washington with a piece which began, "When I am in a theater and the play becomes too exciting I look at my watch, which reminds me that it is 10:15 and that pretty soon we will all get up and walk out, while back of the curtain the dead will rise and the lovers of the plot will wash up and start for their respective homes without so much as a parting hand squeeze in the alley.

"When I am in Washington I try to bear in mind that out through the country there are all those millions of poor people of whom Mr. Roosevelt speaks. But, as in the theater, I am often deceived by the eye and ear. I forget that there are poor or that there is any world beyond the borders of the District of Columbia.

"It takes an effort which is almost physical to recall that poverty and desperation exist elsewhere and that these people were sent here ostensibly to rescue the stricken. . . . Still it would be foolish to pretend that one and all are here to serve mankind, because everybody knows of people who are taken into the administration in jobs far above the subsistence level merely because they were friends or relatives of deserving Democrats and who have no interest but to keep these jobs. . . .

"Nowhere else but in Washington is it possible to conceive the vast number of politicians and little political coat-holders who live well and, in many cases, become rich off the very people whom Mr. Roosevelt desires to save. They live not only here but everywhere in the land, but at inauguration time they come to the capital in droves, well dressed, well fed and well heeled, to see to their political interests and take part in festivities which drown out all thought of distress. I wonder if Washington—the capital, the town—ever looks at its watch to recall reality and remember that the poor are not merely a political phrase."

Pegler liked to demonstrate that he was still a fine reporter. He respected the tradition of the newsman who did his own legwork as opposed to the system by which an observer in the field telephoned facts to a rewrite man who hammered out copy for the composing room, often relying on stereotyped diction out of haste or habit, so that little life remained in the account that reached the public's eye. The rewrite system had a further evil in its division of labor, which tended to place the brains in the office while the outside men needed nothing more than shoe leather to ply their trade. Thus it came about that the district men or the beat men on the courthouse or city hall might be illiterate and scarcely distinguishable from the tipstaves, judges, and police officials among whom they worked. Many of the beat men were drunkards, and they took petty graft like that which helped sustain Pegler's father in Minneapolis. The damage to good journalism occurred when newsmen became too friendly with office holders. Good old Johnny O'Booze, the veteran political reporter, was no man to expose thievery by his pals the court clerk and the city sealer. But from his earliest days Pegler had never worked on friendly terms with the authorities; even before he acquired personal power, he had fought the press officers around Sims and Pershing. Sports promoters and their press agents had learned to fear him, and now with a national audience to instruct and entertain, Westbrook continued to write his column, as far as possible, from information he himself had gathered. This was the way he worked after the Ohio River floods of 1937.

"Fair Enough" on February 4 was a dispatch from French Lick reporting that Pegler had just come up from Alton, "where the Coast Guard boats tied up in front of the church to spend the night." He went on to write that a young man known as Chig Parr came alongside in a skiff and asked, "Where is the man who wants to get out?" Westbrook said he was the man, and "Chig Parr led off through the mud and up a long hill in the dark along a course which seemed to be a creek bed but proved to be the old road, abandoned ten years ago when the improved road was shoved through. He walked fast and said he was used to it and could keep going all day, and as he walked he talked of fishing and the game to be hunted in the woods around, including 'possum, 'coon, and birds, and of his grandmaw who died recently. Grandmaw Parr was 100 years 3 months and 14 days old when she died of pneumonia after two days' illness. She had lived all her days right here on the Ohio River and had seen some great floods and some history since 1836. She was quick as a bird until her final illness. . . .

"Walking easily through the mud and over tumbled stones, Chig strode through the dark, mostly uphill and through woods and through the graveyard for a mile and a half, to the home of his brother, where his pony was loose in a field. But his brother told Chig the little mare was lame—which was no wonder, for she had made nine trips out and back in a few days, sometimes carrying double—and Chig therefore caught his brother's mules Kate and Frank.

"He threw the pony's saddle on Kate and hopped aboard Frank bareback and led on toward the home of Alvin Hahus, a farmer over at the hard road who had a car and might take a man up to Bedford or French Lick to the telegraph wire. . . .

"Mrs. Hahus and her four children sat by the stove, and we talked of the flood and of Grandmaw Parr until Mr. Hahus came in. He was very courteous, and, though it was bedtime for a farmer, he seemed to deem it a Christian duty to help a stranger.

"Mr. Hahus and his young son, a high school student, gassed her up from a tank in the shed, and as we started he brought up the subject of hawks, which proved to be a great interest of his. Mr. Hahus, in fact, is the inventor of the only discriminating hawk trap on the market which kills the harmful hawk but spurns the types which destroy vermin and are held to be friends of man.

"You bait the trap with chicks about two weeks old, being careful to avoid the glare of the sun, which would kill them, and when the predatory hawk swoops down the trap kills him before he can harm the chicks. So you see it is humane as well as efficient, and it seems a great pity that the government does not take it up, for the indiscriminate killing of good hawks along with the bad is one of the tragedies of wild life in this country.

"But what does Congress do? Nothing. Mr. Hahus has never made a scientific study of birds, but he knows most of the indigenous species by eye and ear, and it is an ambition of his some day to cross Florida through the glades and see those fabulous flocks which darken the sky in their thousands.

"Twenty years ago they ruled him out of the Army with tuberculosis and gave him two years to live.

"The flood was of little interest to Mr. Hahus, for his farm of tired, listless acres is high above the water, but Chig Parr, who works on the river, was nonchalant about it, too. There had been no drownings and floods are routine. They always wash some houses off their foundations and dump some on their sides. Just now in every dry house in Alton people were doubling up with the dispossessed, but not for long.

"As in the long life of Grandmaw Parr, the river would go back; it always did.

" 'One thing about these Parrs,' Mr. Hahus said, 'you can kill 'em, but there's nothing on this earth can scare 'em.' "

Five days later Westbrook wrapped up his flood story in a dispatch filed from Chicago. Someone had complained that newspaper accounts failed to recognize the generosity and personal sacrifice of the people in the river towns who had given emergency relief to flood victims. With this Westbrook agreed, but his final column on the disaster took a Peglerian turn halfway to its end. He started by admitting that "The women of the local Red Cross chapters, just ordinary women of the kind whom the census takers put down as housewife—turned to and cooked and served meals by hand to anyone who crawled off a log, and about the only credential that a human being needed was an appetite, of which there was no lack. They would rig up board tables on carpenters' horses in the basement of the courthouse, if it were high and dry, or in the Sunday school room of the church and start putting out as soon as the refugees hit town.

"In some places the washouts were quartered in empty store buildings or courtrooms, but more were taken into private homes and given some kind of shakedown, and it just seemed to be taken for granted that anyone who had a dry house would shelter as many persons as it was possible to crowd in."

Pegler noted that doctors worked around the clock, and he observed a personal touch in all the relief work that "showed the human race at its best." At this point Pegler decided he had said enough about inherent decency and it was time to pull himself up. This scene of the human race in a good moment was not a grand and unlimited prospect. And so Westbrook went on to say that it was interesting "to observe this indiscriminate kindness and zeal to relieve want and suffering, because in other times many of these people had shown themselves capable of the most malignant cussedness toward their fellow men.

"Southern Indiana, around Evansville, was the point of infection of the Ku Klux Klan, which was Fascism at its worst, and there were people engaged in the most trying relief work day and night for about a week who formerly had stayed up nights scheming ways to gang up on their neighbors socially and economically and stewing in the smelly juice of hatred. . . .

"It developed into a great system of snooping, espionage, anonymous threats and night-riding—always with the odds shamefully against the victim—and it would be a comfort to put it down to ignorance but for the fact that Indiana makes quite an important business of squirting education over the young. It finally flopped when the leaders of a movement which claimed to revere and protect American womanhood were convicted of gang rape of a young woman, who was then left to die, and the head man was sent to prison for life.

"No doubt about it, some of the people who gave the most self-sacrificing service in the flood relief, helping anyone who came along with a tender altruism consistent with the teaching of Jesus Christ, were Klucks in the old days.

"And now that the water has fallen and the dramatic phase has passed the worst of the trouble starts, although probably it will receive little national notice. A flood when it is a flood is something to see, for it is exciting and in a sense clean. When the water goes down, however, it leaves slime and horrible objects on the beach. A man can fall in the water, get wet and dry without loss of dignity, but there is something humiliating about muck, and every man's house and farm are his own problem.

"There is no community effort here. His furniture falls apart, the plaster comes off his walls, his house or garage or barn may be left slaunchwise partly on the lot next door, and all this is his little worry. The militia, the Coast Guards and the visiting firemen and police will be gone, and the community will be back on the old basis.

"Some pretty terrible slums have been washed out, and this would be a break for the country if there were any assurance that the reconstruction would not merely replace the slums with the salvage of hovels that were unfit for human habitation in the first place."

So according to Pegler, some of the kindly people of Indiana, who sent their children to college and reverenced Our Flag, and who had given prompt aid to flood victims, were to be listed among the bed-sheet Fascists who smelled of hatred and tormented helpless victims for want of anything better to do. Pegler was right. And he was right too, when he pointed out that after the visiting firemen had gone, a population not too far removed from peasantry was left in a situation not much different from outright ruin.

By the late 1930s there had grown up a consensus among intelligent readers that Pegler was important as well as entertaining; but no agreement could be reached as to where he registered on the ideological scale which swung from left to right according to the weight of liberal, conservative, or outright reactionary opinions. When Pegler stepped on the weighing platform, one could not predict where the indicator would come to rest: it varied from day to day. One thing that readers and critics demand of a serious writer is that he take a position and stay there, and when we have a columnist preaching to us we want to know what religion he dispenses. At this time Pegler claimed membership among the liberals, but the elders of that sect could never quite persuade themselves that he was sound in the faith. Yet Pegler subscribed in an emphatic way to the basic liberal doctrine of the 1930s, which held that the possibility of a Fascist uprising in this country was a matter of much greater concern than anything the Communists might be able to do. Westbrook stated this conviction as strongly as any certified liberal when he wrote in March 1937 that "Communism will never get to first base in the United States because it is strictly a foreign article and identified with atheism. On the other hand there is a good deal of native Fascism in the American makeup and a strong religious and chivalrous strain. The chivalry is somewhat juvenile in that it sometimes goes out to avenge an insult as a workout, knowing that no such insult was ever offered.

"The tendency toward Fascism has been demonstrated many times in vigilante movements of various kinds, such as the Ku Klux, the Knights of Luther, the Silver Shirts and the Black Legion, and in the domination of many communities by an element vaguely described as the right-thinking, God-fearing, patriotic Americans. This element includes merchants and other businessmen, doctors, dentists and druggists, politicians, overzealous and not very intelligent preachers, and energetic young bucks eager for the adventure of preserving American womanhood and American ideals from nameless or fabricated horrors.

"Individually they are all right, and their Americanism under normal conditions is pure. But bring them together under the spell of secrecy and the charm of a voice in the belief that they are morally better than the non-joiners and you have the nucleus of Fascism. . . .

"It is fairly easy to recognize Communism, because it simply cannot disguise itself as that which we understand as Americanism. . . . It is not easy to recognize Fascism, because it always calls itself Americanism and calls on everyone who calls himself an American to join some band to protect his hearth and altar from the foul invader. This democracy has done an excellent job of providing this protection all these years, but now and again there comes a call for some special deputies to back up the authorities.

"Considering the well-known American appetite for this kind of thing and the suckers we have been for promoters preying on our regard for home and church, I feel that Fascism might be put across some time, especially if we get careless about law and the Constitution. But Communism, should it ever make a break, would be slapped down in a few days. Communism just isn't in the breed."

Thus Westbrook continued in that silver decade of American life that must have been the best time of Pegler's life as well. His unqualified success in his trade had started as the decade of the 1930s began, with the Wall Street panic two months old, and many an average American confronting a succession of anxieties. Millions at the bottom of society were to go through emotional defeat if not physical starvation, while the country saw the disgrace of Hoover and the smoke of supper fires in shantytowns, then heard the bracing words of Franklin Roosevelt's first inaugural address. And there remained a kind of hush on the land, and there was much examining of America by writers, and by regional painters. These authors and artists joined in a romantic celebration of the country's past at about the artistic level of the "Socialist realism" decreed for Russia by the commissars of culture. Stephen Vincent Benét expressed the mood in his story "The Devil and Daniel Webster," a piece of artificial folklore that met with admiration at the time. The story has not aged well and seems almost unreadable today. But Pegler stood apart from such contrived "American" writing, for he worked in the genuine tradition of the American journalistic scolds who wrote under the pseudonyms Artemus Ward, Orpheus C. Kerr, Petroleum V. Nasby, and Mark Twain.* The style goes back to the brags of the riverboat bullies in *Huckleberry Finn*. And that scene echoed in Pegler's mind when he turned his attention to Mussolini on March 25, 1937. German and Italian Fascists had interfered in the Spanish Civil War, thus making a bad matter worse, for anyone could tell you a civil war was one thing that outside countries had best leave alone. Common sense would tell you that. And here was Mussolini threatening the British Embassy in Rome because the English papers had reported humiliating defeats of Italian troops in Spain. Pegler wrote, "For a long time I have felt that these quarrelsome, hypersensitive, wild-eyed dictators remind me of someone or some type I have met before. Now I have it. It is the familiar fighting drunk, known in all saloons, who leans to the bar roaring the most idiotic nonsense as dogma, disturbing the peace of the other customers and glaring into the back-bar mirror in

*For an extended discussion of Pegler's pseudonymous literary ancestors, the reader should consult *American Humor: A Study of the National Character*, by Constance Rourke (New York: Harcourt Brace & Co., 1931, and Doubleday Anchor Books, 1953).

pleased appreciation of his fighting face. . . . There is not much doubt that he will fight if crossed, because he is fighting drunk and spoiling for a scrap, in which he might be pretty difficult, because he is utterly reckless in his condition. . . . He tells himself that he is a perfectly deadly fighter and brave as a lion. . . . In the saloons they sometimes give such a man a Mickey Finn or the bartender bides his time and whangs him on the head with his beer mallet. Or maybe some little guy ups and crowns him with a granite gobboon. At this point, however, the analogy runs out, and I just don't foresee the end of this." The reader will have noted that Pegler follows Mark Twain by introducing a little guy who thumps the braggart.

At the time that Pegler wrote this piece, the encouraging events in the publishing trade of the late 1930s included the evident success and prosperity of *Time* and *The New Yorker,* but there were ominous occurrences in the journalistic empire of W. R. Hearst. In spite of the superficial excitement his papers drummed up, and their distribution in thirteen of the largest American cities, banks and accountants had a feeling there was something wrong. Threading their way through the labyrinthine bookkeeping of the Hearst companies, the men with sharpened pencils gasped when they saw the extent of the owner's withdrawals, leaving nothing in the cash drawers but his own markers for repayment at a future date. It took genius to drain the value out of twenty daily and eleven Sunday newspapers, two wire services, a feature syndicate, six magazines, a newsreel, and the big Sunday supplement, *The American Weekly,* whose distribution with the Hearst papers gave it a larger circulation than any other periodical in the world. Hearst also owned gold, silver, and copper mines, chiefly inherited from his father; and real estate, hotels, theaters, business buildings, and ranches to the value of many millions. With all this in hand, Hearst managed to overspend himself for palatial residences and works of art, which he bought on such an imperial scale that he had no place to put the stuff, and some of it had to stand uncrated in warehouses. The ranch at San Simeon cost so much to build and maintain that it could only be compared to the fabulous mansion in a story by F. Scott Fitzgerald, "The Diamond as Big as the Ritz." Hearst had started borrowing at the bank as early as 1924 and never caught up. After the crash of 1929, he assembled something called American Newspapers, Inc., and took out a boodle of $50,000,000; incredible as it seems, by 1937 he was in trouble again. This time it was a case of the man from the finance company in the outer office, and Hearst going out the back window to confront another bailiff in the alley. They took 95 percent of his control of the main holding company, and put out publicity that the Hearst newspapers would be run on a sound business basis in the future. But W. R. Hearst was still the editorial boss, and in that lay much of the trouble: the newspapers were simply no good. Some of the proudest flagships in the line had been losing money, and the *New York American* was dropping $1,000,000 a year. Brisbanalities had ceased to appear on its front page when Arthur died in 1936, and even with this improvement the paper limped so badly that they closed it down in 1937 and continued its name in the afternoon *Journal-American.*

And when Pegler observed the death of the *New York American,* he took it as a warning that any journalist who forgot his readers would eventually land in the street. Brisbane with Hearst's help had ruined the paper, which after all had filled a certain place in the New York morning field, and could have remained alive to this day if properly written and edited. Hearst had failed to see that Brisbane's vanity and belief that the world awaited his wisdom in one-sentence paragraphs had killed the *American,* and that just putting a name at the head of a daily column would not produce a readable piece: the column still had to be written after the oracle's name went up. Pegler analyzed his occupation and saw a degree of charlatanry there; and he concluded that a columnist was neither by definition nor necessity a wise man. He wrote, "Of all the fantastic fog-shapes that have risen off the swamp of confusion since the First World War, the most futile and, at the same time, the most pretentious, is the deep-thinking, hair-trigger columnist and commentator who knows all the answers just off hand and can settle great affairs with absolute finality three days or even six days a week. . . . The trade or calling of cosmic columnist in American journalism is a new development."

This approach harmonized with Pegler's lampooning style when he considered international affairs and the possibility of war. He continued to warn his readers in 1937 that Mussolini threatened the peace of the world, and yet not drive them away with unreadable think-pieces like those that burdened the *New York Times.* Therefore he presented the Duce as a comic figure. In this Westbrook agreed with Charles Chaplin, who cast the moon-faced comedian Jack Oakie as the Italian dictator supporting his own interpretation of Hitler, who apparently copied the small moustache that Chaplin had made famous all over the world some years before. Pegler deduced that belligerency leading to war came from nothing more important than a bunch of dudes in the various foreign offices suffering hurt feelings over matters of precedence. He wrote on March 26 that these fellows would "sulk and scowl and pull down their lower lips if someone of inferior rank gets more soup or an extra nod from the hostess." It was all foolishness anyway, and Pegler recalled an uproar over social arrangements in connection with the official hostess and sister of a Vice President. It had been "a great dither . . . over the grave question whether Mrs. Dolly Gann, the sister of old Charlie Curtis, a blanket Indian and one-time jockey and, incidentally, the best poker player in town, should go into the dining room before or after Alice Longworth. Old Charlie himself once might have preferred a skillet of eggs on a high stool at the Owl Lunch, but he had become Vice President and people get peculiar ideas after a few years in Washington." The danger lay in the possibility that some foreign dignitary might harbor a grudge after being "nosed out in the rush for the goose liver canapes." The loser in this version of the boarding house stampede would "mark it on his cuff" and some day "the peasants might be called on to die avenging a long and deliberate series of foul provocations."

In 1938 the news of Hitler's continued racial persecutions suggested a parable to Westbrook. He wrote on November 23 about how the peoples of the world first destroyed all the Jews, and then continued the slaughter, killing off each other until "it ended with just two survivors, a man and an old woman in a tent. He was one-eighth freckled, that is to say, he had a few small freckles. She was of the pure, non-freckled strain. So one night she slugged him with an ax as he slept and fell dead from the poison he had put in her soup that evening. And the horses and the asses romped in the field, never again to be overburdened; deer walked in the open, unafraid of being shot by men; rabbits and birds took courage, cities mouldered and the world was purified of cruelty, dishonesty, truckling and greed."

An instinct for destruction working on Pegler's thought processes may have given color to that story of all humanity deprived of life, and lower animals in possession of the world. The concept of a pure non-freckled race in pride of its ancestry reminded one of Mark Twain and his disillusionment with man. And the same kind of hopeless anger lay beneath another piece that Westbrook wrote at this time, which expressed his opinion of the Sunday drivers who made highways dangerous with their incompetence and selfishness at the wheel. He imagined a practical way to dispose of such people, and said to his readers, "I forgot to tell you about the hunting last Sunday, the first day of the legal shooting of Sunday drivers. After all these years of protection, the game was plentiful along practically all the roads, and the highway police, who were in considerable numbers, interfered only to settle disputes such as the time when I got a fine buck in the act of creeping at the head of a long line of cars on a narrow, winding road, and another hunter claimed him." The trooper ruled for Pegler and the other man was a good sport about it, explaining to Westbrook, " 'I had had my eye on that creeper for years, and I suppose I was overanxious. He wrecked a friend of mine on a curve near here seven years ago.' . . . Another hunter got an interesting specimen, a buck riding along, wabbling all over the busy highway driving at about 20 miles per hour, his arm around a doe, who was almost in his lap. This one would take his left hand off the steering wheel now and again to remove a cigar from his face and shake off the ash, and there was half a dozen hunters strung out behind him, anxious to make the kill. The one who got him was in an oncoming car in the other lane. He sized up the situation in a quick glimpse and knocked off the game right under the very eyes of those who were edging along in pursuit, but there was no rancor whatever."

In those days our country's reaction to the Spanish Civil War showed how hard most people found it to dig through the sentiments that propaganda aroused down to the rock of consistent judgment and opinion. For it was not only Pegler who suffered from perplexity, and his views had the virtue of simplicity, although it was fashionable to denounce simplification as a vice. For all of that, the basic questions of life and death were fundamental simplicities in themselves, and Pegler saw Hitler, Mussolini, and Stalin as killers and possible candidates for psychiatric treatment if anyone could ever throw the net over them.

Most of the intellectuals in this country agreed with Westbrook about the Nazis and the Fascists, but could not bring themselves to recognize the same danger to civilization in Stalin and the Russian Communist Party. And at that time, the idea that the United States also could be a murderous criminal among the nations was unheard of except among a small number of radical theorists, most of them American Communists and ready to alter their thinking on short notice whenever there came a change in the party line. The war in Spain lined up conservatives against liberals in North America because the Spanish Church and Army had risen against a Socialist government, and the religious and military people had received help from Nazis and Fascists, while Communist political agents and officers had come in on the government side. Although nominally Catholic, Westbrook wrote in May 1938 that he couldn't see why "working class Catholics" should be expected to hate the Spanish government faction. He asked if Dictator Franco planned to drive the people of Spain back into the Roman Church at the bayonet's point, and noted that Franco had accepted help from

Moorish troops who were Mohammedans, and from Nazis who had no religion at all, only a sort of Wagnerian paganism. "If I were a Spaniard," Pegler wrote, "who had seen Franco's missionary work among the children, I might see him in hell but never in church." Heywood Broun himself could not have put it more strongly.

Broun was leader in the social set that included Westbrook and Julie, centering its activities nine months of the year in Fairfield County across the Connecticut line a few miles from Pound Ridge. Most of the members of this clique were writers, and all of them made excellent money in the good market for members of their craft that had developed in the silver decade. People wanted to be informed and entertained with the same dose of reading, as Henry Luce and Briton Hadden discovered when they started *Time* Magazine. The packaging of words had turned into moderately big business, with considerable profit to the men and women who supplied the words, even though they carried on their backs a towering structure of salesmen, business managers, printers, and publishers. Broun, Pegler, and their writing friends enjoyed the immensely satisfactory sensation of commanding ample funds with which to gamble, drink, and set up as country gentlemen. When collecting fees in Hollywood, William Faulkner observed: "Money in his pocket feels good to a man," and the Fairfield County delegation might have taken that remark for a motto. But even more than their good pay they enjoyed each other's company. Broun's circle of congenial friends included such well-known figures as Gene Tunney, the erudite former heavyweight boxing champion, and George T. Bye, who was Mrs. Franklin Roosevelt's literary agent. A popular young man who frequently came to the parties, or passed the weekend at Broun's farm north of Stamford, was Quentin Reynolds, a highly paid writer for *Collier's* magazine who had started out on the sportside, like Broun and Pegler. A few years before, "Quent" had played football for Brown University, and the newspapers had called him "Rhode Island Red" because of his ginger-colored hair. In fluent professional skill he resembled Broun, and could tap out a short story or an article as fast as he could operate the typewriter. This left Reynolds plenty of time to spend with friends, of whom he had many, for he was extremely likeable. Broun had a guest cottage on his Connecticut farm which Reynolds occupied every summer. Anyone who knew Reynolds would be glad to help him; Pegler used to say he had recommended the young man for the *Collier's* job, and Reynolds also got an enthusiastic endorsement from Grantland Rice. Quentin liked to join in the poker games at Broun's farm, in which the composer Deems Taylor and other distinguished and talented people sat in. They always welcomed Pegler to the game, where he was regarded as "a live one." Reynolds recorded that "Peg could be counted to lose forty dollars. All of us were so fond of him that we made no bones about calling him the worst poker player east of the Hudson."

The late 1930s were the time of the celebrity in New York. There were celebrity hours on the radio and celebrity nights in restaurants, dedicated to the idea that persons of renown were interesting in themselves, and that less notable citizens would pay to see and read about them. And it was not very hard to acquire the rank of celebrity at a time when eight daily newspapers were demanding names to fill the large space they gave to night life, the theater, movies, sport, society, and the writing trade. The papers imparted the feeling of a village to Manhattan by recording as news the intelligence that Bill Jones and Susy Smith had lunched at Ed Brown's restaurant. The ease with which a man or woman could acquire the designation of celebrity put one in mind of George Ade's man on whom a job printer conferred the title of Honorable. The college of heralds for these rankings consisted of the Broadway columnists whom Pegler despised, and their coadjutors the night club press agents, a tribe of elderly young men who sat at corner tables, had the privilege of issuing free drinks, and passed on the news of Bill Jones and Susy Smith to the columnists who made their rounds all through the night. Some of the celebrities, like Broun and Reynolds, were people of worth and achievement, but others attained fame by nothing more than showing up night after night. Pegler found it interesting that debutantes, sometimes only seventeen years old, should be appointed to the rank of celebrity, with autograph seekers, photographers, and restaurant proprietors in their train. The most famous of these young girls received the kind of treatment in New York that the press and public in England lavished upon royalty. Pegler observed that this form of the celebrity game had its foundation in false hospitality at the enormous parties the parents gave to introduce their daughters to society. Before the winter social season of 1937, the *World-Telegram* devoted two full pages to a listing of prospective debutantes, sorting them into two grades of A and B. This must have made the Bs happy. Pegler left the question of relative rank to society editors, and addressed himself to the handling of the money. At the height of the debutante season on January 20, he wrote:

"It appears that the idle rich are by no means careless about their buying when they decide to make the welkin ring, which may be one of the reasons why they remain rich. The provisions are acquired in the most businesslike manner, with discounts for quantity and cash, and though the guests may give their happy spirits full play and do the split and skin the cat from the crystal chandeliers, that does not indicate that the host has yielded too. It appears that on the contrary, the host will be keeping a cold, impersonal eye on the hired help and make sure that none of them sends out full champagne bottles among the dead ones or if he does not wish to check and tally himself he will hire a bookkeeper with a long, thin nose and a Vermont disposition to do this for him. . . . By the time joy becomes unconfined, he can start running in the cheap champagne covered with napkins. . . ."

Although he cast a cold eye on debutante parties, Pegler himself played the celebrity game under the influence of Heywood Broun. It wasn't entirely a matter of nightclubs and dances in hotel ballrooms: on occasion, persons of real or fancied renown also displayed themselves in the country. A typical outdoor event took place in the summer of 1938, when softball teams composed of notables played a match at the Lowell Thomas estate near Pawling, over the New York line. Thomas captained the Nine Old Men and Gene Tunney led the Connecticut Nutmegs. The players included the sporty department store magnate Bernard Gimbel, Harold Ross of *The New Yorker,* Reynolds, Pegler, F. Chase Taylor, who was known on the radio as Colonel Lemuel Q. Stoopnagle, and the historian Hendrik Willem van Loon, an imposing man who equalled Broun or Reynolds in bulk. Among the spectators was Frank Norris, managing editor of *Time* Magazine. Norris was present as a guest of Thomas and not as a reporter, but he later gave his friends a vivid account of the game. He said it was execrable as baseball even if not intended seriously, and he noticed that Pegler went down to first base with "a funny little old-fashioned high-kneed run." After the game, the purpose of the afternoon came into view when players and spectators adjourned to the cocktail tables set up by various hosts in the surrounding countryside. Pegler entertained a number of guests who came back to Pound Ridge with him. It was fun, and the only thing about it that seems strange today is the amount of attention the gathering received from the press and radio. This marked the high point in the application of a doctrine that no matter how puerile the connection, names make news. The illness in the newspaper industry, creeping toward its brain and heart, would soon enough begin to put big papers in their graves, at last to leave the field of public information to television, which could scarcely find time for basic news, let alone the listing of celebrities in frivolous pursuits. It made its own celebrities, announcers reading copy in big-head close-ups. The TV people have little enough time, it would seem, for basketball and jackpot bowling, cop and hospital shows with authoritarian heroes, greedy kids wolfing candy and hamburgers in commercials, and politicians telling lies so obvious that you expect coconuts to fall on their heads. Even the celebrity copy in the *Journal-American* was more entertaining than this.

Pegler's exhibition of his funny little old-fashioned high-kneed run, in his cavorting with Broun at Pawling, was no indication that a lasting friendship had developed. On the contrary, the two men were approaching an open break because of basic differences that lay in their attitudes toward organized labor. In 1937 industrial relations, now taken for granted as an infinite series of strikes and raised wages, was the most hotly discussed issue on the domestic scene, and many people thought it was not yet settled and could go either way. How one felt about the labor question at that time might reveal fundamentals of personality, and high-voltage emotional discharges, not to mention physical combat, could be the result of aggressive picket lines or rough argument by hard-bitten union chiefs against employers who did not like to hear it said that they had been greedy when they held the upper hand. Now the Roosevelt administrations had brought about an adjustment of power between the labor force and the managers who employed it. Time-honored classical economics had held that labor was a commodity, and like any other commodity must be sold at the market for whatever the sellers might be able to obtain. This doctrine took no account of the fact that when the price of labor went down, the eating money of the laborers also diminished; and theoretically, at least, when it diminished to an absolute nothing in hard times, the workers and their families might then conveniently meet the situation by ceasing to eat. American labor unions had given some protection to skilled workers since the time of Samuel Gompers, who organized the American Federation of Labor in 1886. But it remained for the Roosevelt government, by new legislation under the approval of public opinion—except for the opinion of most employers, a small minority—to encourage and strengthen unions that gave heavy bargaining power to unskilled workers who had previously stood, often enough, in anxious shabby lines at the hiring gates, to be turned away without ceremony whenever need for their services was no longer felt. Pegler saw the new industrial unions, with thousands of unskilled people under command of aggressive leaders, as a threat to freedom rather than as a weapon that little men must have if they are to come out on top in fights with big men. In January 1937 Pegler wrote that the typical union head was part ham actor and part Tammany chief. "He knows how to pour it on the boys in meeting and create false presumption that they are dirty finks if they vote against his proposition, however wrong they know him to be. He also knows all the smart parliamentary fast ones, the art of concealing a sleeper in the language of a resolution and something about timing and the inertia of the rank and file who go to meeting only when they suspect something is up. He doesn't show too much respect for their intelligence. . . ."

But it was hard to think of Broun as a typical union head. He was still perhaps the most admired columnist in the country, and Pegler recognized his talent with envy. Five hours of work went into the usual Pegler column, and it was work that he found harder than wrestling with containers of pig meat at the stock yards. Westbrook said that Broun had a "beautiful gift," and he could "play the typewriter like a honky-tonk piano." It seemed to come with such slight effort that Broun sometimes gave the impression of failing to take his position seriously. Heywood wrote, "I had an ancestor at the feast of Bel-Shazzar. He sat at the press table." And it looked as though Broun harbored some notion of getting away from the press table and becoming a maker of news instead of one who offered comment on it. He had founded a union among the workers in an important trade, who supposedly could not pull together well enough to organize—and now the Guild was a power to be reckoned with, and Broun its international president, and possibly planning another run for Congress. He might have made it this time, but without the blessing of Roy Howard, who did not wish to see *any* radical in Congress, and certainly not a leftist with the brains and eloquence of Heywood Broun.

Not Socialists but Communists were the troublemakers in the Guild, and Broun's problem of guiding the union along a rational path grew considerably harder in the summer of 1937 when the organization moved from the American Federation of Labor into the Congress of Industrial Organizations. This change had the support of the disciplined party fraction, for it took the Guild out of a federation that looked after skilled craftsmen into a congress where unskilled labor was the source of strength. This meant that clerks, typists, and elevator operators would be joining the Guild along with reporters and rewrite men. The party fraction grew more arrogant, and it seemed plain enough that these Guild members were ready to sacrifice their colleagues' hopes for better pay and more advantageous contracts whenever it suited the mysterious convolutions of the party line. The non-Communists in the Guild learned the manipulation of union politics from the disciplined hard core, and set up a secret activist group of their own, which they called the Anti-Stalinist Caucus. Its members came to meetings prepared for battle, and eventually gained control of the Guild. Oliver Pilat was among the founders of the caucus, and he tells in his biography of Pegler how Westbrook got hold of their circular, *The Guild Progressive,* and used it to prove his contention that Communists were as powerful in the Guild as they were, at that time, in many CIO unions. Pilat says Pegler's support horrified the caucus members, for while their purpose was "to organize a national anti-Communist coalition in the Guild," they were "fussy about being called Red-baiters, a term then more dreaded by some liberals than being called Reds." All in all, Pegler's help was most unwelcome, Pilat records, and "his uninformed opinion rolled back and forth across the country like Victor Hugo's rollicking cannon aboard ship. Many good unionists still read 'Fair Enough.'"

Unionists following Pegler's columns often got the feeling that he was dubious about collective bargaining in general, but not always wrong when he lashed at the men of power in the labor movement. There was no question that some of the union heads were ordinary hoodlums too friendly with employers, and that they used or tolerated violence, so that honest labor leaders sometimes ran risks that included assault and death. In the same year that the Guild entered the CIO, President Norman Redwood of the Compressed Air, Subway, and Tunnel Workers fell dead from a volley fired by persons unknown. A big contractor had threatened Redwood, but the New York police were never able to trace the killers. Rank and file union members by scores and hundreds began writing to Pegler with accounts of meanness and abuse of power by their elected representatives. By telling about the betrayal of helpless dues payers, and attacking the party fractions, Pegler found material for exciting copy, and he did a certain amount of good in discouraging some abuses of union members in cases where their officers sold them out to the employers, or ordered goons to slug them for talking up in meeting. He would also expose such abuses as the theft of vacation funds and expulsion of members who criticized union policies.

Roy Howard must have found it hard to applaud Westbrook when the columnist expressed approval of events in South Chicago that all other writers referred to as the Memorial Day Massacre. These newsmen followed Webster in defining the term as "promiscuous and wholesale slaughter, especially of those who can make little or no resistance," and that was what had happened when police fired into a crowd of strikers outside the plant of the Republic Steel Corporation on

May 30, 1937. Ten people died on the spot, and two more in hospitals. Newsreels showed the police peppering the crowd at will, bringing down seven with bullets in the back as they ran for their lives. In the face of this photographic evidence, on which a Senate inquiry determined the police had no reason to shoot, Pegler wrote of the affair in the spirit of an apoplectic retired Indian Army colonel denouncing the Meerut mutineers. Give the beggars a whiff of grape, sir. Pegler thus made himself a target for caricature, but the writer who might have aimed the most effective mockery was Broun, and at the time he had trouble enough on his hands without attacking Pegler. Moreover, Westbrook continued to present a baffling problem in identification for liberals who wanted his eloquence and fighting qualities on their side.

Pegler could still show sympathy when he could bring himself to visualize a human being in distress. A column of that year revealed Pegler's feeling for an economic royalist named David Lamar who had landed in jail. There may have been memories of the prisoners in Minnesota to whom he had brought water as a child in Pegler's mind when he wrote that while Lamar might make the best of imprisonment, it was a bad thing to undergo, and a quite hopeless thing for one sort of inmate: "The colored boys in the Northern jails where there is no Jim Crow segregation usually huddle together anyway, and face the future with less show of anxiety although that may only be an appearance, due to the fact that nobody cares much about what happens to them. Even when they are out of jail what does the future offer them?" Pegler gave thought to the actual experience of being locked in cells. The nights were the worst time, "broken by mutters and nightmare cries, and the sight of old wiring nailed along wooden beams puts a man in mind of fire in the dead of night when the cells are locked and the guard, a minor policeman, is down in the alley eating the best cuts off a side of beef from the chill-room and knocking over a few bottles of beer with a friend. . . . Call it a rest cure, an experience or a retreat, jail is just what the word has always meant and always will. That is why we have them."

In spite of sympathy for certain inmates, Pegler had his candidates for jail, and often lined them up in print. Leading the procession through the prison gates would be the members of the country's Union League Clubs, fortresses of wealth and privilege in which only Republicans could obtain membership. Wealthy patriots had founded the League during the Civil War, contributing money to the cause rather than their own appearance on the field of battle, and by Pegler's day, their large grim clubhouses were conspicuous in New York, Philadelphia, and Chicago. These institutions gave off an odor of complacent selfishness which stirred opposition in Pegler's soul. In fact, Westbrook saw Union Leaguers as the reincarnation of Theodore Roosevelt's favorite villains, the malefactors of great wealth. Behind their high, thick walls they planned nothing good for ordinary people, and Pegler wrote that these men had odious accomplices in fleecing the public and leading it in the wrong direction, "a combination of Huey Long, Father Coughlin, and the Reverend Gerald L. K. Smith, and all the brutal and reckless enemies of national peace and understanding that ever troubled the country, and the enemy of that public order which it loves so earnestly in its old age. Old age—that is just it."

Broun and Pegler had begun a performance of the classic staircase story in which the characters pass, one on the way down, the other going up. Broun was descending: he still had his "beautiful gift" as a light essayist, but he was no longer as sure of his place within the walls of the conservative establishment as he had been when Howard first brought him to the old *Telegram* in 1929, before its acquisition of the *World*. Publishers of big papers saw that organizing the Guild and marching on picket lines was a different thing from writing graceful pieces about the brotherhood of man and opening job registries for the unemployed in the depression year of 1933. Five years later, publishers and other business administrators were sure they wanted no Fascists about the place, but left wingers were bad fellows too—and Broun was an ornament of the left.

As Thomas Jefferson wished to be remembered for founding the University of Virginia, Heywood made it clear that he considered the Newspaper Guild his greatest achievement. He had forced publishers into concessions they would have thought beyond possibility only a few years before. He had power: newsmen who did not support a Guild strike in Seattle, for example, faced the physical threat of CIO longshoremen when they tried to enter the plant. But this was not the kind of influence that advanced a career on the *World-Telegram*, or made an employee popular with Executive Editor Lee Wood, who hated paying good money and especially disliked Broun's high salary. Moreover, the ease with which Broun turned out his copy gave the impression that he was giving small effort to the earning of his pay. Here they were, paying Broun big money and he seemed to spend more time trying to tear down the newspaper business than working on the job. He was everywhere except at his typewriter. Sooner or later this would have to stop, according to Lee B. Wood. But Broun had nailed up his colors, and in the fall of 1937 he put his talent as a light essayist into the service of his political convictions to explain how he had arrived where he was: "'Tell me, Mr. Broun,' said the young lady to my right, 'how did you happen to become a Red?'" Broun replied that "It was Professor Carver of the Harvard faculty and Tris Speaker, centerfielder of the Boston Red Sox, who closed the door and left me locked in the hall of heresy." It seemed that Professor Carver gave a course in political science which allowed each philosophy of government a guest lecturer to expound the particular doctrine. The students heard from an Anarchist, a Socialist, a Syndicalist, and other radical theorists during the Fall and Winter terms. Come Spring, and the conservatives were to have their turn in Carver's own lectures and on his rostrum. But it happened that the Boston Red Sox had a fine team that year including Tris Speaker, just up from the Texas League to star in the greatest outfield ever seen. "Speaker was batting .348," said Broun, "and Carver wasn't hitting the size of his hat." Therefore Broun attended all the games at Fenway Park and missed the lectures in political science, so that by the end of the term he had heard arguments for all the radical theories, but never got around to hearing the answers. And he left Harvard a "fervent follower of all things red, including the Boston Red Sox." It can be inferred without difficulty that the Chicago White Sox had exerted no such distraction on Westbrook when he was absorbing conservative doctrine from his Jesuit tutor by the lake.

At the start of 1938 Pegler had begun to wage war on Heywood Broun. He harped on the presence of Communists in the Guild, although these disciplined agitators were now conducting a campaign to oust Broun from office. This had resulted from one of those mysterious directives out of party headquarters on Fourteenth Street, orders that were inexplicable to anyone who had not studied the unreadable texts of Lenin and the paralyzing political writings attributed to Stalin. Any attempt to read the stuff all the way through put one in mind of Mark Twain's definition of the Book of Mormon—chloroform in print. The theorists of the American party would instantly alter their line when Moscow so ordered, and everyone knew this, but as Oliver Pilat observed, to question the party's good faith might bring charges of Red-baiting, a grievous thing in the intellectual climate of the day. At any rate, left-wing Guildsmen were distilling chloroform for Broun's career at the same time that Pegler was complaining of Communists in the newsmen's union and lampooning Heywood as "the old Mahatma." Thus Pegler managed to mock two public figures with one appellation, and perhaps to call up a mental picture of a corpulent Broun in the loin cloth of Mohandas K. Gandhi. Max Beerbohm could have drawn it very well, with his graceful line, but in print the idea conveyed nothing more persuasive than a sneer.

It is not to be recorded, however, that Westbrook devoted all the space at his command to criticism of Broun and the Guild. He scanned the horizon for targets and had something to say about state governments in 1937 that remains true in 1974. What he had to suggest was nothing less than abolishing the forty-eight states because their "governments are pretty bad, as all of us have known for a long time. They are not really governments in the true sense, but political organizations which use the public money for the payoff and load.up with all the no-account uncles and inebriate brothers-in-law of the party workers, and stick them away in the county and city governments—which needs a thorough delousing, too." The levying of state income taxes today and their vanishing in questionable schemes administered by thieves and morons, gives melancholy emphasis to Westbrook's remarks. When he was right, he could be devastating in putting facts on record, and could achieve permanency in his words.

That same week, Pegler inspected the U.S. Supreme Court and found it "extravagant in its cold and stately vanity, considering that the Justices do most of their celebrating at home. . . . There are solid marble pillars as big as the stacks of an ocean boat, and white marble benches like those in a stylish graveyard, where no one sits, because it wouldn't seem right. . . . There is plush enough for an old-fashioned Keith-Orpheum, and even in the big marble lobby the tourists speak instinctively in whispers, as at Washington's grave, and the men snatch off their hats and wear a look of uncomprehensive awe. It does give a man a feeling that justice speaks out of a cloud and an almost irresistible impulse to purse the lips and blow a rude and impudent raspberry, just to see whether the clergy were well informed about the hereafter or merely speaking from hearsay. For surely that would be the end of the world, and the building would vanish in a puff of dust and all present would stand naked and embarrassed before the judgment seat." Again Pegler was right as can be. The architectural grandeurs of Washington surround ordinary men who would do better work in plain office buildings, and so far as the Supreme Court is concerned, it ought to be set up in some clean Western desert, with a law library and comfortable quarters for the judges and their families, away from the stink of Washington. The judges should have $100,000 a year with raises to meet inflation written in, to receive their salaries during life unless jailed for gross criminality. In return they should agree to retire at sixty-five and until then take no more than three drinks a day except on weekends, and to refrain from publishing books and pocketing side money by delivering addresses at public gatherings or convocations of university students, most of whom should be driving cabs or waiting table at the Ramada Inn. That is, to be sure, my own prescription for the Supreme Court, but I reach it after prolonged immersion in the works of Pegler, and feel certain that these would be his findings. Was he ever entirely serious? He wrote of this period in his career, "I found myself fascinated by enormities the people either knew not or, knowing, didn't appreciate."

It is necessary to note that for all his independence of spirit, Pegler was not immune to infection by popular and conventional ideas. He could do his share of parroting unsound doctrines once they took root in the popular mind. For example, he had swallowed the idea that the city of Los Angeles was a bad place and subject to condemnation by all civilized, right-thinking people. He did not examine Los Angeles, and so failed to see its beauty, its possibilities, and the human quality of its neighborhoods. His error came from the scorn that eastern writers in the movie industry heaped on their adopted town. Homesick, subject to the strains and pressures of their trade, and forced to contend with producers who were admittedly subhuman, the harried scribblers began to dream of a nonexistent high civilization back east, like the realm of Prester John, and to proclaim an estimate of Los Angeles that could not have pleased the Chamber of Commerce. Frank Lloyd Wright, who should never have been encouraged to talk in public, had given his opinion that the country had tilted on its southwestern corner so that all the ugliness ran down into Southern California. And Pegler fell into line in his productive year of 1938 when he wrote that Los Angeles County would be a lot better off if "that big, sprawling, incoherent, shapeless, slobbering civic idiot in the American family of communities, Los Angeles, could be declared incompetent and placed in charge of a guardian, like an individual mental defective." Warming to denunciation, Pegler went on to say that "Los Angeles is the source of more political, economic and religious idiocy than all the rest of the country together, and a concentration point of shiftless and inefficient culls, who, being too lazy or lacking in ability to make good in their native regions, drift in expecting to be fed from heaven or the public pantry." In this connection Pegler showed that he shared another popular delusion, to the effect that the pretty little toy city of San Francisco was a center of enlightenment: somehow or other, Pegler wrote, San Francisco was "the victim of the infantile giant to the south."

When the late 1930s arrived, life had become pleasant for those who had extra money to spend, and there was a certain quiet elegance to be seen around New York City, while Philadelphia and Chicago seemed to be asleep in a kind of shabby magnificence left over from the 1920s which made them delightful places in which to pass one's time. But Pegler had pointed out an undeniable element of cold calculation in the public entertainments of the rich. And it had to be admitted that some of the wealthy people, especially those who had recently acquired their loot, had developed a peculiarity of conduct that was distressing to persons of taste. This grinding solecism was an obsessive hatred of Franklin Roosevelt that went far beyond criticism of his obvious faults into the relishing of rumors that he was violently insane, or making him the central figure of clumsy and obscene stories in the ancient and traditional mold of the dirty joke. It was hard to see what Roosevelt had done to deserve such treatment; in all probability his New Deal had pulled the country back on its wheels when it lay in the ditch, perhaps not to move again under capitalist power. The Union Leaguers and other metropolitan clubmen may have owed their comforts and soft living to the very man they were traducing; learned professors have yet to study this matter and tell us why they acted as they did. But the meanness of it was plain to all who had any sort of independent judgment at the time, and Pegler gave his views on the subject in his column for May 13, 1938:

"At the risk of seeming self-righteous, I would like to propose a cloture on dirty or insinuating stories about the President and Mrs. Roosevelt. People who tell such stories are bores, anyway, and in telling them they are guilty of an imposition which justifies rebuke. They are asking for it. They assume that others share their own foul taste and indorse their disrespect for the office of the President and for a woman whose detractors, in the main, would be reduced to smears in any direct comparison of her character and conduct with their own. . . . I have noticed that this form of humor about the Roosevelts is favored mainly by men and women who seem to be doing very well notwithstanding the New Deal. . . . Whatever their origin, they are an affront to the intelligence, patience and loyalty of Americans who respect the Presidency and decent women."

In the same week Pegler wrote additional praise of Mrs. Roosevelt, even though she had become a competitor by syndicating a column entitled "My Day" with its New York outlet in the *World-Telegram*. A few days before his rebuke to the traducers of Franklin, Pegler paid his respects to Eleanor in commenting on "My Day" as having described "another routine day in the life of one who is stingily described as the 'most remarkable' and 'most energetic' woman of her time in the country, but who deserves more than that. I think we can take the wraps off and call her the greatest American woman, because there is no other who works as hard or knows the lowdown truth about her people and the troubles in their hearts as well as she does." Pegler went on to say that Mrs. Roosevelt had recently given a fine lecture on international peace, which was all the better because "she works in the strait-jacket of diplomatic and political restraints. . . . Mrs. Roosevelt has been before us for five years now. We know her better than any other woman, and she knows the country better than any other individual, including her husband, and the profit is all on our side."

Not long afterward, Pegler gave his readers the flavor of "My Day" in a friendly parody: "Yesterday morning I took a train to New York City and sat beside a gentleman who was reading the 1937 report of the International Recording Secretary of the World Home Economics and Children's Aptitude and Recreation Foundation of which my very good friend, Dr. Mary McTwaddle, formerly of Vassar, is the American delegate. This aroused my interest and I ventured to remark that I had once had the pleasure of entertaining a group of young people who were deeply concerned with the neglected problem of the Unmarried Father. It turned out that the gentleman himself was an unmarried father so we had a very interesting chat until he got off at Metuchen."

Pegler then returned to his attack on the leftists in the Newspaper Guild when he told an interviewer that not even Earl Browder, head of the American Communist Party, had gone so far as to call him a Fascist. "No," said Pegler, "I believe I am still a Liberal." But "direct democracy" could be a dangerous thing; and so far as the Guild was concerned, he would like to see it a professional group. As it was, the Guild would sometimes destroy jobs rather than protect them as a trade union is supposed to do. This kind of trouble always came up when "Bolos" obtained influence—that was their idea of playing the game, throw people out of work, then pull down everything.

It now appeared that Broun was looking ahead to a time when he might no longer be writing for the *World-Telegram*. No question but Roy Howard was giving him the treatment that customarily overtook a star journalist falling out of favor with the management—curtailment of space, and poor location. Howard allowed Lee Wood to treat Broun like the headwaiter in a snob joint discouraging a Shriner in a Palm Beach suit. He pushed Heywood into the lower left hand corner of the smorgasbord page, and told the copy butchers, squatting on the rim of their huge U-shaped desk, to cut deep in making Broun's contribution fit the daily layout. Pegler was moved to the top of the first column, above Broun; and it caused little surprise, in the spring of 1938, when Broun started a weekly paper of his own, which he called *The Connecticut Nutmeg.* If it succeeded in attracting readers, this publication would make a good base for Heywood's future career in politics, or as a labor statesman. By the following spring, the weekly's name had changed to *Broun's Nutmeg* and he used it, on June 10, for a reply to all of Pegler's tormenting criticism in a piece called "Square Peg." Westbrook had acquired a habit of referring to Broun as "Old Bleeding Heart," and the victim conceded that "if a man went around forever crying out, 'observe how my heart beats for humanity,' he would undoubtedly be set down as a fool or a hypocrite. And he could be both. But how about the fellow who encases himself in triple brass in the pretense that he has no heart at all? His would be the deeper folly. It may be a good idea for a columnist to keep his shirt on, but that is no reason why he should insulate himself like a telephone wire.

"The tragedy of J. Westbrook Pegler consists of the fact that by nature he is not the man he pretends to be. His native sympathies are wide and deep. When he is aroused about some ancient wrong he can be more eloquent than any newspaperman I know. . . . Some day somebody should take the hide off Peg because the stuff inside is so much better than the varnished surface which blinks in the sunlight of popular approval. . . . Frankenstein fashioned a rough guy who destroyed him. Peg's monster didn't have to go to that slight trouble. When the last clay tonsil was modelled by this syndicated sculptor he said in high artistic pride, 'Why, this is me to the life,' and proceeded to cut his own throat under the theory that in a troubled world one Westbrook Pegler might be sufficient. . . .

"I have said that Pegler's worth as a newspaperman has been compromised by his increasing felicity as a writer. When a commentator's chief concern is finding the right word rather than the just cause he isn't a reporter any more. He has gone around the corner and become one of posterity's children. . . .

"Newspapermen must come back from the city of dreams. I wish Peg had the energy which possessed him in the days when he covered the beat from Gondrecourt to Chaumont. I wish he would stop writing out of the side of his mouth and quit the effort to be a Damon Runyon version of Peter Pan.

"This job of being a professional clay-foot shooter may be a worthy one. But the gun should not be handled by a lad who can't seem to distinguish between plaster and solid bronze at twenty paces."

Chapter 5

The moderate tone of this piece made it all the more effective, and Pegler did not attempt to reply with an entire column on Broun. But he kept Heywood in mind when he contemplated the crimes of the Bolos; and these rascals sent their American liberal friends a shock like a slap of electricity along the party line on August 24, 1939, when Nazi Germany and the Soviet Union signed a ten-year nonaggression pact. Those who had expressed sympathy for "the great Communist experiment," or thought Lincoln Steffens made good sense by saying he had seen the future in Russia, "and it works," now fell on evil days. And Pegler wrote of Broun in November like a man closing in for the kill. He reported that Broun had uttered some superficial expressions of disappointment in Moscow but "never an outright recantation." That word carried poison: to make *recantation* of some viewpoint would imply a full and formal previous endorsement of the abandoned position, like a man publicly turning from religious faith and belief. What it boils down to is asking a man if he has stopped beating his wife; more and more often these days, Pegler was finding himself unable to pass up this method of putting someone in the wrong.

Broun had come to the end of his contract at the *World-Telegram* and it was not renewed. He wrote his last column for that paper on November 27. Two weeks later he told the readers of *Broun's Nutmeg* that he had been fired three times in thirty-one years—in the Spring, Summer, and early Winter, and that his "farewell conference with Roy W. Howard passed off in entire peace and amity." Howard had said, "'I've talked it over with my associates and we've decided not to make you an offer. . . . The price of newsprint is going up and we think the place to cut expenses is among the high-priced specialists in order to protect the run-of-mine reporter.'

"'Roy,' I said (all Scripps-Howard executives are known by the first name even to the humblest employee), 'I can't possibly make any squawk about that because I've made the same speech myself at dozens of Guild meetings.'

"And so we shook hands and had a drink and everything was very pleasant. But I still think it is better to be fired in the Summer."

It soon became apparent that Broun would not have to depend on the weekly *Nutmeg* alone, when the publisher of the *New York Post* signed him to a daily contract. The *Post* was politically more liberal than the Scripps-Howard papers, and Broun hoped to find it an appropriate medium for what he had to say. He had just passed his fifty-first birthday, and looked forward to many good years. But Pegler was still attacking: he had discovered that the *Nutmeg* was not a Guild shop, and made the charge that Broun had set rules for publishers that he himself did not feel obliged to follow. These reproaches ran in tandem with a labored proposition that Broun had not taken a stand against press censorship in Soviet Russia. The implications of hypocrisy and dishonesty were reported to Broun as he lay sick with a cold, and Heywood's biographer Dale Kramer recorded that the sick man, dosing himself with gin, said to his friends that Pegler was calling him a liar. "Why does he do that?" Broun asked. "He knows I'm not a liar." Broun's first column in the *Post* appeared on December 15, 1939. He discussed the possibility of Franklin Roosevelt running for a third term, and decided that Roosevelt would do what was best for the country. That enigmatic conclusion was not to receive further development: the cold that had put the writer in bed turned into pneumonia, and he died on December 18. And Pegler wrote no epitaph or elegy for Heywood Broun.

During Broun's last days, in which the staircase story came to its closing scene, Westbrook started on what was to be his most successful journalistic enterprise. Although he had failed to see the charm and importance of Los Angeles, Pegler could not overlook the fascinating business on the movie lots of Hollywood and other places in the metropolitan area. A concentration of talent in this enormous enterprise of story telling had satisfied public hunger for entertainment in a way that made the control of a movie company the same as enjoying ownership of a diamond mine. From early times the magic of acting, of the theater, had fascinated the American people. Miss Rourke has written of ranting troupers under canvas in the remotest bogs and swamplands, who drew crowds long before the Civil War, and thrilled them by the power of dramatic conflict on the stage. When it became possible to present fine actors in smoothly functioning playhouses, the draw was irresistible. Any management offering the likes of Julia Marlowe, William Gillette, Maude Adams, John Drew, or Mrs. Fiske had a fortune ready for banking. But the best show played only one house at a time until we had movies, which could give the same play in a thousand theaters simultaneously, ten times a day. Attendance at movie houses became the favorite relaxation of the world, and the motion picture tycoons made it impossible to fail by compelling exhibitors to take inferior films along with the good ones. The amount of money that came back to the studio owners from rentals to exhibitors throughout the world was enormous, and the profit margin was large.

This prosperity drew the attention of labor organizers, for the making of pictures was a true industry with thousands of workers employed on a factory floor. Some of the organizers were crooks, and by the late 1930s these racketeers had friendly relationships with the studio heads, to the detriment of the unskilled studio labor force in Southern California. Into this scene now came two rogues named George Browne and Willie Bioff, who got control of the International Alliance of Theatrical Stage Employees and Motion Picture Operators, commonly called IATSE. Their aim was to exploit some 15,000 studio workers in the lower ranks who clambered to the grids to throw down artificial snow or turn on sprinklers for "Singin' in the Rain," dragged the cameras in and out for dolly shots, and generally made themselves useful. Their job classification had colorful names such as grip, gaffer, and juicer, and moving pictures could not be completed without them. The studio owners in Hollywood were tightfisted men, some of whom had known what it was to dismantle a peddler's pitch and run for the alley when the cops came in sight; they were on the whole both disgusting and intimidating to civilized people, for they had that street-bred pathological need for money and power which prohibits fair dealing and recognizes no rule but devil take the hindmost. This inveterate greed and dishonesty led the Motion Picture Producers Association to make a secret treaty with Browne and Bioff which resulted in a closed-shop contract that locked in every grip and gaffer who wanted to keep his job.

Pegler heard of the treachery in the IATSE and began to investigate Willie Bioff's background. There were plenty of people willing to furnish leads, and a tip led to Chicago, where Westbrook found records that Bioff had left prison on March 24, 1922, still owing the State of Illinois five months of a six-month sentence on a conviction for pandering. The column carrying this news appeared on November 2, 1939; the authorities compelled Bioff to return and serve out his time, while Pegler commenced an inspection of his partner George Browne. Westbrook proved that he had been a common gunman, the charges mounted up, and Browne went to jail. It began to appear that Pegler had awesome powers, for soon afterward he managed to dig out the criminal past of George Scalise, who headed the Building Employees Union, and get him sent to jail for extortion. When he heard the sentence, Scalise put a phrase into the language by exclaiming, "I've been peglerized!" No matter how much the victims deserved their fate, there was an element of harshness in peglerization, something near savagery at times. Perhaps Westbrook was thinking of this in the first month of the attack on Bioff when he wrote about some wretched migrant workers he observed on one of his trips across the country. He saw the utter poverty of these ragged people who traveled the back roads in their lurching jalopies. At the day's end "they kindled their little brush fires beside the road to warm the children while the weary man wheedles the engine or tapes a tire. It is a sight to make the devil weep and shame or scare the most complacent. If it is left to the Communists to exploit this misery that will be just too bad, for there is still time, though apparently not too much, in which to cure it decently in a land where oranges are dumped into dry creek beds by the ton to wait for rain to wash them into the sea." Pegler charged the big farming combines and organized employers of these people with greed and brutality that amounted to native American Fascism.

When he destroyed Browne, Bioff, and Scalise, Pegler was working in the journalistic tradition which Theodore Roosevelt had called muckraking; at a later time and under the name of investigative reporting, this method of research and exposure was to bring down the great rogue Nixon and his crew. But in spite of Westbrook's successful attacks on Scalise and the two IATSE racketeers, organized labor as a general force now entered on days of power, when the weight of government came down on the workers' side, and employers had to keep in the good graces of Washington as best they could, and thousands of Rooseveltian officials set out in posses to harry them. Union leaders could be seen going into legislators' offices, not taking the trouble to make an appointment but barging right through the door of the inner sanctum.

The greatest of labor men around Washington was Sidney Hillman of the International Ladies Garment Workers, who served on commissions with other bigwigs and enjoyed the full treatment—the limo, the three secretaries, the statements to the press, the direct access to Roosevelt. Mister Hillman's car. Mister Hillman's table. Call for Mister Hillman. The only other labor man of comparable public standing was John L. (for Llewellyn) Lewis of the United Mine Workers, who differed from Hillman when he denounced and cursed Roosevelt after a falling out, but continued to be a power in the land. Lewis had the most grateful and loyal of all union men under his command, miners who had suffered inhuman exploitation and would tell you, "Lived lak a dirty dawg till Johnell come." They would kill for old Johnell, as they had done in 1925 at Herrin, Illinois, when twenty members of an unrecognized union met death by gunfire and public torture at the hands of Lewis's men—and women. Johnell himself would never hire a goon to thrash a critic, as Hillman and the others would do, but hammered on dissidents until their skulls rang like gongs, with his own rocklike fists. At the age of sixty, Johnell went so far as to knock another labor statesman cold on the dais at a national convention. He was a tough one, and he left the CIO as his monument, although he pulled out in 1940. Connoisseurs of oratory took delight in his work and said it was a pity we couldn't turn him loose on the Nazis and Russians; some even put Lewis up near Daniel Webster in the windjamming department. Be that as it may, the power that Lewis and Hillman wielded throughout the country made it plain that Pegler would never be able to destroy the labor movement, and the columnist frequently took occasion to explain that he opposed racketeers, not unions as such. But he would keep on the subject day after day, and extend his account of some minor scoundrel's misconduct to tiresome length. The trouble was that journalistic investigators must expose an *important* victim if it is to hold general interest for more than an edition or two. And some of Pegler's friends became restless because they felt they were not getting the good stuff he used to serve them. The California novelist Charles G. Norris, for example, wrote in early 1941 to ask if Pegler "had to do this." Norris said there had been a time when he had devoured every word because Pegler "wrote so goddam swell." But now he skipped the column because he was "sick of the subject." He closed by begging Westbrook to "think about this, will y'u?" Later in that year Roy Howard showed how he felt in a memo to Pegler: "If you will occasionally chasten your proud spirit with a dash of your own sense of humor, your efforts during the next two or three years are, from the standpoint of journalistic accomplishment, going to top anything you have done to date. . . . Let me once again urge on you a change of pace. . . . There are a lot of good Christians who don't want to be saved every day in the week. . . ."

Pegler had not come to this implied rebuke from his employer entirely by subjecting him to the tedium of reading at tiresome length about a succession of unimportant victims: the columnist had also embarrassed Howard by denouncing a rival publisher. For Howard had intensely disliked reading in early 1940 that W. R. Hearst was "a never to be adequately damned demagogue and historic scoundrel." The statement was true, but there existed a professional courtesy among publishers, and such attacks were supposedly not permissible. Old Man Hearst had a thick hide, but if he wished to he could order a character assassination of Howard that would start in the next edition and continue until his wrath was appeased.

Howard also found reason to worry, a few months later, when Pegler ended his era of good feeling toward Mrs. Roosevelt by exposing a deal to exploit the White House in a coffee promotion scheme. The unedifying spectacle began with the removal of the Pan American Coffee Bureau account from the Kudner agency to another advertising firm as a favor to David Hopkins, Harry's son, using Mrs. Roosevelt as the lure for a broadcasting contract. Pegler had obtained a copy of the sales plan, and revealed the ad men's promise to the client that Mrs. Roosevelt would tell the radio audience "how the presidential cup of coffee was prepared, and, of course, it would be made with a heaping tablespoonful and one for the pot." This was hilarious in view of the fact that Mrs. Roosevelt had appointed an incompetent housekeeper, and the President's coffee was known to be the vilest brew in Washington; Harold Ickes said he choked on the stuff. The ad men continued their pitch with the promise of "personal contacts" in high places, and added that they would tie it up with a prize designed to "associate coffee with endurance in sports." The nine countries supporting the Pan-American Coffee Bureau were to give a large silver coffee cup, through the Amateur Athletic Union, to winners of each year's endurance records in running, walking, and swimming. Pegler wrote that when he "read that to Gene Tunney, a repository of all the old Verbotens against alcohol, tobacco, tea and coffee for athletes, he gibbered like an actor at a New Deal rally and the Fordham seismograph recorded that old William Muldoon, over there at Valhalla, spun like a bobbin for forty minutes in his grave." Roy Howard disliked this flat accusation by Pegler that Mrs. Roosevelt had allowed herself to be used as a shill in an ad man's bunco game; after all, "My Day" was a valuable feature of the *World-Telegram* and hot sales item for the syndicate. But Pegler was riding high, aware as he was that Howard did not run the only game in town. And first-rate book publishers continued to find material in "Fair Enough" that merited reprinting. A second book of newspaper pieces, *The Dissenting Opinions of Mr. Westbrook Pegler,* had appeared, this time under the imprint of Charles Scribner's Sons, the firm that published F. Scott Fitzgerald and Ernest Hemingway.

Westbrook Pegler believed in getting the facts, and if he subjected himself to scrutiny at the close of the silver decade which had seen his country make partial recovery from its great depression, he would have to admit that he was looking at a fortunate man. He could call his shots, he could stand up to his boss, and he could make way against many complaints and considerable dislike. His strength lay in his hold on readers, which remained steady in spite of numerous ill-natured columns and some, of the repetitive sort, that approached the region of dullness without quite crossing the frontier. He could not be completely dull: he was one of those writers gifted with a speaking voice in his writing, and one would hear it, and be aware of its unmistakable tone, whatever the subject. If Pegler could have presented himself as a folk artist on the order of Carl Sandburg, rather than as a commentator on the world's affairs, things might have gone better at the end; but in early 1941, we looked to Pegler for guidance, we knew him as people in the TV age know the big-head-closeup news talkers—come in tight on Cronkite and hold, that's it—and for better or worse, Westbrook had talent and verbal inventiveness of a sort the news jockeys do not display. Here in America we hoped for another ten years, and then at least another ten in which to complete the building of something that had begun to look like a civilized country. We saw what was going on in Europe, and knew it was not the Second World War, but Act Two of the good old original World War that had furnished starring roles for Black Jack Pershing, General Nivelle, Field Marshal Haig, and other brass hats of high rank and low intelligence. There were crazy people running this war, too: Hitler had followed up his nonaggression pact of August 1939 and the attack on Poland which got him into war with France and England, by attacking his Russian friends less than two years later. Evidently he had not read *War and Peace*. And in America we were hoping that the Russians and Germans would destroy each other like the snake swallowing his tail; but we knew that this could not be. We looked long at our skies in that summer. And we knew that things would never again be as they were, in that little period of happiness that followed the silver decade. They had another Subway Series in baseball and the Yankees beat Brooklyn, four games to three.

March of 1941 found Westbrook and Julie in the Great American Desert at Tucson, Arizona. Few people ever visit Tucson or the country around Phoenix without making plans to live there for the rest of their lives, or at least wishing it were possible to do so. The Peglers had a suite at a quiet but luxurious ranch resort, and from their balcony they could enjoy the Arizona dawns and sunsets. When day breaks, out there, you are first made aware of it by noticing that somebody has turned rose-colored spotlights on the mountain peaks, and that is very fine. But the end of each day is so overpoweringly lovely, when "withers once more the old blue flower of day," that it calls for whiskey to deaden the beautiful pain—it is clean and clear and cool, and the sky turns deep blue like a Warner Brothers cyclorama, and at last to black and those stars come on. At this time American whiskey is best, Jack Daniel's or Jim Beam.

Tucson city was a friendly place and aware of Mr. Pegler's importance, and on March 29 reporters found him taking lessons from a riding master, and in a gracious mood. The newsmen described him as a big man of sandy complexion, with noticeable eyebrows, penetrating blue eyes, and a square jaw. Pegler looked fine with tan on his face, a modified Western style hat, and fringed buckskin jacket. He stood with feet slightly apart, as though expecting that he might have to fight off a physical attack. But when they asked Westbrook if he recently engaged in fisticuffs, he said a man of his age should have enough sense to "stay out of that sort of thing." The reporter from the *Arizona Star* called Pegler the "possessor of the most articulate growl in the nation" and put up some targets for him to growl at. Satisfactory roars rang out at the U.S. Army ("in terrible shape for battle at the present time"), labor unions (which "harbored too many thieves and crooks among the leaders, and subject members to the tyranny of an unchecked, unofficial government"), and Harold Ickes ("a frightful old windbag and one of my favorite subjects; I have this number pasted in my hat"). The *Star* man wrote that Westbrook was sincere and added, with keen perception, "he has a touch of the evangelist." If Tucson approved of the Peglers, they heartily returned the good feeling, and showed it by arranging to buy La Cholla, a forty-acre estate that included a house, caretaker's lodge, and swimming pool with a splendid view of the Santa Catalina Mountains in the background.

On their return to the East, Westbrook and Julie felt that the place near Tucson was to be only a winter residence. But they were spending their last days at Pound Ridge; Pegler had decided to go in for farming in a serious way and was negotiating for property a few miles outside of Ridgefield in Connecticut. He might have felt some lingering and perhaps subconscious impulse to imitate Broun, who had frequently written about his Connecticut farmstead; but a more direct influence had been that of John N. Wheeler, the leading promoter of syndicated writers at the time. Although Pegler was in the Scripps-Howard stable, Wheeler maintained cordial relations with him because in the syndicate game, you could never tell what might happen. He had just discovered Ridgefield and recommended it to Westbrook with enthusiasm.

In May of 1941, however, the Peglers were spending most of their time at the Park Lane; and it was here that Westbrook received a piece of news that was almost too exciting to share with Julie before preparing her for it, like a message of death or destruction. Although Julie tried to lead a normal life, for Westbrook's sake, she was a cardiac cripple and she had to keep nitroglycerine tablets handy in case of angina pectoris, an agony stabbing the big muscle of the heart. And behind the door, as friends knew, the oxygen tanks stood ready. But this news could not keep, and Pegler blurted it to Julie as he put down the telephone—"They've given me the Pulitzer." And Julie keeled over in a faint.

Westbrook Pegler's doubting state of mind extended to the granting of formal awards, but for a newspaperman the Pulitzer Prize was something special, like an Academy Award to a member of the movie industry. Old Joe Pulitzer, the publisher who made *The World,* had set it up in his will when he died in 1911. There were a number of prizes, to be given each year under authority of the Columbia University Trustees on recommendation from an advisory board. The categories included literature, music, and drama, but the most important awards were those in Pulitzer's own field, and at the time Pegler was honored, they were given for reporting, public service through journalism, commentary, editorial writing, cartooning, and foreign correspondence. In later years the significance of these prizes in journalism was lessened when the trustees added five more categories, while the awards for literature and drama scored more misses than hits. But the 1941 award for reporting, based on the destruction of Browne, Bioff, and Scalise, was a genuine distinction, and recognized Pegler as the head of his craft. With the honor came a check for $1,000, real money in those days. Pegler said he planned to invest his thousand in "awning striped shirts like Roy Howard's."

There was a long Indian summer that autumn of 1941. We had now gone so far toward entering the war that we knew it was only a matter of a few weeks or months, and we would be in it. We had fired on German submarines, and probably killed one or two, or sent them off wounded; the Germans had sunk our destroyer *Reuben James*; young reserve officers could be seen in the restaurants and nightclubs of New York, escorting girls who were so beautiful it would break your heart. And the band at Larue's played show tunes by Cole Porter and Irving Berlin. The whole thing was running on emotion and everybody knew it, for that is always the way it goes. It was not our hatred for Germany, but our love for each other that made us want to be at war. A hinge of history turned on December 7 when the Japanese came in fast and shot up Pearl Harbor. We were in and it was the kind of tailormade war this country likes best, with England setting the example and no danger whatsoever to Muncie, Indiana.

6

THE QUINTESSENCE OF PEGLERISM

WESTBROOK HAD A GOOD PLACE FROM WHICH TO SEE HOW FAST things could move in Washington when a war cancelled the usual procedures. The first thing they did was establish censorship over the press and radio; then on December 8 Mr. Roosevelt told the nation where it stood. This was the statement about the "day that will live in infamy." Franklin Roosevelt knew how to address the American public, and could measure out to its exact limit the dose of official utterance they would accept on any specific occasion. In this instance, he got on and off with dispatch—no time to stand around talking, have work to do. My fellow Americans. Always remember the character of this onslaught against us. No matter how long it may take us. I ask that the Congress declare. And so on. . . .

Not even Pegler could bring himself to write that the speech was a lame effort, and that it contained nothing about the folly and incompetence of bunching the greater part of our Pacific fleet in one of the fattest targets ever offered to a determined attacker. And Pegler could not know until a long time afterward that men in Washington had obtained advance knowledge of enemy plans from decoded Japanese cables. And the amount of damage was kept secret; all we carried away from the first wartime speech of our commander-in-chief was the impression of his scolding, indignant note of vexation at the Japanese for their unfair tactics. Roosevelt sounded like a headmaster announcing that because of deplorable misconduct by certain boys, there would be no holiday for the Deerfield game. Although this was plain enough, Pegler praised Roosevelt's "wisdom," and said we needed a strong leader, now that we were at war. At the moment, there was nothing else to say.

A President whose country has blundered into war, or one who has led his country into war, enjoys a sweet racket provided at least two-thirds of the people are in favor of that war. Roosevelt came now to the most satisfying days he ever had, after the shock of Pearl Harbor wore off and he realized that he was absolutely and without question not just Mister Big, but Mister Biggest—Number One, El Supremo, with power to sink ships, blast cities, and incinerate men, women, and children without argument as to his authority or limit to his commands. Admirals and generals crawled before him seeking promotion and grants of power; Congress did his bidding and the press ceased carping; for the time being, the newsmen considered it their mission not to publish the truth, but to market propaganda in the guise of news, because the overriding consideration was to win the war, and propaganda was part of it. Winston Churchill soon arrived in Washington to turn his charm on Mr. Roosevelt, and they renewed the friendship they had started at the time of their first meeting that summer on a battleship at Placentia Bay off Newfoundland. Here they had unveiled a statement of Four Freedoms as a promise of good times coming. Churchill was eloquent and brave, but a strange boy-man playing with ships and soldiers, wearing eccentric costumes and sitting up all night sucking on the brandy bottle. Nobody in the American press corps reported Churchill's excessive drinking, or that his view of history and politics seemed to be formed on the works of an esteemed author of juvenile fiction, G. A. Henty. The leader of our great fighting ally a brandy-head who wrote speeches that sounded like something out of *Ivanhoe?* We could not have tolerated such a statement at the time, simple fact though it was. And our leaders would have instantly silenced such talk; happy as they were giving orders and waiting for body- and city-counts, at the middle of their hero sandwich lay a sliver of cold fear: such was the ferocity of this war that they could already sense what waited at the end for the leaders of losers—the gallows.

What did Pegler think of this? It did not take him long to find that he still had within himself the fundamental objection to authority that had always motivated his will and directed his talent. In Pegler's first war, President Woodrow Wilson had seemed impossibly far away, a comic figure dressed like the Lawyer Marks of a Tom show in bulb-toed shoes and swallowtail coat. Pegler had fought with Wilson's men Sims and Pershing, who had tried to take away his livelihood. But in this second war, the military brass were not so important to Pegler, and it was the White House that symbolized unchecked authority and touched the motivating instincts of Westbrook's personality and put him on the alert like Rikki-Tikki-Tavi scenting the cobra in the garden.

There was no prospect of Westbrook going to war; he was beyond the age of military service. Pegler saw many young men enlisting as volunteers, mostly young fellows from the colleges who had been brought up to think this the thing to do. Generally speaking, they held reserve rank or received direct commissions, and were all we had to offer in the way of an elite corps like the British public school boys who had committed military suicide in the 1914 war. In the matter of combat deaths, we had gotten off lightly before, compared to the losses of our enemies and allies, but this time we were heading for heavy casualties, and had already acknowledged the necessity of conscript armies to do the thing right. Out came the press gangs just as they had in Woodrow Wilson's time. When the draft law went through and started working in the summer of 1941, Roosevelt had burbled that this was nothing more than the old Continental observance of the muster, apparently hoping to put us in mind of the "Concord Hymn" by Ralph Waldo Emerson. In actuality, some of the worst people in each community signed on to administer the draft law—club bores, professional jurors, retired chiropractors, failed lawyers, and elderly men who were glad to have something to do. The obscenity of such tribunals sending young men to face danger and death did not escape Pegler's notice, and his feeling of outrage against conscription began to grow. But he was a noncombatant, and as such, a sharer in the prosperity that had come with the war. Like the workers in war industries, he had more material than he could process in each day's work; the growth of the unions brought on an incalculable number of complaints from workers who found that union bosses would kick them around as severely as employer bosses had kicked them in days of yore. What it boiled down to was, it was no good being a little man or woman, the big people only let you have so much; and they measured out what they let you have after taking their own cuts off the top, and if you didn't like it, you might get a punch in the mouth. Pegler's problem therefore was not the finding of material for his columns about the workers' troubles, but deciding what to omit, what to put aside among the things he simply did not have room for. He filed hundreds of letters which he could not get into the columns, and they may be seen today at the Hoover Library. The pain and anguish, bitterness, and frustration of the letters contrast with the benign countryside in which the library sits.

Navigators who knew the journalistic heavens could now have charted collision courses for Mrs. Roosevelt and Westbrook Pegler. Not forgetting the praise Westbrook had bestowed on Mrs. Roosevelt, we must keep in mind that he had spoken the kind words before the country went to war. And some who fought it, and still used their minds, observed that nations at war came to resemble each other, their political leaders and generals blending to mirror images. At night all cats are gray. None of this ever occurred to Mrs. Roosevelt, who had become excited at the approach of war. Having returned from a trip to England on December 3, Mrs. Roosevelt went on the air two days after Pearl Harbor to deliver a report as "Mother of the Nation" to the mothers of America over 136 stations of the Blue Network, anchored on WJZ New York. Mrs. Roosevelt appeared under sponsorship of something called the Council on Candy as Food in the War Effort, an ad man's publicity setup, and a pointless one—for it was obvious that the government would ration sugar if we ran short of it, and until that time children would continue to eat candy bars, and throw away the wrappers as they walked to school. So far as Mrs. Roosevelt's message was concerned, the network would have been happy to carry it as news. But then there would have been no fee.

Although her four sons had volunteered, the idea of conscription intoxicated Mrs. Roosevelt. After the volunteers went on duty, why shouldn't everyone be a conscript? Surely that would be the best way to administer our great common cause, the war effort. She wrote in "My Day" early in 1942 that it would be fine "if we were all drafted and told what to do." It was the only way Mrs. Roosevelt could see "to get the maximum service out of our citizens." Some high authority would "tell us where we can be most useful and where our work is needed."

The idea of bureaucrats plugged in at the White House and telling everybody what to do was as repulsive to Pegler as it was delightful to Mrs. Roosevelt. And it was at this time that Westbrook began to feel the need of a second self, a journalistic ventriloquist's dummy, to express some of his resentment of authority and things in general. Thus he hit on the idea of George Spelvin, American. The name Spelvin was a concise statement that it was really Pegler who spoke, for tradition in the theater had made George Spelvin the assumed name of an actor doubling in a small part. Spelvin played messengers, butlers, second detectives, and burglars who went out the window early in the first act. For Pegler he was to enjoy a long run in a part that altered as Pegler grew older. In an early appearance, on July 17, 1942, Spelvin appeared as a worker who had not shared in the general prosperity and had some questions to ask:

"George Spelvin, American, has been laid off his job, what with priorities and all, so he has been looking around for something in the war industries, but with unsatisfactory results. He had read quite a long time back, where Mrs. R. said she thought everyone should be ordered what to do by the government and he has been reading also where Paul McNutt* says this and Paul McNutt says that about how people have to fit themselves into the effort or else. . . .

"Well, so he has been scouting around for a job, but every place he goes some guy tells him, well has he got a union card and old George says well he used to have one years ago in his old home town and they always tell him that doesn't do no good. He has got to join a new union and some of them want up to $300 and some want a racket of $2 a day for a permit and some don't want so much, but they are so bossy that he just says Bigod nobody is going to make him join anything whether it is the Elks or the Moose or the Mice or the Muskrats or whatever. It is the principle of the thing with George and, moreover, being a native American and a veteran of the last war, he has a rather narrow prejudice against being ordered around by guys who talk like they just got off the boat. A lot of Americans are narrow-minded like that.

"One place George went the company couldn't even see him at all without he had an okay from the union, so he went down to the union joint and hung around half the day until the head guy came in and by that time there was about 50 guys waiting. Some of the guys they crowded up to the head guy and asked could they speak to him confidentially and after they spoke to him they went right out, apparently well pleased and Spelvin got an idea from the way they acted that they had slipped the head guy something. . . . At last the guy got around to Spelvin and told him it would cost him $75 to join, but he could pay it 10 bucks down and the rest $2 a day until he was paid off and George says: 'What the hell do I pay you 75 bucks when I got my ever-loving to support and what do you figure to do for me for the 75 bucks? I would rather buy war bonds.'

*Paul McNutt was a war bureaucrat in Washington.

"Well, that is the way it goes everywhere and nothing but arguments and George Spelvin, American, still wants to win the war, but they can throw him in the can for life before he will shower down, but the union guys keep calling him a lousy traitor or a fifth columnist and they say when he gets drafted for a job they will give him the dirtiest kind of work at the lowest pay and they will not let him leave the union, but they will just hold back a certain amount of his pay so the union can slip it to the New Deal and preserve the unity of our beloved country and the precious heritage of democracy."

Strikes aroused even stronger emotions in wartime than when the unions first started to acquire power. The public had become used to scenes of violence in grainy black and white newsreel films of drab-looking people milling around on the outskirts of town. But now the pickets had taken to appearing in front of department stores, supermarkets, and other Main Street establishments, and sometimes they harangued or even threatened and attacked persons attempting to enter the struck premises. Indignation and resentment resulted from the actions of such noisy and aggressive picketers, whatever the facts of the case might be. Mrs. Roosevelt had a simple solution: she would respect all picket lines without inquiry as to what was at stake. She put this policy on record by writing in June of 1942, "I can't cross the picket line, fair or unfair." To Pegler this was evidence of a self-esteem so insensitive that it did not need to know the right and wrong of any question, but could settle it according to personal bias. His comment took form in a set of savage verses, which began, *"Goons, goons, goons! /I'm the patroness and priestess of the goons! / Lady me, Lady I, / Lady I, I, Me."* After that, there were no more expressions of good feeling between Pegler and Mrs. Roosevelt.

That year of 1942 was the year in which the country settled to the reality of war and the long, fatal sickness began; an economic boom was gathering force to ride on war prosperity into the shattering explosion of inflated prices and vanishing values that was likely to be the last illness of the perishing republic. The emotional disturbance of realizing that the country's finest days had passed went very deep with Westbrook Pegler. He searched within himself for the ultimate simplifications that greed caused inflation and fear caused war, but never quite reduced his thought to that pair of stark equations. His thinking went that way, although he held to the conviction that the only thing worse than winning a war was losing it. Shortly after Pearl Harbor he wrote that "in a brawl with Adolf Hitler who is, after all, the principal enemy, it is well to have a man in the White House who will not bother to break clean or keep his punches up." Pegler looked back on Roosevelt's aid to the British, which had included the gift of fifty destroyers, not to mention our battles with German warships, and decided that Roosevelt "was right all along and doggedly brave at times when he fought almost alone to make the people recognize their enemy." This was the liberal line. A few days later, Pegler fired on old Johnell Lewis, and said the President should consider the benefits that would come to our side if old Johnell were "jailed away for the duration." We were in this thing on the same side as Russia, and that country had tremendous fighting power. But they were Commies, and that was bad. Westbrook's thought was, "The Russ is our ally and we're lucky to have him. But don't try to pretty him up." This was *not* the liberal line. Our official picture of Stalin at the time showed a chuckly, pipe-smoking Uncle Joe, a Russian version of Cap'n Andy in *Show Boat,* but Pegler warned, "these people are killers."

Those who commanded an audience in print or on the air felt that they had a continuing obligation to the war effort, but found it hard to get the war into their performance day after day when life seemed to go on pretty much as usual, except for the erosion of decency and fair play in dealings with customers in stores and passengers on trains and airplanes. Pegler first became aware of this on a trip to New England in November 1942, and his reactions caused his friend Bill Cunningham, a Boston columnist, to write that readers might well take Pegler to be "a cold-blooded cobra or a word-slinging scorpion." Westbrook went out to dinner with Cunningham and wrote to him after returning to New York, "I fell into sin after that dinner and could be convicted of first-degree sitting-uppery. God, how I suffered the next day. God, how I still suffer to think how I suffered. I must ask God to make me a better boy. . . ." Westbrook added that he envied Cunningham and Quentin Reynolds their ability to write pieces straight off with no trouble at all. It was obvious that the five hours of pecking and paper-crumpling that went into a Pegler column must have been hell on hangover days.

An additional reward for the labor of turning out columns came in 1942 when Scribner's issued *George Spelvin, American, and Fireside Chats,* Pegler's third book of collected newspaper pieces. Roosevelt had called his radio speeches fireside chats, and Pegler's title represented the jester apeing the king. Nothing can be more satisfying to a journalist than to see his transient writings between book covers, but Pegler kept his ego under control, and indulged in self-ridicule from time to time, as though saying to himself, "Westbrook, you can only fool them for so long and then they'll get on to you, so don't let success go to your head." A typical Pegler burlesque of Pegler occurred when he presented George Spelvin as witness before the Committee on Peace, with Senator Nilly (Ind., Ind.) in the chair. On being asked "'What about Quisling and Laval?' George answered, 'Well, I think like you do on that, and I certainly would burn them down, but when you are out after traitors, why the way I see it as an American, why there was a lot of other traitors there in France and they did their worst to louse up France so Hitler could walk in, and it was the same in our own country but now they call those bums patriots, excuse me, I don't know whether you are a Democrat or not, but President Roosevelt he lets those dirty rats, no-account, low-down, Communist traitors get jobs in our government, like the Dies Committee said, and now they are all mixed up with Sidney Hillman's outfit and so'—(By Senator Nilly): 'The Committee thanks you, Mr. Spelvin.'"

After that Senator Nilly often summoned Spelvin for testimony in which Pegler appeared to satirize both senator and witness, yet occasionally gave George a penetrating remark. On the whole, these two characters represented what Pegler thought about citizenship and government, the one scarcely enlightened, the other unworthy of trust. George had a spark of humanity and a trace of self-awareness, but Nilly remained a fool for whom there was no hope at all. And day after day the pages of the *Congressional Record* documented Pegler's case. These underlying disillusionments touched similar feelings, largely unexpressed, in all sorts of readers who were supporting the war effort in one way or another, and yet had instinctive knowledge that their lives had passed from individual control, and much that had been promised for the future would turn out wrong. But Pegler felt his personal fortunes must be secure when in 1943 a letter came from Joseph B. Connelly, who stated that Westbrook was "the most powerful columnist in the English reading world today." Since this Mr. Connelly was a high executive in the Hearst organization, his letter made good reading. Another interesting letter was the invitation to Hearst's eightieth birthday party at San Simeon on April 4, 1943. Spies brought word to Roy Howard that Pegler was among those paying tribute to the Chief, who warmed his enormous vanity with 200 movie stars, successful authors, and political celebrities about him. Howard's spies may not have been present, or eavesdropping, when Pegler was summoned to a little private talk. Westbrook recorded the scene in his manuscripts: knowing that his people had approached Westbrook, Hearst had chosen to overlook Pegler's published insults, and he came quickly to the point, inviting Pegler to "sign up" then and there. Pegler replied that he "had a moral debt to Roy Howard for promoting and advertising his work. At that, Mr. Hearst put out his hand and in his gracious and always courteous way, remarked that we might get together at some future time." Not long afterward, Pegler also heard from executives of the *Chicago Tribune,* informing him that he would be welcome at their syndicate whenever his Scripps-Howard contract ran out.

In October 1943 the National Maritime Union threw 1,000 pickets around the *World-Telegram* building to protest what Pegler had written about union seamen who drew high wages on the Atlantic run. It could not be denied that Navy gunners on the same ships got less pay, but the Maritime pickets refused to debate this point and shouted "THROW—PEGLER—OUT! THROW—PEGLER—OUT!" as they marched back and forth. Westbrook wrote his copy uptown and so did not see these demonstrators, and Roy Howard persuaded the union leaders to call them off. But the incident disturbed him. The Scripps-Howard papers were presenting themselves as liberal voices raised in behalf of organized labor, and Pegler's persistent attacks on unions had much greater literary power than the platitudes of the editorial pages. It was more than a question of allowing a dissenting voice—the voice drowned the editors out.

In the spring of 1944, Westbrook ran into trouble of a sort to make Howard even more uncomfortable when he looked at Pegler's space in the *World-Telegram,* which was now filled most of the time with attacks on organized labor. But one day Pegler got off that subject and caused an uproar by a personal attack which raised resentment at a powerful newspaper in Chicago. The embarrassment came when Pegler mauled Colonel Frank Knox, one of the country's official Great Men, the Republican publisher of the *Chicago Daily News,* who had gone into Franklin Roosevelt's cabinet as secretary of the Navy. Knox had accepted the post in 1940, and Pegler did not get around to him until May 1944, when he roughly upbraided the colonel for letting down his side by serving under Roosevelt. Though far from a radical sheet, the *Daily News* had felt uncomfortable with Pegler for at least a year; and when he referred to Knox in an insulting manner, they announced Westbrook's last column on May 22 with a note that ended, "Good-bye, Mr. Pegler." This caused Roy Howard considerable pain; he did not like to see a fellow publisher kicked around, and Knox added tragic emphasis to the affair by dying of a heart attack on the following day. Howard also felt financial pain because the *Daily News* had been paying half of Pegler's basic contract, which was due for renewal in December. Howard therefore negotiated a release and the column for Saturday, September 9, began, "This will be my last piece for the *New York World-Telegram,* and in parting I should like to say something about Roy Howard." Westbrook went on to report that he had found Howard a liberal publisher, "one who permits the expression of views contrary to his editorial policy in his newspapers. Often I have written matter which I knew to be in disagreement with Howard's ideas and have seen it in print nevertheless; and Heywood Broun was, for all practical purposes, an enemy of Howard and was allowed to have his say down to their parting, a few days before Heywood died." Pegler said that enemies had pressed Howard to censor or dismiss him, but the publisher had refused to give them Pegler's hide, or any scrap of it. There had been one case of outright financial intimidation, when the Italian Line pulled advertising, but Howard never mentioned it to Pegler. The column ended with a one-line paragraph, "Seventy-three and thirty." An editorial note explained that this was the oldtime telegraphers' code for "Best regards and good-bye."

And so the "Fair Enough" column closed down. Roy Howard and his friend Bud Pegler had seen some exciting days together—the labor at the old UP downtown, the San Jose uproar, the many columns that had made people believe they heard Pegler's voice speaking to them alone, the crusades against the figureheads of power, and the Pulitzer Prize. In the Pegler manuscripts, Westbrook gives his recollection of the parting, after he had accepted the offer that took him to his third principal employer, the King Features Syndicate, which he called "the Hearst package goods department." The manuscript note on the change of publishers continues, "Joe Connelly wanted to announce our deal in a release to the United Press and Associated Press but I put it to Joe that in fairness I had to be first to tell Howard. That was the way it was, then. Julie consented to my new adventure, notwithstanding terrible moral doubts about the Hearst people. But 'All right,' she said, when I insisted, 'if you are going whoring I will go with you.'"

The change was news to ordinary readers who had no notion of the dissatisfaction in Roy Howard's office and at the *Chicago Daily News.* Howard made a gracious statement about his admiration for Pegler's talent, and good luck in the future; and when reporters asked Pegler if there had been friction at the *World-Telegram,* his answer was, "Nothing of the sort. I have simply landed a better job." All the news stories emphasized Pegler's acerbic quality, and some writers phrased their comment in words that were none too respectful, but this was Westbrook's own manner. The press section of *Newsweek,* for example, said that "Pegler's gadfly now will buzz for Hearst." Since he himself was the gadfly, this was an imprecision that Pegler would not have committed, but readers got the point. The magazine estimated that Pegler had 10,000,000 readers, and the King Features salesmen multiplied this figure by three and by four, depending on the amount of chilled alcohol in their bellies when they gave the pitch to prospects over tables at lunch. For the most part, King Features clients would be happy to pick up Pegler, but there again they sometimes indulged themselves in mockery like that which the columnist dispensed; one publisher sent in his signed contract with the note, "Pegler is the flea on the journalistic dog, and I suppose we have to have him."

Pegler had left Scripps-Howard on Saturday, and on the following Monday, September 11, 1944, he ran outside the *Journal-American* in a double column at the left side of Page One with the heading, "As Pegler Sees It." This put his name on the top line while retiring along with "Fair Enough" any lingering idea that Pegler might trouble himself about fairness when public interest was at stake—readers could take it as he saw it, or pass him by. This opening column for Hearst made no mention of appearing under new management, but got right to business, as though Pegler had always worked this stand, with some comments on James Cannon, Jr., a Southern Methodist bishop who had recently died. Cannon had made big tracks in his day, and had looked like one of the most powerful men in the country during the life of the liquor prohibition law. When legal booze came back, people stopped taking orders from the bishop, and office boys were told to give him the gate when he showed up at editorial rooms where he used to walk right in, announcing his views in a voice so deep and resonant that it rattled the windowpanes. When Cannon died, nobody respected or feared him any more, and only his family mourned the passing. From this Pegler made an adroit transition to a closing paragraph expressing the hope that bullies of the James Cannon type now infesting the labor movement would meet with a similar fall, which would be on the day when the unions, at last, were run right. It was irresistibly readable, it brought forward nothing new, and was a good average Pegler column.

Critics of the press, and those few readers who relished newspapers like movie fans who preferred even a bad movie to none at all, were unanimous in their agreement that Pegler had landed in the right place as the brightest star of the Hearst newspapers. Against this shabby background Pegler's talent would shine brightly. But historians of the press are willing to admit that there were a few other *Journal-American* features that provided entertainment. One was the daily cartoon, "They'll Do It Every Time," by Jimmy Hatlo, which had succeeded "Tad's Indoor Sports" when T. A. Dorgan died. Another humorous artist, Gene Ahern, contributed "Our Boarding House," which had developed a large following for Major Hoople, a fat braggart who wore a Turkish fez and loafed around telling lies while his wife did all the work. And there was a weekly piece by George Jean Nathan, witty and spirited critic of the theatre.

Westbrook set himself an easy pace in his first months with the *Journal-American,* and gave readers the feeling that he was wound up to keep going for an indefinite time. When he looked back on his life in the late 1960s, he said that the ten years beginning in 1944 had been his best. Before the end of 1944 he had again stated his major themes which were the crimes and follies of the Roosevelts; the corruption of labor unions; and the destructive malice of various Bolos, professors, and hop-heads who were tirelessly working to cancel the Constitution and bore holes in the ship of state. Pegler would give occasional relief from these heavy themes by presenting a column in verse, usually with a tone of self-mockery, or by reminiscences of his early days. Readers and editors greeted these columns with such delight that Pegler might have concluded he did best as a humorist. He often brought forward George Spelvin to help answer the question of how to present serious convictions in an amusing way. Spelvin came up in the world; once a laborer or handy man out of work, George got his share of the war money, and rose from blue collar to middle management, marriage to his high school sweetheart, a mortgaged house on Dudgeon Heights, and membership in the Bosky Brae Country Club.

In early days on the *Journal-American* Westbrook took occasion to show his continued interest in reporting away from the office, and by September 25 was out on the campaign trail with Governor Thomas Dewey, who hoped to defeat Franklin Roosevelt in November. Pegler made good use of this material in columns that were detached, shrewd, and penetrating. He observed Mrs. Dewey burdened with an onerous schedule, and asked, of politicians in general, "Why does the wife have to go?" A good question, which was still being asked some years later when we were told that DICK AND PAT MAKE NEW FRIENDS IN FAR-OFF LAND. Pegler said that the politician is the person we wish to meet and know, and presenting his wife to the public results in nothing but tedious, manufactured, woman's-angle copy. "And, except for Mrs. Roosevelt, who is a phenomenon beyond understanding, the wife must be elaborately polite, and able to make news of her nylons." After his first appearance, the *Journal-American* ran the column on its opposite-editorial page with inconsequential Broadway gossip and King Features boilerplate material; but after the first Dewey piece, the editors spread "As Pegler Sees It" on the first two columns of Page Three, the obvious position of honor for their best writer. You picked up your paper, glanced at the front page, leafed over—and there was Pegler looking stern in the column's title, a double-decked heading for the day's piece, and then the piece itself to the bottom of the page, set in two-column measure and varied down its eighteen inches with boldface type to emphasize meaning and rest the eye. Paragraphs started with extra indentation and a block initial letter two lines deep; the effect was stunning, and made the Pegler typography of Scripps-Howard days seem feeble by comparison.

This year of 1944 which began that decade of what Pegler called his highest achievement brought him opposition and hostile criticism along with the excitement of moving to King Features and Hearst. For one thing, the farm near Ridgefield turned out to be more trouble than it was worth. Wartime shortages made it impossible to get anything right, and the agricultural operations were disastrous. Pegler had hoped to produce meat and vegetables on his 100 acres as a patriotic gesture to increase the food supply, while easing his tax burden through operating losses. But the farm produced neither food nor tax remission in any sizable amounts, although the trouble was enormous. And Pegler became unhappy when a nearby suburban newspaper launched an investigation of the farm, intending to prove that he was using rationed materials acquired in the black market. Word of the suburban paper's project reached the *New York Post,* whose editors took up the investigation, only to drop it when their man reported, "No story." Pegler resented the hostility of these papers, and their readiness to assume that he was not a patriotic citizen. Perhaps the emotional strain caused the gastric ulcer that began to pain him. He called the illness an "internal gum-boil," his graphic imagery of a lesion in mucous membrane which would form a crater. At that time ulcers were fashionable in the best medical circles, and Pegler went to Boston, the Lourdes of the American rich. Here he entered the Lahey Clinic for observation and treatment by Dr. Sara Jordan, who turned out to be one of the select group of human beings, aside from Julie, for whom Pegler had no critical or belittling word. Dr. Jordan told Westbrook he was anxious and emotionally tense, a typical ulcer personality according to current medical lore. All at once it was obvious that the time had come to shake the aggravations of hostile newspapers, and the tiresome work of trying to run a farm, and take refuge under the impersonal skies of Arizona. Accordingly Westbrook put the Ridgefield property on the market and moved to his La Cholla estate, making Tucson his official residence and registering as a voter in the Democratic party.

Westbrook's plan was to travel as a reporter half the year, writing on the road, and to spend the other half-year on the desert, getting in material by mail and telegraph and turning out five or six columns a week in the little writing-house on the La Cholla grounds. Although the travel time grew gradually less, he would hold to this schedule for eighteen years, and his love for Arizona scenery and climate never wavered. They say you don't begin to feel the full beauty of it until you have stayed out there for at least six months. And it took Pegler about that long to become accustomed to the plants and animals that flourished in his part of the Great American Desert where you might conclude, at first glance, that almost nothing was alive. But out in rough terrain bobcats could sometimes be heard calling at night, their sound like the cry of a house cat, only louder and more unnerving. At sunrise or sunset one might catch a glimpse of desert cottontail rabbits who stayed in hiding all day long; and on rare occasions the piglike peccary might be seen, bolting from his shelter in some desert wash and heading for a water hole. These creatures weighed as much as sixty pounds.

And in the nearby mountains there were bighorn sheep, and mule deer, the bucks weighing up to 160 pounds and carrying heavy, many-pronged antlers. And everywhere, if one knew how to find them, were smaller animals; several varieties of skunk, the little rock squirrels that would colonize any vacant house, the spotted ground squirrel, the porcupine, the raccoon, the gopher, the coyote, and the gray wolf—the kind that reared Mowgli in the *Jungle Books*. Pegler was fascinated not only by the animals, but by the plants and flowers of the desert, for one of his seldom-confessed enthusiasms, numbered among "the things I really like," were flowers. Once in Chicago friends had seen him ordering yellow roses in a hotel florist shop, giving a room number for delivery, and when the salesman asked who the flowers should be addressed to, Pegler muttered, "Nobody—I mean, they're for me." On an impulse Westbrook once sent a bunch of sweet peas to Jesse Jones, the imposing Texas banker who ran the Reconstruction Finance Corporation. Pegler explained that the sweet peas had looked so beautiful in the shop he thought Jones might like them. He added, "Pansies are a good flower too." So it was not to be wondered at that Westbrook learned how to recognize the flowering plants that came up to the sun from the gray-green reaches of the desert valley that he inspected when riding out from Tucson toward Magee Road with the Rincon Mountains in the distance and the rolling foothills beginning to vary the flatlands as he approached the La Cholla spread.

There was much to see and identify, beginning with taller growths dominated by the weird-looking saguaro cactus which put out a white blossom in season on the upthrust tips of its hideous crocodilian limbs; other growths such as the yucca and the buckthorn looked like something designed by Heironymus Bosch, their horrible need for water giving them an appearance of plants on the bottom of an undiscovered sea. But the yucca in its season put out a white flower, an explosion of bloom at the end of a skinny arm that projected from a nightmare shape on the ground. The staghorn bloomed in crimson, a plant called hedge hog produced a crimson flower, and something called devil's fingers, that grew almost flat on the ground, yielded lavender blossoms; the sturdy little ironwood leafed in green, and the palo verde blazed like forsythia when the time was right. On his own ground, Pegler liked to gather Queen Anne's lace, which he said was a weed in the Northeast, a flower in Arizona. He also fancied the tall occotillo plant, which bloomed in purple, and rejoiced in oriental poppies and oleander at his door. Pegler said, "Any man who doesn't like flowers is a fool."

Early in 1945 Pegler began to assess the meaning of the war and the prospects for civilization at home and abroad. After stating in 1941 that Franklin Roosevelt was the strong man we needed in war, Pegler thought better of it, his doubts about Roosevelt returned, and he decided that a war which we had entered behind an unsound leader would be a war that would lead to disaster for his country. Pegler foreshadowed George Orwell in the idea that the growth of feebleness in language, the destruction of idiom, was also a destruction of ethics and a destruction of trustworthy government. This is not by any means a foolish theory, and the insipid ghost-writing of orations for world leaders made Pegler angry. But he was happy that Churchill's public statements were "hand-rolled, because Churchill is a writer, a great professional, much too proud as an artist and a man to call on anyone for a word or phrase whether of scorn or corn. Can anyone imagine Churchill calling in a British Sam Rosenman, a Tommy the Cork,* a Robert Sherwood and a lot of political gag-writers to do his speeches for him? Long after this old growler dies, some of his messages to his

*Roosevelt's nickname for an aide, Thomas G. Corcoran.

countrymen will be classed among the greatest orations of all time. . . . Beating history to the punch, it is my decision that Winston Churchill has it all over our Commander-in-Chief. . . . And finally, there is the matter of oratorical delivery. To us, of course, Churchill has an 'English accent' but, to his own people, it is the genuine language and inflection of a cultured Englishman who speaks as one who knows them from association and not as a highly superior being who has been kind enough to rule them.

"But what is that Roosevelt Choctaw, anyway? It isn't real Harvardese nor Bahstonese nor Grotonese nor the language of New York, the South or the West. What other American ever pronounced the word 'again' as Roosevelt has pronounced it again and again and again?" Along with his complaint about accent, Pegler was referring to a Rooseveltian campaign promise that no American boys would be sent to a foreign war.

Westbrook was beginning to sense the last part of something in American affairs, an end to the period in which, as we made partial recovery from the great depression, we had come to believe in a usable past and a perfectible future. And now we were learning that wartime needs had furnished an excuse for slovenly work in every line of civilian endeavor, and surly abuse of the public. The vast gap between what was advertised and what was delivered began to open, the first long step toward the present day when a great deal of advertising is nothing more than fantasy, not connected in the slightest way with the goods or services supposedly provided.* Transport began to break down, and in the same month he issued the Churchill piece Pegler announced that he was happy to cooperate in the matter of keeping off trains, as the government had requested. In his youth and early maturity, he had loved the trains and it had taken a long time to satisfy a longing "that was aroused back in Minnesota when I hung around the water-tank down by the depot and heard those marvelous stories of their tours hither and yon from the bums who dropped off there to rinse out a shirt and catch a little sleep in the bushes by the right of way. It took hundreds of days and nights between here and Chicago and Detroit and the South and the West Coast, but I am cured and, in fact, my trouble nowadays is not keeping off the cars but in getting myself going when I know I ought to go somewhere and see some people, personally, about something." It wasn't even safe. Pegler said he "happened

*For an example of fantasy in advertising, note the airline copy which sells the physical allure of a stewardess, or the color of an airplane.

to know a couple of railroad presidents, too, whose last thought as they drop off to sleep at night is a dread that the phone will ring and the office say that the big train has piled into a freight or hit a curve a little too fast somewhere and tumbled down a mountain." Even though service was deteriorating, there was much unnecessary travel, Westbrook reported, and he said that we read of "big union officials tripping down to Miami and New Orleans for discussions that could have been conducted by phone, and out to San Francisco for the Peace Conference which was no more their business than it was the business of the Elks or the retail druggists and say to ourselves that if this travel was necessary, so was ours. But I assure the Office of Defense Transportation that I will not press my right to stand in a red-hot train corridor for 100 miles to catch a sorry meal dumped on the table by an overworked and exhausted waiter or to cling to the furniture as some dashing jockey up front does his best to straighten out a curve. I will waive."

But when compelled to travel in those insufferable trains of wartime, Pegler observed the young brides, often with babies, who followed their men around the country to live near training camps, where rapacious landlords would charge exorbitant rent for miserable quarters. Yet there was an unconquerable brightness in these girls who had been playing with dolls not many years before. Westbrook thought this cheerfulness beyond praise. They had youth on their side, and in most cases the interest of traveling for the first time, and they were just great. Pegler decided that one good night's sleep would be all these girls needed to recover from the most exhausting trip. But older people had to have at least two full days of rest after such journeys. Westbrook could usually arrange to get the necessary physical rest, and his mind never stopped working anyhow. But what about the men and women who could not control their schedules, and had to travel say twice a week between Chicago and Washington, or St. Louis and New York? There were many such, and they were running tired out, using up their reserves, and eroding their nervous systems.

Westbrook had grasped the truth that work in itself never killed anybody. The great addicts of work, such as Henry Ford and Thomas Edison, were healthy as horses. What tore you down was aggravation and strain in getting *at* your work, without having to sustain a series of attacks on your peace of mind. The meanness of travel, for example, was magnified in the conduct of hotels now that rooms were in demand and overbooking an ordinary practice. It was during this period that the great downtown hotels laid the foundation for their ultimate ruin by treating guests like prisoners lined up for entry at a county jail.

Chapter 6

Pegler wrote on October 25 in 1945, "I tell you honest, I just went into this hotel because I had a date for lunch with an old friend, and I was just waiting there in the lobby, causing no disturbance, when the manager he came up with a halfbrick in his hand and he said, 'Be absent,' he said, 'be missing,' he said, 'because we haven't got any rooms and we are not taking any reservations and I am getting sick and tired of people coming in here trying to rent rooms and offering us $25 a night for a little $3.50 flea-bag and a $100 bonus for our kindness because it is bums like you throwing money around who are making life miserable for honest hotel men and it is nothing but inflation and you ought to be patriotic and stay the hell home. . . . We have got you covered and you make one move toward that registration desk or you try to pull a sneak up the back stairs and the house dicks will be all over you and moreover I had to hire 20 of the most insulting, crooked, nasty-talking clerks, telephone operators and waiters so I figured the Labor Relations board was the logical place so I went down and got me a slew of their best agents and most of them are Communist lawyers trained for years in acting under-handed and naturally they figured there was a wonderful chance to louse up our reputation with the public and bankrupt the investment. . . . 'What for do you do the customers that way, anyway?' I asked him. 'You used to treat the customers real nice here.' 'Because why don't they stay home where they belong instead of everybody coming to New York and crowding up things so you can't get a taxi and people walk all the way from Grand Central carrying heavy baggage and we have to spread cots in the dining rooms and not a night goes by but a dozen war veterans and their little wives and sometimes a baby even, and their home-folks are bunking in chairs in the lobby. That is why.'"

The ideal America, a civilized land of good humor and good manners, continued to recede before Pegler as the war approached its end. As in all wars, the wrong people were getting killed, and the wrong people were getting rich; and although the President's sons were in uniform and facing hazardous duty, there had been a certain air of dubiety about Elliott Roosevelt's career in the Air Force. He had entered as a captain by direct commission and there was some question as to the military value of his contribution to the service, in which he rose to the rank of brigadier general. Granted that little buck generals were very numerous in the Air Force, Pegler found it impossible to give Elliott the respect that may have been his due. Early in 1945 a story got out that the Air Transport Command had assigned an "A" travel priority to Elliott's dog, which bumped three enlisted men off an airplane at Memphis,

Tennessee. When Pegler questioned Headquarters Air Transport Command about this, they answered, "No comment." On January 29 Pegler wrote, "What do you mean, 'no comment?'" He went on, "The thing to do now is to call up Gen. Harold L. George, of this command, make him click his heels before a committee of Congress, stand at attention and answer questions. . . . And while the subject is warm there is occasion also to check the priorities on commercial transports which have been practically monopolized by the Government with civilians outside the privileged class imposed on with delays, expense and hardship. It is no justification to say that civilians should not travel unnecessarily. The law is that they have as much right to travel as Mrs. Eleanor Roosevelt. . . . They have as much right to travel in the best accommodations to be had as Elliott's latest wife. . . . They are no less entitled to go to conventions, whether of antique dealers or the Sons and Daughters of I Will Arise, than Mrs. Roosevelt, Sidney Hillman and a thousand others were to occupy train space to Chicago for the purely political convention of the CIO. . . . Mrs. Roosevelt remarked apropos her own restless wanderings that she traveled 'because the people want me to,' a mandate that must have been written in invisible ink inasmuch as no such proposition has ever appeared to the naked eye on the ballot or in any of her party's platforms. From the time when accommodations became a problem before Pearl Harbor and since, Mrs. Roosevelt's mileage has exceeded by thousands of miles, within the United States alone, that of the most itinerant non-professional wanderer. . . ."

There was tension now between Pegler's picture of himself as a good American and his disillusionments with war, and presidents, generals, kaisers, and kings. William Faulkner had said it at the end of a story of the first war, when the American pilot dives the Handley-Page at the chateau where the German generals are lunching, releases bombs and zooms away thinking, "God! God! If they were all there—all the generals, the admirals, the presidents and the kings—theirs, ours—all of them." Pegler suffered that same loss of faith, and shared George Spelvin's thoughts in the column for August 23, 1945, with Germany defeated, the end in sight, and Spelvin in one of those moods when he "locks the doors and draws the blinds of his soul and goes over his secrets like a fugitive from a chain gang who has changed his name and lives in fear of denunciation.

"At such times he bats himself over the head with reminders that the only Indian treaties which his own country did not violate, in a manner that would have been the very pattern for Adolf Hitler's penetration and the ensuing rescues of his oppressed minorities of Germans, were the last ones. . . .

"But then he turns to the British and French and Dutch empires and wonders by what right these European peoples, his gallant allies in war and strictly peace-loving, nonaggressive members of the new family of good nations, ever acquired those properties and for what purpose beyond that of improving the condition of the natives. It couldn't have been profit, could it, and the exploitations of the labour and the products of little brown people and yellow people and blue people and, by the way, did those peoples definitely ask these Europeans to come in and set them right or was it a case of spontaneous and altruistic sacrifice for the good of the backward breeds? . . . Spelvin sort of twitches when he comes to the perfidious sneak attack of the Japs on Pearl Harbor because he does regard it as a dirty trick and hates Japs for their ferocities to prisoners and their arrogance in momentary victory.

"But, in the privacy of his own mind, he harks back to that little, insignificant dispatch out of Boston thirteen days before Pearl Harbor which attributed to Sen. Claude Pepper, of Florida, a flat statement that our side would start shooting without warning the instant the Japs should cross an undefined line, apparently in the Pacific. . . .

"Was this just a case of a flannel-mouthed irresponsible talking big and loud or was this a responsible statement by an informed public official of the American government announcing our repudiation of international law? If he was right in warning the Japs that we would start a war with a sneak punch, didn't that give them the right to beat us to the punch?

"It is one thing to whoop it up in parades and damn the Japs regardless, but for personal consumption, Mr. Spelvin wants to be sure he isn't kidding himself about his own country and her record and the present motives and past performances of the other good countries as compared with the conduct of the bad ones. It hurts but George Spelvin, American, feels that these little secret sessions do him good, at that."

The shortcomings of the world's leaders and the insanity of their policies, more drift than long-range planning, had caused many an intelligent man and woman to abandon hope for humanity. Mark Twain had given up on mankind some years before, although he did not release the most pessimistic of his writings; and Twain in the closing years of his life had kept up a front as entertainer with that white suit, and that pool cue, and that Oxford degree, and that mop of white hair, and those cigars, until he died. In the same way Pegler often delighted his audience with humor throughout the 1940s although the indignation within him frequently boiled into print. Because the angry columns outnumbered the gentler ones, Pegler had acquired an undeserved reputation of personal bad temper and belligerence. He was capable of much kindness to friends, visiting them when they were sick, sending flowers to hospital rooms along with new books from Brentano's, and baskets of fruit from Sherry's for convalescents. Westbrook was good about answering letters from friends, and, what was even more appreciated, would supply recommendations for those in search of jobs. And if any friend told him a change would be welcome, Pegler would pass the word when he heard of an opening. His usual manner except with people he knew well was diffident; and the contrast between Pegler in his private life and the stern investigator and accuser who produced the crusading columns was so remarkable that one of his friends wrote about it. This friend was the novelist Homer Croy, who visited Julie and Westbrook in Tucson and wrote in a magazine article that Pegler's "Heart is soft as churn butter, and almost anyone who comes along with a hard luck story can get a loan from him. . . . His sense of humor runs through him like a wick through a candle." Croy also gave a flashlight portrait of Pegler's appearance: "He has reddish hair and is as freckled as a turkey egg." This freckled, soft-spoken, generous man was great company, Croy said, at cocktails on the terrace at La Cholla. When the cool air came down from the mountains Pegler seemed happy and at peace. And Julie was there.

And in June of 1944 Gene Fowler wrote to Julie, "No matter what fire is directed on Westbrook I am in his corner. I have never left it. . . . I am remembering the man I worked with, the bright, gay intelligent, gentle and forgiving fellow of many years ago. He was a grand person then and he could not change in essence. . . ." Fowler was the kind of friend who came on for life, but the old crowd in Connecticut had fallen away; this was mostly because of the manner in which Pegler had treated Heywood Broun. Some said Pegler had showed execrable taste in attending Broun's funeral, and took him off the list of cronies; others like Quentin Reynolds continued to be civil but there was no more warmth where once there had been comradeship and laughter. Reynolds was now a celebrity, having become friendly, during his days as a war correspondent, with Admiral the Lord Louis Mountbatten, Churchill, and Roosevelt. He was making big money writing and broadcasting, had married a beautiful actress named Virginia Peine, and lived in a spectacular apartment on the 19th floor at River House, overlooking Blackwell's Island, Queensborough Bridge, and the Pepsi-Cola sign in Long Island City. Reynolds had grown stout, and his curly hair was gray. He looked the way U.S. senators ought to look. Any cab driver on the late watch in mid-Manhattan who saw him would call out, "Hi, Quent!" and perhaps be rewarded with a five-dollar bill, a "fin," for a few blocks' ride. Westbrook saw Reynolds occasionally at the luncheon meetings of the Dutch Treat Club, which took place at the Park Lane. The two men would exchange pleasant greetings, but that was all.

The death of Franklin Roosevelt on April 12, 1945, served to justify the statements that Pegler had made to the effect that the President was in no condition to rule in a fourth term which he would not survive. These statements had caused consternation, and some said Pegler's attitude in the matter had horrified Roy Howard. At the time millions of people were devout president-worshipers, hypnotized by the phrase "this great office," and regarding its holder with superstitious awe. Tribal beliefs ran strong that it would be fatally bad juju to think, or at any rate to say, that the Leader had human limitations. The sky might fall or the world come to an end. Roosevelt's associates later revealed that he had suffered months of "heart trouble," that he had kept a heart specialist near him, and had looked so bad before the 1944 elections that his people thought he might die at any time. Nevertheless the White House staff hushed all talk about presidential health, and put out publicity that everything was fine. The medical authority was one of those uniformed doctors of the kind that presidents always seem to have in attendance. A doctor of that sort is not going to bring bad news.

At any rate, they carried Roosevelt to Boot Hill, and the question before Westbrook's readers was, how would he handle Harry S. Truman, who became President immediately after the word came in that Roosevelt had collapsed and died in his cottage at Warm Springs. Truman's arm went up like a semaphore, they put the Book on him, he said "I do," and there he was President, a man who looked like a guest at a Times Square hotel. But there had been things about Truman that appealed to Westbrook: during the First War he had served in the line with Missouri troops hauling guns around and firing them at the enemy, and "we grow good people in our small towns, with honesty, sincerity, and dignity." Pegler may have forgotten that he had written at the time Truman was nominated for Vice President that "this Truman is thinlipped, a hater, and not above offering you his hand to yank you off balance and work you over with a chair leg, pool cue or something out of his pocket." Truman had been a smalltime political chiseler around Kansas City during one of its most corrupt periods, and he had taken orders from Tom Pendergast, who got to Mass at 7:30 every morning for thirty years, and had so corrupted local law enforcement that the Federal Bureau of Investigation made sure it never shared information with the K.C. cops—it would be the equivalent of calling the crooks on the telephone and reading it to them or putting it on the six o'clock news broadcast by Lowell Thomas. Pegler wrote of the man who taught Truman his trade, "Unlike most of the bosses of the same general type, ironically known as Honest Johns, he let little of the graft trickle down to his underlings." Pendergast's way of running things at its logical end "would mean either dictatorship or revolution." That line of thought led Westbrook to a conclusion after the dropping of the atomic bomb on Hiroshima and Nagasaki, August 6 and 9, 1945. Estimates of the dead ran from 120,000 to 374,000; whatever the kill of Japanese, it was the greatest slaughter resulting from a single military order in modern times—and Truman had given the order. Pegler decided it was the deed of "a vulgar Kansas City commissioner playing God Almighty with a swagger." By September 1946 when the Pearl Harbor Report came out, Pegler had Truman squarely in his sights. He wrote that for some reason Truman seemed to hold the American people responsible for Pearl Harbor, which was a typical demagogue's trick. And Truman was "ruthless toward helpless men," the admiral and general in charge of U.S. forces out there when the Japanese made their attack. Doggedly loyal to Pendergast was Truman, faithful to the "corruptioneer" who had sent him to the Senate. Westbrook charged that Pendergast had tried to block the confirmation of an honest U.S. district attorney named Robert Milligan, who was "wrecking the machine and sending to prison some of Truman's old associates." Loyalty to such men was "a bad trait in Mr. Truman, more expressive of the underworld code than of decency, and his greatest weakness."

Another favorite tackling dummy in this period was Harold Ickes, a man who resembled Truman in noticeable lack of charm, but who differed from him by being capable of achievement in ordinary life. As we know, Secretary of the Interior Ickes was one of Franklin Roosevelt's ablest associates. But there was something about him that set Pegler's teeth on edge. "That Ickes is for me," said Pegler, "and I can take him any time." Westbrook had written in 1944, "Hey, Ickes, you penny-ante moocher, tell us about the two times you put yourself away in the Naval Hospital in Washington, for $3 a day, all contrary to law, and you a rich guy able to pay your way at the regular hospitals as all other sick civilians have to do. . . . Why you cheap sponger, you couldn't rent a hall-room in a pitcher-and-bowl fleabag for three bucks a day.

You know who paid the overhead for your hospital bargain, don't you? Well, I did. And George Spelvin. We paid it."

Some people deprecated the abusing of a cabinet member, but there was a mean streak in Ickes and Pegler sensed it, and in the following year he exposed Ickes as a man who would confiscate the widow's mite if he could get away with it. The matter had resulted from the tragedy which occurred when Mrs. Ickes was killed in the wreck of a car driven by a hired chauffeur. Ickes sued the chauffeur for damages, but the man died, leaving $696, and the court placed this money beyond Ickes's reach because he didn't get law papers filed until after the man was dead. The money went to the widow and her five children. Pegler wrote of this $696 estate, "The thought that Mr. Ickes might have had it for himself but for an error of timing is one that wrings my own great and mushy heart for him."

In the fall of 1945, Pegler made what was for him a reasoned and moderate statement on the manipulation of labor unions, taking the text from his experience in the Newspaper Guild. Here he managed to give his views on Heywood Broun without setting him down as a direct agent of Moscow, but coming at him on the side where Broun himself had admitted he was weakest—his desire to be a public figure. Pegler made his approach by way of Milton Kaufman, a former official of the Guild who had called a press conference, on October 25, for a left-wing lawyer named Nathan Witt. Pegler wrote that he used to see Milton Kaufman "doing his stuff in the meetings of the *World-Telegran* unit of the American Newspaper Guild and they had a wonderful team, too. Old Broun had taken some elocution lessons on the sneak and had learned to shake his William Jennings Bryan hair-do at us poor, bewildered editorial saps who, to our cost, had given him our confidence, and glare and spatter sweat over the front rows, as he howled for a strike which would throw all hands out of work and smear the paper and send a little circulation over to the *Evening Post* which was where he was going when his contract ran out. . . . They may have been only junior varsity parliamentarians in the Union Square League, but we, after all, had no experience whatever and they were champions by comparison. So most of the time we didn't know the score or whether we were discussing a motion, an amendment or a strike to reinstate some drunken Bolshevik in Boston. This Kaufman was what they called the executive secretary which in those days didn't mean much to me although I presently learned that in the Communist scheme this office in a union corresponds to that of minister of the interior in a European cabinet. . . . I somehow thought he must be a newspaper man like, you know, rewrite, headquarters, city hall, general assignments or copy-desk and the Bolos of course said, oh, to be sure he was, except that he worked on some garment trade paper which didn't seem real newspaper to me, and, not that I am any way snobbish, but just clannish if you will, I kept wondering how a cloak-and-suiter got to be so important in our lives, when so many of us had been in the business so long and had met just about everybody but never before had heard of Milton Kaufman.

"Just all of a sudden there he was, the head man, with old Broun for a front and Broun always insisting that all this talk about Communism in the Guild was nothing but Red-baiting and probably the work of the Nazis.

"I decided to take the fence soon after a long meeting which the Commies dragged out until many of the Americans had gone home to catch some sleep and the rest of us were groggy from the smoke, in the hope that they could out-vote us because their side never gave up, maybe they weren't allowed to go home. At any rate, they put up a fellow from some of the mechanical trades, which had firm contracts with the paper, who said that if we struck and put pickets around then he would consider that an unhygienic working condition and perilous to life and limb and call out his men too. Not a sympathetic strike you understand. No strike at all, on their part. . . .

"That was when I decided that Broun was a fake friend of labor, perfectly willing to inflict all this distress on fellow-workers in the shop much less able than himself to live a spell without pay or find new jobs, just to build his reputation as a professional bleeding heart. That was when I decided that unions were as dirty in their way as the corporations ever were and, finally, that the rank and file had no chance under the present law and the New Deal hypocrisy which persecuted and oppressed them through union bosses while pretending to befriend them, and I wasn't wrong either. . . ."

Two months later Westbrook showed that his strongest suspicions lay against bureaucrats rather than ideologues, when he had George Spelvin say "Although I bet if I was to meet some Russian and we could speak some language to get along together why I would find he was a pretty good egg because they say they like to drink and as far as Communism is concerned why that seems to be strictly export goods because it seems like there is a small bunch of head bosses and they live on caviar and highly seasoned viands like our New Dealers and you can't tell me those ordinary Russians enjoy getting their gizzard blown out just because the big guys decide to take over China or Turkey. . . . Our government has been going all over the world since long before we even born, telling the Germans, Russians, Italians, the Mexicans, the Chinese, 'you guys are just dumb backward serfs and ignorant peons and your trouble is you do not have candy-bars and beautiful tooth-brushes; look at those crude suits you guys wear, they went out of style in America fifty years ago; no nail-polish on your girls, no glamor, big old fat babes from hoeing turnips and carrying the hod. You are backward because you do not think right. Your only hope is you have got to act like we Americans and you will have radios and hi-fi, electric kitchens and wonderful plumb pudding in cans. . . .'"

In the same piece Spelvin mentioned an unsavory episode in the Roosevelt story that Pegler had first brought to light in his column of June 10, 1945. What Pegler had to reveal was an accusation of fraud on the part of the President and his son Elliott in the matter of extracting $200,000 in cash from John Hartford, the chain-store grocery king. Elliott had applied for this sum as a loan in 1939, offering stock in a Texas radio chain as security. Since Hartford was under threat at the time from a New Deal congressman who was working to cut him up by passing some law or other, he felt, as he said later, that Elliott put him in a peculiar position by coming in with his hand out. Elliott got his father on the telephone and introduced Hartford, who was embarrassed to hear the President say anything he could do for Elliott would be appreciated. Hartford then came through with the money. Three years later, Franklin Roosevelt sent Jesse Jones to settle up, and Jones told Hartford the most he could offer was two cents on the dollar. Hartford accepted $400 as payment in full, and returned the radio stock, which later proved to be worth $400,000 when it went to one of Elliott's wives in a divorce settlement. Pegler said he thought he should have received another Pulitzer award for this story, which was vouched for by Jesse Jones, who also published it. But the affair was so grotesque that it is still hard to take in: here we had Elliott like the roper in a confidence mob bringing a sucker to the inside man and taking him for $200,000—an amount that served the victim as a tax deduction, thus loading part of the loss on other taxpayers. Many a time thereafter would Pegler return to the tale, once referring to Elliott with mock compassion as one who had to live by the motto of the little Broadway chiseler who said, "I look to do the best I can." Worshippers of the presidency found the publication and reiteration of this story more than they could bear. They cursed Pegler for calling Roosevelt a con man, but he replied, "If the gradual disclosure of the truth evokes abuse of the truth itself, as ghoulish attacks and mad rantings, that may be only evidence of the depth of a great moral and ethical decline, between 1933 and 1945."

There was no question that *something* had broken down. The successful novelist Edna Ferber gave unconscious testimony to the decay of civilized instincts by recording a party that took place in the studio of a popular illustrator on January 10, 1946, at which the guests drank a toast in champagne wine to the crew of *Enola Gay,* the American airplane that delivered the atomic bomb to Hiroshima. At the same time an important American writer lay captive in Washington, and Pegler took his part. The author was Ezra Pound, a poet of great influence in American literature, who believed that the paying of interest, or usury as he called it, was responsible for the trouble in the world. Pound lived in Italy for years, and during the war he broadcast pro-Axis propaganda. At the end he was arrested by the kind of military authority that moves in after the fighting has stopped, and they charged him with treason to the United States. They didn't have the nerve to shoot him, and locked him up in St. Elizabeth's, a mental hospital in the District of Columbia. They said he was crazy. Although his theories of finance could be disputed, Pound was sane, and so far as mental powers went he loomed over his psychiatrist-jailers like Gulliver over the inhabitants of Lilliputia. Pegler got on to the story and his indignant writings on the imprisonment, to which he returned from time to time, may have helped bring about Pound's eventual release in 1958. Pegler gave no evidence of having studied Pound's verse, which was so erudite and allusive that "few persons profess to understand his stuff and those few may be faking." But Westbrook would have applauded these lines from Canto LXXXI:

> Pull down thy vanity
>   How mean thy hates
> Fostered in falsity,
>   Pull down thy vanity,
> Rathe to destroy, niggard in charity,
> Pull down thy vanity,
>   I say pull down.

In his comments on Pound's imprisonment Westbrook came straight to the point—it couldn't be doing Pound or anyone else any good to confine him in extreme discomfort among roaring madmen when he would be quite harmless back at his study in Rapallo. His war broadcasts, said Pegler, had been "nothing but babble, anyway. . . . He was just not like other people, which is a challenge to compulsory conformity. . . . Assuming, however, that Pound is crazy, is his poetry any worse than Einstein's maths and is lunacy sufficient ground to haul a man home from Rome, where he got along all right, and lock him up in bedlam?" Pegler was none too respectful of psychiatrists, and especially suspicious of those who locked people up for taking an unpopular stand. He defended another agitator of this sort when a Mrs. Lucille Miller landed in that same District mental hospital for opposing continuance of the conscription law in time of peace. Mrs. Miller had argued that compulsory military service in absence of war was the same as slavery and therefore unconstitutional. This made too much sense, and they put her in St. Elizabeth's, which aroused Pegler's indignation. His defense of Mrs. Miller earned him abuse from those who needed the comforting thought of armies to defend us from being murdered in our beds. Also, questioning the authority of government to do *anything* was disloyal, or heresy in the religion of patriotism, the only religion that really moved most people. *I pledge allegiance to my Flag*. . . .

In the year 1947 Pegler combined his talent as an entertainer with a substantial piece of public service when he drew the country's attention to Henry Agard Wallace and the famous correspondence known as the Guru letters. Wallace was the grandson of an old Iowa scissorbill who had founded a newspaper that later became *Wallace's Farmer*, the leading agricultural journal of the country. The publisher's son, Henry Cantwell Wallace, had been secretary of agriculture and it therefore seemed fitting that Henry A. Wallace should hold the same position in Franklin Roosevelt's cabinet from 1933 to 1941. It was hard to describe Henry Wallace, for he lacked crispness of outline, though he seemed to be a decent sort of man, with a strain of mysticism that perhaps qualified him for the definition of harmless crank. Wallace had a taste for symbolism, and persuaded Treasury Secretary Morgenthau to adorn the one-dollar bill with the mystic pyramid from the Great Seal of the United States, which carried a gigantic surrealist eye at its apex. Although cabinet officers had not been taken seriously for years, many people thought that Wallace might accomplish some good, but changed their minds when they saw what he decreed as rational policy in the official destruction of millions of tons of food, and making payments to farmers from the public treasury to grow no grain and send no meat to market. This resulted in the renowned little pigs who gave their lives for no discernible benefit to anybody. Most of the money went to big agricultural operators, and the little men, especially the sharecroppers, got only the crumbs that fell from the rich men's tables. Many of the croppers suffered from empty bellies and fought gun battles with sheriffs who came with law papers to put them off the land. You couldn't convince the beamish Henry Wallace that there was something wrong here, and when he served as Vice President, from 1941 to 1945, there always existed the possibility that he would be running the country, for there he sat, the traditional heartbeat away from the presidency, with Roosevelt in bad health, and the ever-present chance that a sniper might kill him. And Wallace had all those wild notions revolving in his head. As history records, Roosevelt survived that term, got rid of Wallace, and replaced him with Truman as second in command. And it was Truman who succeeded to the presidency when Mr. Roosevelt died.

We may note without reprehensible digression that the papers solemnly listed Franklin Roosevelt as a war casualty, who had knowingly tired himself to death in his country's service on a sort of political kamikaze mission. In fact the President's health had broken from natural causes, as happens to any elderly man when his time draws near. All this seemed obvious to Pegler, who found nothing acceptable in any claim that Roosevelt had fallen like a man in battle. Nor did he care much for Harry Truman, whom he took to be cocky and ignorant rather than bold and wise with folk wisdom, as the official propagandists would have it. Nevertheless, Truman looked better to Westbrook than Wallace, and he felt that there was danger in the possibility of Wallace being nominated for President in 1948. And in advance of the conventions Pegler started an anti-Wallace campaign.

On June 2, 1947, Pegler announced he had discovered that seven years before, Wallace had been "staggery and in a spiritual haze," and had sought counsel from a man named Nicholas Konstantin Roerich, a guru or teacher of the occult who was now believed to be somewhere in Southeast Asia. In 1930, Roerich had promoted financing to build an Oriental museum at 310 Riverside Drive, and this building was "nothing but a 25-story joss house." Senator Wagner had spoken well of it, but "Old Wagner never was anything but a common Tammany Club house politician and judge," so his recommendation was worthless. The "gigantic joss house" was the sort of place that would look like a repository of esoteric wisdom to Henry A. Wallace. Now it had become known that during his time in a cabinet office, Wallace had been a disciple of Roerich and had written him a series of letters that indicated a degree of imbecility unacceptable even in a Washington job-holder. Pegler admitted that "Wallace is indifferent to personal disparagement. Call him a crackpot and you are the crackpot, making fun of a holy man." Westbrook had nothing but admiration for Roerich, "the old guy with the two-legged beard and the squint eyes who looks like Chu Chin Chow and is regarded as a master intellect."

Some of the information on the Riverside Drive joss-house had come from Representative Sol Bloom, a man Pegler respected as an oldtime carnival showman, street-smart and still able to take to his heels rapidly if cops came in sight. Sol had worked the Midway at the Chicago Fair in '93, and "had seen the best of them, close up, fortunetellers, hypnotists, phrenologists, astrologers and all." Bloom told Pegler that "a hypnotist might make a fellow take off his pants in public without knowing a thing about it. They used to do it at the state fairs." So he would never let Roerich draw a bead on him. Pegler thought Wallace might have been hypnotized when he organized an expedition to Mongolia for Roerich, which was all right except for the matter of expenses, all of which went to the American taxpayer, "and you can't wiggle off that hook, Wallace." The secretary had indeed wasted time and money on the Roerich expedition, which produced nothing of value. They were looking for a new kind of drought-resistant grass seed to replenish the dried-out American plains, but the rain came back and the seed wasn't needed even if Roerich had found it. Westbrook said the Republicans had conspired to souse the plains, and blow seed in on the north wind just to discredit Henry Wallace. The letters showed that Wallace accepted Guru Roerich as guide and teacher, and Pegler wrote of the doctrines ruling the Riverside Drive lamasery, "they say God lives in the Himalayas and is some kind of Chinaman." As he did in all his big running stories, Pegler gave painstaking research to the guru series, and made many efforts to reach Wallace. All he got from the secretary's office was a standard publicity handout about the Wallace farm, which Pegler answered in an open letter serving as a column.

"To hell with your farm, your chickens and your strawberries," he wrote. "For two months I have been calling at your office and telephoning to ask whether you ever were a disciple or pupil of Nicholas Roerich. . . . I have been trying to corner you to make you answer whether you wrote Roerich a lot of idiotic letters and whether you regarded him as a god or supernatural master of mankind as many of your associates in the cult did. . . . Wallace, you are nailed on most counts. You certainly did mess around with old Roerich at the joss-house. You were seen there." Henry Wallace made no reply.

Westbrook had the kind of courage one needs in the business of making enemies, the procedure that James M. Whistler called a gentle art. But he did not like to face in person the miscreants he attacked in print. The hesitancy was caused by Pegler's lack of ability as a debater; he disliked getting on his feet before an audience, and he marshalled his thoughts best in his workroom, with plenty of paper to rip from the typewriter and throw on the floor. Nevertheless, Pegler felt he must openly confront Henry Wallace in the preliminaries to the national elections of 1948, and he forced himself to board a train at Pennsylvania Station early in the morning of July 22, bound for Philadelphia and the press conference Wallace had called to explain his purposes in seeking nomination by the Progressive Party. Pegler had recently shuddered in print over what might have happened between 1941 and 1945. If Wallace had inherited the presidency during this period, "He could have called in some fortune-teller or Himalayan faker to tell him what to do. Hitler heard voices. He obeyed his instinct rather than his generals and plowed ahead into Russia and plowed under the entire German race." If Wallace sat on the throne, would he plow under the entire American race in some unforeseen disaster? With that question in mind, the men and women of the press had gathered to interview Wallace in a hotel ballroom, and Pegler took a seat near the front.

Like any politician whose claim to good sense and honesty is not clear, Wallace opened the meeting with an attack on the press. The newspaper people listened patiently while Wallace told them to mind their manners and mend their ways. In the course of his talk, Wallace said he had received a letter of support from George Polk, a reporter who had died under mysterious circumstances in Greece, probably the victim of right-wing government terrorists. Pegler like many of his colleagues thought this irrelevant, and "a *faux pas,* too, for it introduced the subject of letters." Pegler's account of the proceedings said that after Wallace called for questions, "a tall, not unhandsome chap arose, a man of spiritual mien and prematurely gray, to declare: 'My name is Westbrook Pegler, Mr. Wallace. You twice referred to the subject of letters in your remarks and you have reminded us journalists of the important duty of getting all the available facts. Therefore, I ask you whether you did or did not write certain letters to Nicholas Roerich, addressing him as Dear Guru, and his wife as Modra?'" Wallace flushed and his voice tightened as he replied, "I do not answer questions put to me by Westbrook Pegler." Thereupon Martin S. Hayden of the *Detroit News* rose and asked the same question. Wallace said, "I don't answer questions put to me by a stooge* of Westbrook Pegler, either." Boos and cheers were heard, and "the stately H. L. Mencken" raised his hand. Pegler recorded that "Mencken, being an atheist, was ready to swear on the Baltimore city directory that he put only his own questions." Mencken asked, "Mr. Wallace, do you consider me a stooge of Westbrook Pegler?" Wallace laughed nervously and said no such thought had ever entered his head. Mencken thanked him, and went on, "Then I should like to hear, did you or did you not write the Guru letters?" Wallace said, "I will never engage in any discussion whatsoever with Westbrook Pegler." Mencken said, "But what about the letters?" Wallace answered, "I will handle that matter in my own way, at my own time, and not here." Warren Francis of the *Los Angeles Times* now put the question and got the same answer. Dan Lundberg of KXLA-Pasadena took the floor to remind Mr. Wallace that he had made Pegler a present of the slogan, "Stooges of the world, unite!" and the news people present might act on it, so what *about* those letters? Wallace rebuffed Lundberg, and asked for some "sensible questions." Now a woman reporter stood up. She was Mary Spargo of the *Washington Post* and she said, "So far as being a stooge is concerned, I don't know Mr. Pegler and I don't like his column but I should like to hear you say you did or did not write those letters." Again Wallace shouted that he would answer in his own way and time. Mencken said, "Why not answer now? We are all here." Wallace shouted, "It has no importance—suppose we get on to something important." The goons in Wallace's bodyguard had been growing restless and one of them now yelled, "If you stooges don't like this why don't you get out of here?" In a short time there were no reporters in the hall except those from Communist publications. The press had treated Wallace roughly, but he was an obvious nut and had demonstrated that if he could not even control a news conference he was no man to put at the head of the entire country.

Photostat copies of the handwritten letters reached editorial offices, and the Paul Bloch, Scripps-Howard, and Hearst papers called in experts, who agreed that the writing was that of Henry Wallace. He never came clean on it, and wrote to Paul Bloch that "a member of a great minority group should not be responsible for opening that door." After

*A favored slang term of the day, "stooge" had originated in the theater where it denoted a low clown, drubbed and kicked by superior artistes to get laughs; by extension, any low confederate who accepts abuse from a patron or employer.

that Wallace was no longer taken seriously and he faded from the scene. His nemesis Pegler continued to flourish, but with excesses of accusation and hostile portrayal that caused uneasiness among his better sort of readers, the old regulars who had discovered him on the sportside and never missed a word he wrote. One of the brightest men on *The New Yorker,* Wolcott Gibbs, was a connoisseur of Pegler's writing and an accomplished parodist. Just before Christmas 1949, Gibbs gave readers a version of a famous editorial as Pegler would have written it. An editor of the *New York Sun* had once assured an inquiring little girl named Virginia that Santa Claus existed, and according to Gibbs, Pegler would have given the same assurance and further identified Santa as Comrade Jelly Belly, "after a poem composed about him by an admiring fellow-traveler, now under the sod." It seemed that Mr. Claus was "understandably" a reticent man, but Pegler had information that he was a porchclimber who had been born in Red Hook "under the appetizing monicker of Sammy Klein." The parodied Pegler told little Virginia that it was "a matter of common knowledge that his burglary rate never fails to hit a peak at Christmas. No one has ever been caught for any of these misdemeanors, but the evidence in each case is always the same—a few shoddy toys in a stocking on the mantelpiece, and a mink coat or a pearl necklace missing from the hostess's effects. One victim I know said she wouldn't mind so much if the toys were any good, but they are just cheap, tasteless junk that crooked labor unions have been turning out ever since the Great Brain decided to sell out this country to the lazy and incompetent. . . ."

There came now the turning of the hinge that set Pegler's life on its decline. One might ponder at length the question of whether or not every life has such a turning point, but Pegler's discernibly did, and the reason for it lay back in 1939 when he made his last attack on Heywood Broun. The literary historian Dale Kramer published a biography of Broun in 1949, and the editors of the *Herald Tribune* book section gave it to Quentin Reynolds for review. Kramer had recorded the savagery of Pegler's attack, and had described how Broun took to his bed when he read it. It was the closing scene of the biography, and also of Reynolds' review. He ended the piece by writing that "Broun couldn't relax. He couldn't sleep. And he died."

Although this was not quite a direct accusation that Pegler had caused Broun's death, it certainly did not imply that he had shown consideration or mercy to a former friend who had come on bad times. Pegler took mortal offense, and struck at Reynolds in a column of maniacal vituperation. Without mentioning the review which had offended him, Pegler told his readers that Reynolds had been a war profiteer, that he had faked his reports as a correspondent, that he had been fired from *Collier's* magazine, and that he was a notorious coward—his protuberant belly contained no guts. This was only the beginning. Pegler wrote that Reynolds was a moral degenerate, one of the "parasitic, licentious lot" that Broun had organized, and so lost to shame that he "paraded his mangy hide" naked on public roads in Connecticut. Among other crimes, the cabal of Broun and Reynolds had been responsible for the seduction of "a susceptible young white girl" by "a conspicuous Negro Communist." To wind up the column Pegler wrote that Reynolds had displayed such atrocious lack of taste as to propose marriage to Connie Broun, Heywood's widow, while accompanying her to the funeral.

The shock of this extraordinary attack dazed Reynolds so that he hardly knew what he was doing for three days. He later wrote in his memoirs *By Quentin Reynolds* that "Pegler's column seared my family, my friends, and myself." When Reynolds was able to think clearly, he consulted the well known trial lawyer Louis Nizer, who told him that he had grounds for a libel suit, and that bringing such an action would be an exhausting ordeal. Reynolds told Nizer to go ahead.*

What made Pegler launch an attack of such mindless ferocity? So far as Reynolds was concerned, there were resentments that had begun to form in what had seemed to be carefree days in Connecticut; Pegler had envied both Reynolds and Broun their facility in writing. And when Pegler began to realize that he had become an outcast from the inner circle after Broun's death, his anger burnt deep, like fire in a mine. And finally, Reynolds had been an unabashed hero-worshiper and court journalist to Franklin Roosevelt. As Pegler saw it, Roosevelt had bought Reynolds by giving him a few compliments and calling him by his first name. Thus Reynolds earned Pegler's professional contempt, a form of contempt that may be the most virulent of all.

Westbrook's lawyers would come from the Hearst legal department, headed by Charles Henry, who had gone through a good deal of libel work in his time. He knew the basic defense to any accusation of libel is to prove it true; in hopes of this he began an exhaustive pretrial examination of Reynolds, and on the other side Nizer began to study Pegler's writings and question him for hours at a time about his work and background. Early on, Charles Henry found himself not the happiest or most confident lawyer in New York. His client was the Hearst Corpora-

*For detailed accounts of this case, see Reynolds' book, *By Quentin Reynolds* (New York: McGraw-Hill, 1963), and *My Life in Court*, by Louis Nizer (New York: Doubleday, 1961).

tion, and yet he was working for Pegler, who had proved to be touchy, and unreasonable in his estimate of their problem. On March 27, 1953, Henry sent Pegler eight pages of single-spaced typing in which he tried to explain the trouble they were in. Pegler had told Henry that Reynolds had given evidence of cowardice in his books, but the lawyer had not been able to find such evidence. Henry said that Pegler seemed to think Reynolds had been under some obligation to place himself in dangerous positions, but this was not so. Henry next pointed out that Pegler's contention that Reynolds had "run all the way back to the United States" at one time during the war meant only that Reynolds had been granted a vacation by his employers, and there was nothing wrong with that. Furthermore, there was no use hoping that Reynolds would go to pieces under examination. He would not. And it was improbable that the Reynolds suit was the result of a plot, as Pegler wished to believe. Charles Henry said people bring libel suits for only one reason—they hope to get money, and in the present case the plaintiff expected a large amount if the defendants failed to prove the charges Pegler had made. In the last paragraph of this noticeably cool letter, Henry gave Pegler some advice. Pegler had said he was not satisfied with the Hearst legal department's work. Therefore he might give thought to hiring his own counsel. He was not too poor to do it. But if Pegler did bring in his own lawyer, Henry warned him that nothing would be gained by waiting until the last minute and then employing counsel to state that he would prove Pegler's charge of cowardice by quoting from Reynolds' writings. It just wouldn't work. What they needed was someone to stand up in front of judge and jury and state under oath that the charges were true. And whether or not they could produce such testimony, the case would come on in about a year, during the early part of 1954.

The men in charge at King Features and the Hearst papers had been worrying about Pegler for some time before he caused the Reynolds suit. They felt he was worth money, but they feared what he might do, and had each column read by members of the legal department before publication in the *Journal-American* and release to the syndicate wire. This meant night duty for staff lawyers and an editor who must be of sufficient rank to approach Pegler if anything had to be changed. In spite of these precautions the Reynolds attack had gone out, and after that, relations between writer and publishers were always under strain. Pegler suspected the editors and executives of planning to take the bite out of his copy and make him resemble any other writer who did nothing more than fill space. The Hearst papers had a dozen of this sort, and Westbrook vowed he would never make one more of that crew. In the entire Hearst organization he now placed full confidence only in Ward (Jimmie) Greene, the editorial chief at King Features, who was a sympathetic friend, and Maud Towart, an efficient and loyal secretary who had started working for Pegler in 1947. William Randolph Hearst died in his eighty-ninth year on April 12, 1945, and this removed an element of strength from Pegler's position; it had been known that the Chief had disregarded Pegler's insults and kept after him until he joined King Features. But with old Mr. Hearst in his grave, Pegler was no longer untouchable. And with all this to consider, the Hearst editors were delighted, early in 1951, when Pegler gave them the most popular column he ever wrote.

The piece had to do with the dish called chili con carne, a stew made with chili beans, ground beef, chili powder, tomatoes, and various condiments, which is one of the best liked dishes in this country. Pegler's mention of chili, as the dish is generally called, included his last friendly reference to President Harry S. Truman, who had patronized Dixon's Chili Parlor in Kansas City. The President had perched on a stool and "put himself outside a bowl of chili along with a scuttle of beer fetched from yonder, Mr. Dixon having no beer license." This started Westbrook on a discussion of chili, which had been a staple of his youth as a wandering newspaperman with a big appetite and a small salary. "If time would turn backward 35 years I would be able to take you to chili parlors in St. Louis, Dallas, Fort Worth, Omaha and Chicago where you could get a big, white bowl of chili-con or chili-mac for 15 cents. You could live high on a dollar a day in chili parlors." Westbrook then considered how the dish should be prepared, and closed by recommending the canned products of "a firm called Gebhardt's in El Paso," which was "no sneak ad because I deem it my professional duty to my fellow countrymen to inform them of those superb vittlements." He could not be charged with trying to hustle a free case of the stuff, because to his "morose regret" his "duodenal gum-boil" precluded his ever again "savoring this delight."

The letters that immediately came in gave much satisfaction to Pegler and his publishers. Along with scores of recipes, and discussions of how chili should be prepared, came hundreds of reminiscences about famous chili parlors of the past, or recommendations for parlors still in business. Many of the correspondents took a tone of pretended belligerence in denouncing what they called heresies in Pegler's column. Some said chili should be made with tomatoes, some without; the grinding or nongrinding of the meat, the presence or absence of onions or garlic, whether to serve with crackers or bread, and many similar matters were considered. In reply Pegler wrote that he "had no inkling of the feeling among the devotees, who fell on me in numbers, by telegram and mail. I don't want a fight. I am just a mild fellow anxious to please everybody." In conclusion he said that a New York friend had reminded him that chili could be had at the Alamo on 47th Street and El Rancho on Seventh Avenue, "where our family traded years ago. Notwithstanding my duodenal bunion, I might give El Rancho one more play. You can only die once." After that, so many letters came in that Pegler had to send a form letter in reply: "There has been such a tremendous response to Mr. Pegler's columns on chili that in the pressure of getting off on his Western trip, he is not able to dictate individual replies, much as he would like to. He has found it an enlightening discussion and thanks you sincerely for writing him."

President Truman did not get back in Pegler's favor with his bowl of chili and scuttle of beer. In August 1950, two months after we got into a fight with the North Koreans, Pegler was writing that the futility of this war could not be concealed, and that we should get out at once. The trouble had started at the top, where we had a mean little crook as president; we had big trouble so far as quality in the White House was concerned. There was something in this. Truman and his people had put us into a very bad war out there, a model for the war in Vietnam a few years later. And on the personal side, Truman did much to distress the fastidious. He talked in a nasal whine, and when he hit the Bourbon jug he would write nasty letters to people he didn't like. An example of this occurred when Truman's daughter Margaret presented herself as a singer, and a Washington critic reported that she had neither talent nor voice. Truman wrote the man a letter in which he threatened to kick him in the crotch. When Pegler said this was a hell of a way for a president to behave, Truman retorted that Pegler was nothing but a guttersnipe. In challenging Pegler, Truman went out of his class, as he discovered on May 23, 1952, when Pegler published one of the best of all George Spelvin columns:

"As George Spelvin, American, waited for the light to change at the corner of Elm and Spruce, he became casually aware of a jackass standing by the curb. He paid no special attention until the jackass said:

"'I have got a good mind to seize the press. I have got the right to seize it, you know.'

"Mr. Spelvin was so stunned that for a moment he couldn't offer any comment.

"Then he said: 'Can you talk? A jackass?'

"'Sure, I can talk,' the jackass said.

Chapter 6

"'But,' Mr. Spelvin stammered, 'excuse me all over, but I mean it is so surprising! I didn't know jackasses could talk.'

"'That is just crazy,' the jackass said. 'All jackasses talk. Most of them, that's all they do. Some of them even get to be Ambassadors and go around telling other countries what we are going to do to them if they don't run their Government like we do ours. Some get to be Secretary of Labor or Secretary of State. Sure, we can talk.'

"'But,' Mr. Spelvin insisted, 'I mean, why, if you will just sign on the dotted line with me, I can get you on the radio and, boy, will we clean up!'

"'Control yourself,' the jackass said, 'I have been on the radio hundreds of times. I just have to say the word and I get a national hookup. All the big networks and a hundred million Americans sit and listen to the wisdom of a jackass.'

"'But, an actual jackass talking like you do!' Mr. Spelvin gasped. 'You would be terrific. Sensational. I will be your manager and we will clean up. I will put you on television, too!'

"The jackass peeled his lips back off his teeth. . . ."

Here Mr. Spelvin realized he had seen that grin before—on Inauguration day 1949, right in front of the White House when the President had "stared back with a glassy glare in his spectacles and peeled his lips off his white teeth in a snarl at one of his enemies." Mr. Spelvin looked again.

"'You are wearing glasses,' he ventured . . . 'and a bow tie, too.'

" 'What have you got against bow ties?' the jackass demanded. 'What prejudism is this? Bow tie bigotry? Wait till I report you to the President's Committee on Civil Rights. We will pass a law to put your kind in prison for discriminating against the minority group who wear bow ties.'

"'Don't get me wrong,' Mr. Spelvin said. 'I am not prejudiced. It just seemed odd—'

"'You are a dirty guttersnipe,' the jackass said. 'You are a Fascist-minded tool of the special interests . . . You labor-baiting, rat, scab, fink. You and Taft, and MacArthur.'

"'Gee,' Spelvin said. 'I am going to hurry right home and write all this down. I don't want to forget a word of it. Amazing experience!'

"'I can write too,' the jackass said. 'I get alone in my study at night and write nasty letters. I threaten to kick guys and wreck them. Below the belt I threaten to kick them.'

"'Darndest experience I ever had,' Mr. Spelvin said. 'Am I asleep? Dreaming? Because everything you say reminds me of things I have read and radio speeches I have heard.'

"'You certainly are asleep,' the jackass said. 'The whole 150 million of you are asleep.'. . . The scene began to fade and the jackass blurred, all but the glint of the glasses and the necktie and the snarl on that mouth.

"'. . . Before I go, tell me, What is your name?'

"'If you don't know, it's you that is the jackass,' the jackass said. 'George Spelvin, American, what a jackass.'"

The case of Reynolds *v.* Pegler, the Hearst Corporation, and the Hearst Consolidated Publications came on before Judge Edward Weinfeld in May 1954 at the United States District Court in Foley Square. Pegler sat at the defense table heavy and forbidding, and when Reynolds glanced at him he thought of his "mother's high opinion of Peg—how she admired him for being a good Catholic, for the sweetness of his nature, and for the graciousness of his wife, Julie. In the old days, it had seemed to me that Peg and Heywood had a trait in common. Both, in their way, were puritans. . . ."

Louis Nizer opened by stating that he was willing to put his client under a microscope but intended to "take the same privilege with Mr. Pegler." One of the first things Nizer established was that Reynolds owed Internal Revenue $40,000 at the end of the war, which was supposed to refute the profiteering charge. It came out that Reynolds could not have faked the locations of his stories, because they had to go through military censorship at the point of origin. He could not have asked Connie Broun to marry him on the way to the funeral, because she was under sedation and dozing all the way. Her stepson and Monsignor Fulton Sheen were also in the car. Nizer then came to the charge of cowardice, and displayed documents and military photographs establishing that Reynolds had seen hazardous duty at Montmeidy and Bauvais, on Atlantic convoy, in the Libyan Desert, on the Dieppe raid, in Sicily, and at Salerno. Nizer also proved by witnesses that Reynolds had behaved well during the air raids on London. Reynolds was relaxed on the stand, and convincing in his answers. He said he had often been afraid under fire but had never run away, and in such situations there was no place to which he could have run, even if he had been willing to.

When Charles Henry took over for cross-examination, he began to drive at the question of malice, and tried to establish that the Hearst executives and editors were old friends of Reynolds who would not wish to do him harm. So if there was malice involved, it must have been on Reynolds' part, in bringing suit for what was nothing more than an exchange of criticism between literary men. It was hard to understand how he expected the jury to believe that the *plaintiff* was malicious, and Henry must have wished he had not opened this line when Reynolds gave an answer that brought him up short like an exploding cigar: "I don't know the complete meaning of malice in its legal sense. All I know is that Pegler made the bullets and the Hearst papers shot them."

Hoping to make this reply seem unimportant, Henry persisted, "Is it not true that in the ordinary sense, then, that the malice is between Pegler and you?" Reynolds now made reference to the answer which the Hearst Corporation had issued when he first entered suit. He said that he was astounded to find, on reading this document, that his supposed friends in the organization had supported Pegler's attack. The fact was, although not mentioned at this point in the trial, that they had published a *second* Pegler column about Reynolds, also filled with charges of immorality, cowardice, and espousal of Communism. This had come to print through the same legal inspection by house lawyers as the first attack. How this could have happened is still unclear. But at the trial, Reynolds said that he had been horrified to find that the formal reply to his suit, in effect repeating and endorsing Pegler's attack, had been signed by "three top executives whom I knew, and who knew me and who knew better." Reynolds stood down after eight days of cross-examination. A number of reputable witnesses followed to affirm Reynolds' good character, reliability, and presence at scenes of danger in the war. With obvious indignation, Connie Broun testified that Reynolds had not asked her to marry him at the funeral. She denied that Broun's friends had been licentious, and said that they had not walked around naked and helped Negro Communists seduce white girls. She listed some of Broun's visitors at the farm: Herbert Bayard Swope, Paul de Kruif, Harry Guggenheim, Averell Harriman, Joseph Patterson, Gene Tunney, and Harry Hopkins—all these eminent men accompanied by their wives. She said Catholic priests came socially to the farm, and that Franklin Roosevelt had written Broun a fan letter. Without reproof from Judge Weinfeld, Connie Broun cried, "To speak of these people as a licentious and parasitic lot is as low a use of language as I have ever encountered." Charles Henry did not cross-examine, and the jury and audience settled down to hear from Westbrook Pegler.

For three days Pegler testified under questioning by Charles Henry, repeating his charges against Reynolds, and stating that Connie Broun herself had told him Reynolds went swimming nude in the lake at the Broun farm. According to Pegler she reported that she had been out rowing, and Reynolds had climbed into the boat without his swimming trunks. This introduction of hearsay was permitted under a statute applicable to libel cases. After three days of it Henry was finished, and "almost casually," as Reynolds recorded, "he said the words we had waited almost five years to hear: 'You may cross-examine, Mr. Nizer.' "

There were a number of remarkable things about the long examination. One was the extreme nervousness that Pegler displayed. He did not relax and fall into a rhythm of reply as Reynolds had done. On the contrary, he gave the impression of a man beset by almost unbearable tension and anxiety. At one point he cried out to Nizer, "Don't come near me!" as though he feared or loathed Nizer's touch. The lawyer read certain statements about Communism not being dangerous to the United States, and when Pegler identified these sentiments as the party line, Nizer revealed that Pegler himself had written the passage. He also cited Pegler's statement that hates gave him more satisfaction than friendships.* And he brought up the subject of personal honor, and asked Pegler to define it. Pegler replied, "Honor is each man's rag doll, to do with as he pleases." After seventeen days of it, Nizer ended his examination.

Now was the time for the witness Charles Henry had hoped for, the man or woman of good repute who would swear to direct knowledge that Pegler's picture of Reynolds was correct. But no such witness appeared. In the line of permitted hearsay, Julie Pegler testified that she also had heard the story of Reynolds in the lake from Connie Broun. But she admitted that in all the times she had visited the Broun farm, she had never seen Connie in a rowboat; and after the alleged incident, all concerned continued to be friends for years. Then came an admiral and a general, but before they got through they had helped Reynolds rather than Pegler. After eight weeks, the case went to the jury. At this point a disinterested observer would say the Hearst-Pegler defense had been inept and unconvincing—or perhaps from a lawyer's point of view, a capable effort in behalf of an indefensible cause. You can't tell about juries, but this one took only fifteen minutes to find the defendants guilty and order the payment of one dollar to Reynolds for loss of income, plus $175,000 in punitive damages. This gave Pegler the distinction of being responsible for the largest amount awarded up to that time for punitive damages along with so small a compensatory award. Pegler's contract made his employers liable for the entire sum, and they paid it, with interest, after losing their appeal.

Pegler and his employers were uneasy in each other's presence for some time after the Reynolds trial. The legal department suffered the chagrin that lawyers must feel when they lose a case, granted that this case was hopeless from the start. The editors and executives had felt

*See pages 106 and 130.

the regret of men who did not foresee conclusions that now seemed easily predictable. They were too high up to be fired, and too weary to hunt for a scapegoat lower in the organization. And so they tried to decide what it was that they had in Pegler, and what to do about him, now that ominous weaknesses were discerned in the Hearst financial structure, and doubts were beginning to arise about the future of all big newspapers. The decision on what to do about Pegler was a sensible one: they would close ranks around their damaged star and put on a promotion campaign of unprecedented vigor. The first move was a lunch at the Waldorf, "honoring" Pegler with an award by something called the Banshees, which was a publicity front of King Features, modeled on the lines of such convivial social groups as the Friars, the Dutch Treat, and the Circus Saints and Sinners. The Hearst organization picked up the check for between three and four thousand Martini cocktails plus lunch for 1,000 free-loaders, and gave away to each person a magnificently produced souvenir program, one of the most expensive promotion pieces ever seen. The book weighed twenty-five pounds and had a figure of Pegler in high relief on the cover, clad in armor and holding a real pen as a lance.

Syndicate sales held up, and W. R. Hearst, Jr., along with his top executives Richard E. Berlin and J. D. Gortatowski, decided that Pegler at the age of sixty looked like a man with plenty of good writing left in him. And to lessen the danger of offending advertisers or blocs of readers, Pegler agreed that from now on he would do at least one George Spelvin piece a week. These would deal with Spelvin in his finally evolved form of a youngish householder at 22 Juniper Terrace, Dudgeon Heights. He was now in middle management, something having to do with plastics, and was more likely to go on in praise of his wife, whom he called Dreamie, than to identify a U. S. President as a jackass. George loved Dreamie and could never find fault with her, because no matter how ridiculous he made himself, she always mussed his hair, kissed him, and told him he was great. This manifestation of George Spelvin made a hit with readers and pleased the executives at Hearst headquarters. But the other question, of exactly how Pegler could be defined, they found insoluble.

In fact there was no way to frame a definition of Westbrook Pegler, except to say that his was a personality of warring opposites, which never completely canceled each other out. Sometimes one aspect of his personality would come through in the column, sometimes another very different one would give his writing its point. He was, for example, a friend of the underdog, yet the spectacle of labor disputes could rouse his anger at underdogs, especially if disorderly pickets made an appearance. He wrote that such people "should be clubbed senseless." His remarks about Milton Kaufman showed his sense of brotherhood with reporters and deskmen in the newsrooms, and yet from about this time on, when King Features arranged for Pegler to visit a client paper, he would not appear in the city room but would receive owners and publishers at his hotel suite, and dine at their homes. But he remained a hero to many newsmen. Perhaps rather than make any attempt to define Pegler, we might try to define something called Peglerism, calling to mind the victim who complained that he had been peglerized. And this thing, I believe, was the instinct that makes a dog bark at strangers, or a conger eel lunge for anything it sees moving.

The quintessence of Peglerism was attack; and when he had once placed a person or institution in enmity, Pegler could be unscrupulous in his choice of weapons. And having gone on the attack, he often used his skill in words to embed among his sentences a shift of meaning which altered the picture of his opponent from that of someone possibly in error to that of a malefactor who had committed a crime. It was syntax in the service of character assassination, and not at all pretty.

An example may be found in Pegler's treatment of a man named Theodore Brameld, a member of the faculty at New York University. For years Pegler had displayed animosity toward college professors, and his dislike of such people fitted in with time-honored Hearst policy. Before Hearst abandoned Chicago, his papers had conducted an endless feud with the university, so that RED PROFS HIT FLAG was kept standing in type on the composing stone. In the first scene of *The Front Page,* Ben Hecht and Charles MacArthur had a Hearst reporter, played by Frank McHugh, on the telephone: "Madame, is it true that you were the victim of a Peeping Tom? Did he look like a college professor?" There were, indeed, legitimate targets for satire on the faculties, especially in the departments of education and what were called the social sciences, where many pretentious quacks belabored the obvious in an unreadable jargon intended to give their proceedings an air of authority and mystery, the modern version of the alchemist's stuffed crocodile and the astrologer's pointed hat. And in Theodore Brameld, Pegler thought he saw an example of a social scientist wandering from his field in a reprehensible way, for Mr. Brameld had acted as spokesman for an academic gathering that had condemned "Anti-intellectuals," and singled out Pegler as a dangerous example of the breed. Pegler didn't have to take it, and he launched a counter-attack.

Chapter 6

It happened that at this time someone had invaded the lodgings of a New York University coed and stabbed her to death. It was a common occurrence in the city, a routine sadistic murder worth only a few sticks of type so far as news value was concerned. But Pegler noticed that the girl had been studying human relations. Some time previously, in Minneapolis, Brameld had been vice chairman of a conference on human relations. And Pegler wrote that he would like to know if the dead girl had ever studied with Brameld in New York. The reader would infer a possible chain of connection where there was none. Brameld taught political science, not human relations, and anyhow, the girl had never studied with him. The police caught the murderer, an ordinary psycho from Brooklyn. Brameld left the NYU faculty, eventually pulling up at another large university. What had he done to Pegler? Nothing, except criticize him in terms of severe disapproval, something Pegler himself did to all sorts of people nearly every day. Pegler's philosophy, if he had any at all, appeared to be that of the crazy French generals who worshiped the principle of attack above everything. If all you want is a machine for biting, the conger eel is a beautiful thing. All teeth in front and the long body nothing but muscle. Tear you to pieces before you know what hit you . . .

Pegler had begun to indulge himself by writing intemperate letters, worthy of Harry Truman, that should never have been mailed. He had a grievance with the drugstore at the Waldorf-Astoria over returning some unsatisfactory goods, but before he was through, Pegler had written to the manager of the hotel and denounced him as a crook who operated a fleabag and tourist trap where the rates for bad accommodations were the equivalent of highway robbery. A case had come up to the Supreme Court in which a woman in Texas had protested the withholding tax on domestic servants' pay. The court turned back the plea and Pegler wrote to Chief Justice Earl Warren as follows:

Dear Judge:

I see by the papers that your gang of loafers has refused due process to Mrs. Carolyn M. Abney, of Marshall, Tex., in the baby-sitters case.

This is a damned outrage, the worse because you bums know damned well that you could not possibly frame a decision on the issues which would confront you which could reconcile this law with the Constitution. You are the lousiest supreme court in the history of the court and laziness is only your second worst fault. Dishonesty comes first.

What are you going to do about Douglas, horsing around Arizona when a judge in his job ought to be doing the work he gets paid to do, accepting gifts of money from political "foundations" and pay for trash writing from *Look* magazine?

How can any honest patriot sit with the son of a bitch who planted Alger Hiss in the Government and trained a lot of other traitorous reds to do their dirty work?

How can you refrain from drawing a bead on Tom Clark some day in open court and telling him to answer the questions or get the hell out?

What a stinking aggregation you are! Yet you have the gall to deny this patriotic woman her day in court.

Read this to those ambulance chasers in open court. Read it into the record.

Yours truly,
WP

Pegler also went on the attack against his employers and suspected that W. R. Hearst, Jr., was an especially dangerous enemy. From the time of the Reynolds verdict, "As Pegler Sees It" began to appear further back in the *Journal-American* than its accustomed place on Page Three. Readers now hunted for Pegler among several columns on the editorial page or across from it. It had been done on orders from the younger Hearst, who had his own plans now that the Chief was dead. The publisher told subeditors that they were free to cut Pegler's copy. This meant that in the home office and out among the syndicated papers a sentence or paragraph might disappear from the column and give the reader a sense that something was wrong. Point-killing editors sometimes cut the last paragraph, weakening a column or making it meaningless when Pegler had aimed the entire essay toward the effect of the last two or three lines. This was what they had done to Broun during his last year on the *World-Telegram*. Pegler wrote in his column in 1957, "I am a great finisher and some authorities will testify that I have written some very high-class get-em-off lines. However, you wouldn't know anything about that because you have not had a chance to read any of them since June 1955. June 12, I think it was. They have a standing order in the composing room to pick up the last five inches of Pegler and throw it in the hell-box to make room for a comic. Pegler is supposed to be vitriolic and the comic is supposed to be funny. But often he isn't and neither is the comic. I have sometimes said why don't you stick that damned comic over in the used-cars, electric-belts and loan sharks? If it is so good, the customers will chase it all over the paper until they find it, and you will lead readership into depressed areas of advertisement. . . . I have said, but why don't you stick me back in the loan sharks? Stick me back in the goiters, but let me do my stuff, let me alone. . . . Don't murder me just to make me look bad. We have the grand jury system of editing in our place. You do a column and a sort of assistant district attorney takes it over to a door and puts it in a mail slot. . . ."

Early in 1955 Pegler had written to Ward (Jimmie) Greene, editor of King Features, "We have changed so disgracefully since the Old Man died." Westbrook had aimed some disparagement at Henry Ford, II, and Hearst had ordered him to lay off. Pegler went on in his letter, "Jimmie, this is plain whoring. The public will buy papers which tell the truth." The legal department had recently ordered some cuts, and Pegler reminded Greene, "My career has been based to a considerable degree on my courageous disclosure of facts which other journalists will not tackle."

Ward Greene decided a trip abroad might make Pegler feel better, and sent him to Europe in the summer of 1955. Westbrook visited the Allied governments in Berlin, and was delighted to discover that the Americans used the acronym HICOG to designate the High Commissioner for Germany, our ranking permanent bureaucrat over there. Pegler thought this made that official the Hicogalorum, and planned to use this mode of address in calling on John J. McCloy, a banker who occupied the post. John McCloy went skiing and "fell off an Alp, and broke a knuckle in his foot, so I had to settle for a pompous, arrogant commissioner for American 'culture' calling himself Shepard Stone, an assistant Sunday editor for the *New York Times*, who was sitting in as regent Hicog and chucking his weight around in enormous hunks. He had never had it so good back home." The associate Hicogalorum had "eight servants, whose wages came from the American taxpayer, a car with driver and fuel, tax-free booze, and groceries at PX rates, less than half the price at home." Beneath the Hicogalorum and his regent were 400 useless American employees, "trying to keep out from under foot." Many of them would be ruined for life by the good pay and pickings for doing nothing at all. This was devastating Pegler copy, and had influence on American readers who began to ask their legislators what good resulted from bureaucratic empires on foreign soil. The empires continued to flourish, but Pegler had the satisfaction of having done his best, and the High Cogalorum was forgotten soon enough.

Westbrook and Julie came to Switzerland in August, and he reported to Ward Greene that internal bleeding had resulted when he "blew a gasket." In October 1954 Pegler wrote to Greene from the Hotel Flora in Rome that after two months of strain and "running on the battery," he and Julie were going to relax and "pull themselves together." Greene answered that he was worried about the Peglers' health, and begged them to recruit their strength. Westbrook was unhappy when he answered this letter; he thought that Hearst and Gortatowski were afraid of what he might say about the new State of Israel, which caused him to write, "I am not going to beg anyone to use my stuff. I am better than the whole goddam gang. . . . Fight? Sure I will fight, but first I want to know who the enemy is."

On October 12 Julie suffered what Pegler called "a very bad and unnatural seizure." Her health had not improved through the years, and she fell and broke a leg in 1949. Both Julie and Westbrook had checked in and out of Boston hospitals several times since then. Perhaps Westbrook became ill in sympathy with Julie when her damaged circulatory system tormented her with weakness and pain. But he also had genuine illness to contend with, for that ominous internal gum-boil refused to become permanently healed. Turning out five and sometimes six columns a week, Pegler wrote too much for the best display of his talent, since many of the pieces were repetitions of something previously established, or laborious efforts to push someone or something into a false category, as in the case of Professor Brameld. Perhaps at this period he was also writing too much for his health—for while the work itself was not harmful, Pegler's travels were exhausting, and the emotional strain of controversy, which he suffered almost every day, is demonstrably hard on the nervous system, and not to be recommended for a man in his sixties. But he felt that somehow he would get through to calm harbors so long as Julie was there. But after July 9, 1955, Julie was gone. She died in her sleep at the hotel in Rome. The attack in October had warned him, but the death stunned Westbrook. He was bitter in his grief and told friends that the "cardiac strain of the Reynolds trial" had killed Julie. The lawyers had shown her no consideration and had sent her from New York to Tucson and back on an exhausting trip with Maud Towart to get records for the court. In a calmer mood a little later, Westbrook wrote to Ward Greene, "Julie did her best in life and she was very tired when she died. She was indescribably good and generous, and I hope she sleeps gently forever." They buried Julie in the Gate of Heaven Cemetery in Westchester County, and by her own request there is no marker on the grave.

Chapter 6

When he came away from the cemetery Pegler was fortunate in one thing only, that he had work to do. The conditions of his work were not agreeable, because of the tension between Pegler and the Hearst management, a complicated and unprecedented situation. Around the midtown lunch restaurants, where wiseguys bellied to the bars and circulated the gossip of space salesmen and press agents, one might hear rumors that Pegler was on his way out of the Hearst organization. That was not the way "Bill" Hearst and his associates saw it. Pegler would lose a paper here and there; he would bristle at "Gorty" Gortatowski or a member of the legal staff, and write long letters to Ward Greene. But nobody talked of breaking off relations; Pegler on one side and the bosses, except for Greene, on the other resembled partners in an unhappy marriage who have not yet talked of divorce. What made the situation strange and peculiar was the King Features promotion which continued to present Westbrook as the world's most influential and widely read journalist, and to praise his vigor and courage in pointing out abuses and attacking villains. Yet at the same time the Hearst front-office men at the uptown headquarters—Pegler called them the college of cardinals—were constantly meddling with copy, and making no effort to prevent local editors from mutilating the column. Before long the legal department began to address Pegler, in writing, as they would an adversary of the Hearst Corporation. And yet from time to time Bill Hearst or Richard Berlin would send Pegler a note congratulating him on an effective piece of writing. Suppose that a theatrical management presented an actor as the greatest in the world, yet frequently quarreled with him backstage about the material to be used, and at the same time sent flowers to the dressing room. It was puzzling and unsatisfactory for all concerned.

A request that sometimes reached Ward Greene when the front office did not wish to argue directly with Pegler was that he "give us a rest about the Roosevelts." Some said that Franklin Roosevelt was not a proper object of attack because he was dead. The living members of the family were well equipped to defend themselves, and Mrs. Roosevelt led several counter-attacks in the space she filled as a nationally syndicated columnist. She told people who wrote to inquire that there was no use paying attention to Pegler, "a poor little creature," far off on the horizon and hardly discernible when compared with the moral grandeur of "my husband," enshrined as he was in history's esteem and his countrymen's affection. Mrs. Roosevelt used her regular page in *McCall's* magazine to advance a theory as to the origin of Westbrook's enmity toward the late president: "I have always thought that it was because he was disappointed in not working for my husband in a position he would have enjoyed." It is interesting to note that in implying that Pegler was turned down for a White House job, Mrs. Roosevelt did not state that he ever asked for such a job. Pegler would have refused any government job, and Mrs. Roosevelt must have known it; her careful phrasing of this small libel is worthy of Pegler himself.

And Pegler kept hitting away at the grotesque cartoon figure of "Old Moosejaw," who had talked in geechee and inflicted terrible frauds and disasters on America. Westbrook was hitting at authority and trying to express his conviction that it is not necessarily a good thing. Those who worshiped Roosevelt, or attributed supernatural virtue and power to "that Great Office, the Presidency of the United States," detested Pegler and condemned him. Westbrook might have tempered some hostile criticism by explaining his methods, but from the late 1950s on he was never in a mood for soft answers or soft approaches to any opponent. He said the thing to do was "get down on the flat of your feet and punch for the belly."

One punch had to do with Mrs. Winthrop Rutherfurd, a lifelong friend of Franklin Roosevelt, who was present when he died at Warm Springs. There had been a romantic friendship years before, when Roosevelt was Assistant Secretary of the Navy, and the lady was Lucy Page Mercer, a delightful young member of the impoverished boarding-house aristocracy in the District. Later on Lucy married the rich Mr. Rutherfurd, he died, and the friendship was revived. It was a pleasant story, which has recently received wide exploitation in print; for anyone not involved to begrudge Roosevelt this comforting presence from his youth would be to show meanness of spirit. But Pegler *was* involved, for he had made the attacking of Roosevelt a cornerstone of his career. He handled the story decorously, aiming for those who had concealed facts, and not referring to Mrs. Rutherfurd in his usual knockabout style. Instead he used the language of ordinary journalism in asking a question about her when one of Roosevelt's secretaries published a book of memoirs and listed Mrs. Rutherfurd as a guest who was in the room when Franklin Roosevelt, sitting for his portrait, slumped in the chair unconscious from a stroke. Pegler's question was, "Why was this not revealed at the time?" He got no answer. Here is a sample of Pegler's usual writing on Franklin Roosevelt, from 1959:

"When, in 1932, the constant moocher was ready to relax from the strain that dieting had imposed he tied loose on a lolloping souse-party on the *Nourmahal** off Miami. The charter cost would have been a quarter-million each time. *Nourmahal,* a private ocean liner, was 264 feet long. She could cruise 20,000 miles. She had a log fireplace in her library. She had a crew of 42. Wages, insurance, food, uniforms, gear and soap cost $125,000 a year, tied up. The additional cost of fuel, food and booze for a passenger list of deserving Democrats would be trivial by comparison, although to millionaires no cost is trivial. That scrupulosity makes millionaires. . . ."

It must be admitted that the Roosevelt family gave Pegler some good material, but he harked back to the unpaid Hartford loan so often that it must be one of the best known transactions of its kind in history. Something along the same line was supplied by Anna Roosevelt Boettiger and her husband John Boettiger when they established a daily paper at Phoenix, Arizona, in May 1947. Their paper was called the *Arizona Times.* It succeeded a small weekly throwaway sheet which Anna and John bought for $25,000. Not all of this purchase price was their own money. After about a year, Pegler reported later, the *Arizona Times* "passed to other hands. It had lost about $400,000 in a boom town and a sellers' market." He continued:

"Roosevelt's daughter and her husband gave a lively imitation of Elliott Roosevelt's financiering and ran through a fortune of sucker money borrowed or promoted from Barney Baruch, Marshall Field, one Walter Kirschner who seems to have been the master-chump, Charles G. Ward, of St. Paul or Minneapolis, and others. The rate of settlement was one cent on the dollar. Baruch went for only $20,000 but he rates priority in the mention because he is Baruch. Why he should have given Anna anything—he was not particularly interested in Boettiger—you will have to guess. Ask him, if you have nothing better to do, and he will either tell you confidentially and tie you up, or give you those oracular bromides about patience and perseverance or the stitch in time. Anyway, he did stand for two bites of $10,000 each and he knew what he was doing. . . . I heard Mr. Kirschner was an idealist who so greatly admired, if one could not say that he actually revered, the memory of the late Commander-in-Chief that he had taken a more or less public obligation to see that none of Roosevelt's loved ones should ever want. That is a big order, as the wants of Elliott alone should have warned Mr. Kirschner. A fatter cat than Mr. K. might have gone scrawny-broke trying to make it good.

---

*Vincent Astor's yacht

"Charley Ward, the other bull-chump, really did owe a debt of gratitude to Old Moosejaw because Ward had a bad criminal record and Roosevelt took him off the hook with a Presidential pardon, which meant that he could vote and hold public office. His old offense was selling narcotics and the judge who sentenced him in Denver left no doubt of the court's immediate opinion of his character. It couldn't have been worse. . . . One of the parties to several of the complex double-shuffles which ensued told me Mr. K. blew up and carried on like a hackey with a locked bumper when he got into the showdowns with Anna and he saw that he was going to get the old Roosevelt proposition of two cents on the dollar but, this time, cut in half. You remember that when the old man finally got Jesse Jones to close the bag on John Hartford and the other rich rubes who bought Elliott's goldbricks, Jesse offered them the strictly nominal settlement of two cents on the dollar. . . . How to explain it I do not know, but there were, and may still be, many rich men who would almost tear their pants off reaching for their money for a Roosevelt. . . . I am a great admirer of the late Moosejaw myself and I can think of no greater honor to his memory than to borrow an awful lot of money and settle for one cent on the dollar. . . ."

These facts were irrefutable and left the victims no way out. And when it came to Mrs. Roosevelt, Pegler had ammunition in the matter of a New York State trooper whom she considered to be a good friend, perhaps in the manner of Queen Victoria and her presumptuous Scotch footman. A fine crystal vase, originally a gift to Mrs. Roosevelt from Finland, adorned the trooper's house. His wife threatened to name Mrs. Roosevelt corespondent in divorce proceedings, but was persuaded to drop the accusation with no public comment from the lawyers involved. It looked very shabby indeed as Pegler presented it, but he scored best on Mrs. Roosevelt when he pointed up the triviality of her style. He defeated himself when he attacked Eleanor Roosevelt with personal abuse. What he could not say was the root fact about Mrs. Roosevelt, that she was a stupefying bore. Once he admitted that, Pegler would have nothing to write about. Before his writing on Mrs. Roosevelt turned completely sour, he achieved some broad effects that came off well. Dubbing Mrs. Roosevelt La Boca Grande was rough but permissible in view of her constant speech-making. And in one reminiscent passage he went back to days in Connecticut when he and Mrs. Roosevelt were still speaking to each other. He wrote in recalling the Hyde Park weenie-roasts that "She used to hop off that board up at her swimming-pool, let out that nerve-wracking whoop, take off above the horizon and come down with the splash of that poor horse that goes off the thing at Atlantic City." Whether or not he meant to, in this case Pegler left the reader's sympathy with Mrs. Roosevelt.

A trouble in Pegler's life had given premonitory symptoms as early as 1949, when he first heard what he called "the reptilian hiss of anti-Semitism." In that year he replied to a correspondent who had asked about prejudice, "I am not against Jews as such, but in a large city one does sometimes comment unfavorably on someone who is Jewish." Pegler was beginning to be aware of something called the Anti-Defamation League, a pressure group sponsored by the fraternal order B'nai B'rith, Hebrew equivalent to the Knights of Columbus. Its title defined the purpose of the league, and its officials kept files on those they considered to be defamers of their people. They complained to editors and publishers who circulated such material and asked them to cease and desist. Many people believed that the ADL had great influence, and its officers could get a hearing anywhere in New York. Their actual influence is probably like that of the Pope—a fiction that lives by custom and journalistic inertia rather than any connection with reality in the present day.

Anti-Semitism is the attribution to the Jewish people of a greater proportionate share of wickedness and malice than is found among the rest of humanity. This is no longer taken seriously except among the dog-brained bureaucrats of the Soviet Union. Among civilized people, prejudice of that sort died after the second war. Hitler had showed that anti-Semitism could lead to mass insanity and hideous crimes that brought a pervading sense of shame to the human race. Then came the founding of the state of Israel under British sponsorship after many years of Zionist agitation throughout the world. Those who have read the Old Testament as history may entertain doubts as to Israel's survival, taking the long view. At any rate, Pegler did not echo the hosannas rising in the United States on the founding of Israel and its recognition by President Harry Truman in 1948. By 1955, Pegler was writing in a letter, "I have never been allowed to discuss the merits of the case for or against Israel." He wrote to Ward Greene that he "considered it a hell of a note that it is necessary for a reporter to submit a scenario or synopsis of a legitimate news story for consideration by our syndicate under an apprehension that the facts themselves will be 'anti-semitic' merely because the offenders are Hebrews and have made themselves conspicuous in a racket. . . . An inhibition has been established which has the effect of warning me to let alone items of legitimate public interest and information. . . . On one occasion, when I referred to Barney Baruch, the qualifying phrase 'revered elder statesman' was inserted. I do not revere him and he is not a statesman but a fourflushing old mountebank. . . . I am not and no harassment will drive me to be 'anti-Semitic.' I detest many individuals who are Jews but not because they are Jews."

The front office people hoped that Pegler's avowed lack of prejudice would be evident to his readers, but they continued to worry. They feared the loss of department store advertising, and their anxiety led them to some odd decisions. One day, Pegler cited Captain Dreyfus and Leo Frank, victim of a Georgia mob, as examples of injustice. Query by front office: Couldn't he substitute Sacco and Vanzetti? And they killed an entire column filed from Germany a month before Julie's death, in which Pegler said that when he saw John Foster Dulles "lending my income taxes and yours to the Sovereign State of Israel so that Israel could compensate Arabs for property which Israel stole from them, it occurred to me that we Americans should demand a look at the books." He wrote in another column, which escaped the blue pencil, that "Roosevelt is thought to be the savior of all Jews and anyone who ever criticized Roosevelt therefore is a Jew-baiter."

Pegler was on solid ground here, but it appears that he came in for criticism by the ADL in connection with the Rev. Dr. Gerald L. K. Smith, an evangelist who published a paper called *The Cross and the Flag,* which contained much sensational material which the ADL found to be anti-Semitic. Pegler had rebuked Dr. Smith, and received a letter of apology from the ADL when he pointed this out. But two years later, in 1955, Pegler took an interest in a man named Edward A. Rumely, a Commie-fighter who had drawn fire from the ADL. Pegler wrote that he thought the ADL, and not Rumely, should be investigated. He pitched it strong: "The ADL has made people walk in fear of its power. . . . It is not good for any organization to be held in fear as though it were a Gestapo. . . . It is time to stop this spying on citizens by self-appointed Vigilante outfits administered by irresponsible professionals and this keeping of 'dossiers' susceptible of abuse or blackmail or boycott. . . . Any organization held in such awe by the chairman of a congressional committee that he is afraid to mention its name is the victim of bad judgment within itself. That certainly was not the original objective of the worthy citizens who lent the prestige of their names to the activities of the Anti-Defamation League. . . ." Two days later the league sent some men that Pegler described as "highbinders" to consult with Bill Hearst. Pegler wrote to a friend that "The Hearst people were in a panic. After eight days of negotiations, Bill and I went in chains down to their national headquarters for 'lunch.' I sat on my hands and refused to break bread with them. I made no apology. But it was clear that they were threatening to kill off retail ads and since then the Hearst outfit has inexorably shoved me back into the clap-ads to appease them. . . ."

There could not be an organization in the country better calculated to arouse Pegler's combative instincts than the ADL; and now that they had tried to get him fired from his job, or at the least, harassed and censored in his performance, it was impossible for him to regard them as just another nuisance, or to attribute decent motives to anything they did. Pegler began to have suspicions about Jews in general: Reynolds' lawyer and the judge on the bench had been Jewish. In his fury Pegler allowed himself to conclude that these men harbored prejudice against him. Within a year of the verdict, Pegler was writing to Ward Greene, "No, I still don't hate Jews notwithstanding the seven weeks of ordeal at the hands of a leering, sneering cabal and the suffering which my dear wife was put to by these vermin. But I do and will hate selectively to my dying breath and I will never forgive myself my error and lack of honest courage in refusing to listen to the case which the Germans had presented to the world in justification of their beliefs on this subject." But he would fight, he would be heard, nobody was going to shut him up.

The list of people with whom Pegler now considered himself at war included officials at the Hearst Corporation, and he retained his own lawyer, William B. Mulligan, to represent him in continual skirmish with the legal department. A thought had come to Pegler, a possible way to escape from journalistic bureaucracy; it involved leasing space in newspapers and subletting to advertisers. Pegler asked Roy Howard what he thought of it, and Howard replied to Dear Bud that it wouldn't work. He added, "a lot of us have profited by your ability to express your opinions over the years."

Pegler expressed his opinion of Hearst editing at frequent intervals to the patient and sympathetic Ward Greene. They were out to get him; they were trying to ruin his reputation for craftsmanship by meddling with copy and sending corrections so late that clients were inconvenienced. If the front office people were so anxious to edit, he asked in 1958, why didn't they give some editorial help on the column of February 24, in which, Westbrook was willing to admit, "certain phases of the whole idea were labored to the point of exhaustion. This is a case in which editing would have been helpful." That kind of help did not appear, and Gortatowski killed a column on civil liberties in which Pegler wrote that "Any honest pastor of any denomination in Harlem would have to tell these people that they could substantially improve their economic and social condition by drinking and gambling less, by working faithfully instead of going on relief at the slightest legal pretext, and mending their personal behavior."

By 1957 the breach between Pegler and his publishers was obviously beyond repair. There came exceedingly harsh letters from Ray McCauley, head of the legal department, who upbraided Westbrook as an insubordinate and contumacious employee. The letters would make one think there was a law suit between Pegler and McCauley's client, the Hearst organization. Three years before, this lawyer had been stung as though by an angry hornet when Pegler sent him a letter complaining of "effrontery" by the legal department. In answering at that time McCauley wrote, "I am under instructions from the management not to let anything dangerous appear in your columns. I shall carry out that order. . . . Because of your adjudicated malice, two Hearst corporations are out-of-pocket well over $175,000, and when it comes to effrontery, your letter is effrontery, contempt of the management of the company which employs you. . . ." If contempt of management were a criminal offense, Pegler would be in jail, for he certainly was guilty of it, and it did not make for happy life at his trade, and Pegler's friends hoped that happier days were in sight when he married Mrs. Pearl E. Doane on May 11, 1959. As the widow of James Doane, a popular Hollywood agent, Mrs. Doane was a member of Pegler's world, and appeared to be in ideological agreement with him, for she had been active in a group supporting Senator Fighting Joe McCarthy, who achieved notoriety as a Commie-fighter before he turned out to be only an irresponsible drunk, and died in obscurity after succumbing to the blind staggers. But Pegler had supported Fighting Joe and presumably would live in contentment with a lady who shared his opinion. Eight months later, Pegler sued for divorce. There was a reconciliation, and then Pearl Doane Pegler sued for divorce, which was granted on October 30, 1961.

The situation in New York was now unbearable for all concerned. Westbrook had written a column on Mrs. Roosevelt in December 1959 which caused some people to ask themselves if he was aware of the impression he produced when he wrote on this subject. The piece compared Mrs. Roosevelt to Medusa, one of the snake-haired Gorgon sisters of mythology, with emphasis on the teeth, which "were huge and projected from her mouth in a way which deteriorated from such natural pulchritude and charm as the Gorgon may have possessed as original endowment." Her devotees "were quite impatient of unbelief and put down with great intolerance dissent from their unsupported dogma that Medusa was the First Lady of all Creation. . . . She was popularly regarded as a roaring or forensic being who roamed widely on unexplained errands, uttering sounds in a form that nowadays would be regarded as speeches or lectures. . . ." Westbrook then introduced the subject of Mrs. Roosevelt's fees and payments for expenses. He said that Homer failed to tell us if Medusa married "and if so whom and how many children they had, if any. He may have thought that by his own moving description of Medusa he had precluded such questions. . . . Truth is stranger than fiction."

In the late winter of 1961 Pegler got word that his father would not live much longer. Arthur James Pegler was almost one hundred years old, but the added years of life had been unhappy, because the old man had not been able to do what he wanted to do, and had not even decided exactly what it was that he wanted to do. He died at Tucson in the early morning of March 7, 1961, with Westbrook lying awake on a cot beside his bed. In the next room stood "the old, woodburning, double-deck Smith-Premier typewriter on which three kids learned their alphabets long, long ago." Eight months later, Pegler's personal life took a turn for the better when he married Maud Towart at St. Ann's Roman Catholic Church in Midland, Texas. The date was November 22, a pleasant time of year in that country. They chose the city of Midland because friends lived there, and the church was available because Pegler had married Mrs. Doane in a civil ceremony.

On August 2, 1962, Attorney Mulligan wrote to Pegler that he was continuing to fight Hearst editors on the question of altering columns, whether produced in Tucson or New York. As a good lawyer should, Mulligan spoke frankly to his client. It appeared that the publishers now had Pegler typed as anathema to Jewish advertisers, who controlled 90 percent of local display advertising in New York. Westbrook had been criticizing the Kennedys, with emphasis on Bobby, and this was dangerous in the editors' view, for they thought the Kennedys an unforgiving lot. Mulligan advised against attacking the U. S. Marines while Colonel Glenn was orbiting the earth. This was the kind of thing that made the editors tear their hair. And Pegler was no longer in the dominant position. Gortatowsky said King Features was losing money on the column, because the list of syndicate buyers had shrunk to 75 papers. But the Hearst lawyers were not ready to pay up the contract and set Pegler free. In order to prevent the killing of columns for "policy," Mulligan asked them to state Hearst editorial policy, which they were unable to do, as no such thing existed. The publishers complained that Pegler no longer kept in touch with them and they sometimes didn't know where he was. But they did know where he was, because he was in touch with Greene, and Maud Towart Pegler was as always conscientious, efficient, and well organized. So in spite of everything, it would be possible for Pegler to have a reasonably satisfactory time of it for the remainder of his contract, which had two more years to run. Mulligan suggested that during that time Pegler would do well to bear in mind that "reflection and writing, rather than litigation, are your strong points." And Mulligan felt it his duty to add a further warning: there had been talk about Pegler's emotional condition. Westbrook was being accused of putting everything on a personal basis when crossed, and some people at headquarters had been describing him as a victim of paranoia.

Anyone who knew what was going on around the Hearst front office would understand why the executives were saying harsh things about Westbrook. He had called the trio of Bill Hearst, Frank Conniff, and Bob Considine "the Rover Boys" after they had jointly received a Pulitzer Prize in 1956 for their reporting from Moscow and other foreign cities. The fashionable concept of team journalism was not for Pegler, and he resented the suppression of a column he had written in criticism of the Pulitzer committee while Hearst and his coadjutors were on their trip. Westbrook suspected that Hearst did not want to offend the committee while engaged on a project he hoped they would recognize.

This among many grievances was on Pegler's mind at the time Mulligan mailed the warning letter, for on that day, August 2, he somehow got up in front of a gathering called the Anti-Communist Christian Crusade in Tulsa, Oklahoma, a meeting he once would have scorned to enter. But the champion of Fighting Joe, and the journalistic hero of the meatballs, was not the man who had defied generals and admirals, and tackled New York with nothing in his pockets. Of recent years Pegler had been far from fastidious in selection of associates, and had resumed friendly relations with Dr. Gerald Smith and other persons holding extreme views. It was natural, then, that Pegler should accept an invitation from the Rev. Dr. Billy James Hargis, the tent-show evangelist who operated the crusade. A bulbous person with a buzz-saw voice, Dr. Hargis had a big following out on the Great Plains, and he sometimes landed on target when assailing Communists. Pegler still retained enough of his critical sense to appreciate Dr. Hargis as a folk artist, and wrote that he could "whinny-whicker like a country auctioneer selling out a widow on the lawn a week after Paw's funeral." His admiration for Dr. Hargis may have contributed to Pegler's acceptance of the guest-star role at the anti-Communist show. Pegler was assured he could speak freely, for there would be no reporters present. But there was at least one reporter in the crowd of 3,500 people at the "Baptist vatican" when Pegler rose to speak, and that reporter wrote shorthand. And on the following day Bill Hearst and his editors, together with most newspaper readers in the country knew that Pegler had denounced his employers in a blast of sarcastic invective, for censoring his copy when he criticized the Kennedy administration. Pegler had told the Tulsa audience:

"Most of our daily press is now under a coercion as nasty and snarling and menacing as Hitler's was in the first year of his reign. I will not speak of other newspapers, but of recent alarming experiences in the Hearst organization. I received insolent, arrogant warnings from King Features that nothing unfavorable to the Kennedy Administration or offensive to any member of the Kennedy family will be allowed out of New York where the censors sit." Pegler praised the late William Randolph Hearst as a "great founding genius" in publishing and said "control has passed to his sons, who lack character, ability, loyalty, and principle. . . . I was forced to suppress a column blasting Pulitzer Prize procedures because after Junior and his Baby Sitters interviewed Khrushchev, Junior immediately set up the petulant yowl of a spoiled brat for a Pulitzer award. . . ." Perhaps his audience would like to know about King Features. Pegler would be happy to tell them that it was "a subdivision of the Hearst empire dealing in comic strips, comic strip books, sweet powders to make soda pop, toys and a very ingenious variety of dingbats for the immature. . . ."

On the next day, August 4, 1962, the head office made a brief announcement that the Pegler column would no longer appear in the Hearst newspapers or be furnished to clients of the King Features Syndicate, because "Too many irreconcilable difficulties on vital matters have existed between the parties to continue a workable relationship." Compensation under the contract, which had until March 1964 to run, had been settled by mutual agreement. In addition to the formal statement Frank Conniff said, "The maximum tolerance is made in this organization for prima donnas, but this had become personal." After thirty years with Scripps-Howard and Hearst, Westbrook Pegler was no longer a daily voice.

7

OVER AND OUT

When the announcement of his leaving Hearst came out Westbrook was at the Park Lane and available to interviewers. It was front-page news in the regular papers and in the weekly trade press, with the dramatic value of any story in which a giant falls. For even with his hacked and doctored copy, and his peripatetic position in the *Journal-American,* Pegler was still a figure of importance on the American scene; had he been a more likeable writer, or the possessor of a winning public personality, he could have been on the verge of becoming an official Grand Old Man, a Bernard Baruch of public commentary. Therefore it did not soothe Westbrook to read in the *Herald Tribune:* "Westbrook Pegler, journalism's angry man, lost his job yesterday." He straightened that out when he talked to Ray Erwin of *Editor & Publisher:* "I did not lose my job. By mutual agreement we terminated my contract. I was compensated. I have plans, but cannot discuss them now as negotiations are under way and I don't want to scare the hen off the nest. I will be a journalist as long as I live. I will continue to write, perhaps not on a daily basis, as that has become onerous. I have a great deal of information which has been inapplicable until now because I could not get it published. The censorship has been going on a long time, just as I said. I simply cannot in conscience accommodate myself to these conditions and accept restrictions and make concessions. I know what I told you is skimpy. I do not want to be cagey, but I can't discuss my future plans until they are all set. Junior and the Rover Boys are not adequate—but I don't want to go into that.

"This is a guilty administration. I do not say the Kennedys are guilty—but their grandfather got kicked out of Congress. An innocent woman was arrested in Washington and held in a mental institution, and yet they talk about civil rights. . . ." The reporter went away with a strong impression of Pegler's "blazing conviction." According to *Editor & Publisher,* the column had been appearing in approximately 140 papers, which was nearly twice what Attorney Mulligan had been told; but that point was not worth argument, for now Pegler was appearing in no papers at all.

As he said to the trade reporter, Westbrook had plans, and they did not include retirement from journalism. He had said to Ward Greene that he could not describe the anxiety he had suffered in his efforts "to cry out through the gag." He told Greene that he had "abundant shocking information all verified" and now he could place facts before the public without censorship—provided he could find an editor who would not try to alter what he wrote. And it appeared that such an editor was at hand in the person of Robert Welch, founder of the right-wing John Birch Society, who published a monthly magazine called *American Opinion.*

Mr. Welch was an erudite, soft-spoken Harvard graduate and student of history who had founded his society as an activist group like the ADL or the political arm of the CIO. As editor and agitator Welch had caused consternation by questioning the integrity of President Ike Eisenhower. Here Pegler was in agreement, for he had said, "I always thought there was something fishy about Ike." And indeed the general left much to be desired as President, for he loafed on the job with his bridge and golf, and made one of our strangest popular heroes with his weak, silly grin, collapsing sentences, and fondness for the company of corporation presidents. The story of how he became a millionaire on Army and government pay has a sort of repellent fascination, but cannot be put in detail here. What concerns us is that Pegler evidently thought anyone who was on to Ike must be all right, and after a talk with Mr. Welch in Dallas, he agreed to become a monthly contributor to *American Opinion.*

All went well during the early months with the magazine up to the end of 1962. The pay was $1,000 per article, which was about half what Pegler earned at Hearst for the same number of words. The statement made to the courts at the time of his divorce showed that Westbrook had acquired an estate of $400,000; and the contract settlement was estimated by persons who should know at around $40,000. So although he was now out of daily work in his sixty-ninth year, Pegler had enough to get along on and money was not the first object. The main thing, as with William Lloyd Garrison, was "I will be heard!" Very well, having been told of "abundant shocking information all verified" the editors expected that Pegler would provide a series of rending journalistic explosions, and experienced a let-down feeling when they saw what he handed in.

Robert Welch has been so kind as to recall the circumstances. He states that the problem arose over "the monotony of Pegler's articles, especially with regard to subject matter. He wanted to write over and over, no matter under what title, on the subject of Earl Warren or Eleanor Roosevelt, or two or three more of his pet personal peeves, and we could not persuade him to do anything else. Or if he could be persuaded or seemed to be, he would change his mind and come through with a new rehash of the same old materials, mostly about the same personalities. And as this went on, he had a tendency more and more to use the pages of *American Opinion* as a means of venting his personal spleen, with comments which he had obviously been wanting to get out of his system for years which no one else would print. . . . At one point in one article he wrote, '. . . and as to Earl Warren, may he break both legs. . . .' This somehow got through all editing and proofreading, and actually showed up in the finished article in the magazine of which the first copy landed on my desk one night just as I got back from Los Angeles. I killed the whole issue, at tremendous expense for us in those days, rather than let any such statement appear in one of our articles in print."

The end with *American Opinion* was now in sight. Robert Welch said that they paid for three articles that could not be used, and "reluctantly severed relations with Pegler." The publisher thought that Pegler would blame him for the failure at *American Opinion* and he was right. As Westbrook told the story, the people at the magazine had tried to subject him to censorship, and he wouldn't stand for it. Pegler said to an interviewer, "For some reason Mr. Welch killed my article. I had enough of that with Hearst. I don't have to take it any more."

Pegler turned for peace and refreshment to his home in the desert, although for several years the city of Tucson had failed to please him. As far back as 1955, Pegler had written that developers were ruining Tucson, and he put his opinion of the local boosters in such scorching terms that the *Arizona Citizen* denounced him as "a vain old man, evidently aware of his waning mental and physical vigor." Pegler had drawn a bad press when he went to court with a complaint about dogs that barked all night near his house. Although two neighbors joined Westbrook in complaining of the nuisance, one newspaper in town published a piece making fun of Pegler as though he and not the dogs had caused the trouble. The case died when the people with the dogs moved away. This article portrayed a complainer and public grouch which was not the real Pegler. He was known in Tucson for addressing students at the University of Arizona, and for occupying the position of honored guest at the induction ceremonies for new members of a literary society at a local high school. The boys and girls of Quill and Scroll entered a darkened hall two by two, carrying candles, and Pegler told them to get a good education, work hard, and tell the truth.

In covering Pegler's departure from *American Opinion,* the papers had said that he planned to write a book "cataloguing his aversions." It was correct to say that a book had taken form in his mind, but Westbrook still longed for journalism, and looked into possibilities with three regional publications on which he felt he might be comfortable as a contributor. He attended the 1964 Democratic convention as correspondent for the *Toledo Monitor,* a professionally produced monthly publication that is not easy to describe. With a circulation of 14,000, according to Dun & Bradstreet, the paper was mostly devoted to business news, but also carried general articles and items on happenings in Toledo. The *Monitor* was a sort of specialized house organ for its owner, D. H. Overmyre, who headed a national warehouse business. When Pegler left *American Opinion,* Mr. Overmyre had suggested that he might be willing to write for the *Monitor* on a regular basis, and there was much cordiality and enthusiasm at the start. The first contribution was a fighting column headed "Pegler Punches Back." The trip to Atlantic City for the convention was a success, but in September 1964, only four months after Pegler had started with them, the *Monitor* asked Pegler, "Please try to stay off the following topics for a while." The subjects they wanted Pegler to avoid were "(1) New Deal and Roosevelts; (2) Kennedys; (3) Jews." Cordiality vanished and they parted after an argument over a voucher for sixty dollars which was delayed between New York and Toledo in the Overmyre accounting system.

The other two papers were published in the South, and it is fair to say that neither would have qualified for approval by the ADL. These were the *Jacksonville Chronicle* in Florida, and *The Councilor,* published at Shreveport, Louisiana. Critics in Northern cities were inclined to dismiss these papers as "fringe publications," but there was something to be said for them; they gave enormous satisfaction to subscribers in the South and Southwest, and also served as rich mines for students of the unrestrained expression of fundamentalist opinion on politics, religion, and national affairs, much of it extremely entertaining to read. There were 225,000 subscribers to *The Councilor,* and Pegler did not have to worry about censorship of what he wrote for this journal, or for the *Chronicle;* with two such outlets, he might have settled to a period of calm and relatively peaceful production. But age and bad health began to close in, and as Pegler wrote to columnist Murray Kempton in New York, he sometimes felt too tired to strike the keys of his typewriter. Advancing weakness showed in manuscripts and letters: where he had once tapped out line upon line of clean typing, wrong strokes would frequently appear, and uncorrected errors. And he felt the brain worker's awful fear that his mind might lose connection with his fingers.

In one of his last columns for Hearst, Westbrook had returned to the attack on Tucson, calling the place "an unsightly sprawl of an overgrown, one-story trade post, with hundreds of crude bars and beer joints filling gaps between second-rate steak houses." This comment deprecated booming growth while overlooking indestructible charm, for it is not possible to spoil Tucson while desert and mountains remain. And out at La Cholla, Westbrook saw no disturbing novelties in the landscape. Nevertheless, his remarks about Tucson illustrate a frame of mind, and what he said could be terrifying, in these last painful years. He placed John F. Kennedy beside Franklin Roosevelt as a villain, a "low-browed donkey with the honor of a pickpocket" and a "mean, ratty, dough-heavy, Boston gang politician." Pegler wrote that we had gone on a national binge of sentimentality during John Kennedy's funeral, "a maudlin orgy of simulated woe." He went so far as to charge that Mrs. Kennedy had played to the cameras by wearing that bloodstained dress all day; and he referred to John F. Kennedy, Jr., a small boy touching the world's heart with a salute at the funeral, as "the little donkey." After Kennedy's death, Pegler thought things got even worse, for the Presidency had fallen to a "high-boot Texan" who was greedy, ignorant and vain, "a vicious and contemptible swine." Pegler also disliked Robert Kennedy, and wrote at his typewriter in the desert that he found Bobby so despicable that he hoped "some white patriot of the Southern tier will spatter his spoonful of brains in public premises before the snow flies." Robert Kennedy's assassination occurred three years later.

When Quentin Reynolds died on March 17, 1965, Pegler wrote that he had been an alcoholic, and a "cheap Communist propagandist who never had the guts to join the party." Reynolds had won a libel suit, Pegler added, before the "U. S. District Court, Southern District of Tel Aviv." He had given up rationality where Jews were concerned, and wrote in his manuscripts, "My detestation of the Jew is considered and mature. It takes more courage to say 'I hate Jews' and why than to palter with cowards and tiresome argumentarians who have never arrived at an honest excuse for the bloody iniquities of these incorrigibles."

Such material can be found throughout the manuscripts that Pegler left as the uncompleted and unorganized work of the years 1963 to 1969. The pages are pieces for the papers, letters, and unfinished chapters of his proposed book of aversions, the autobiography. In these remarkable and deplorable pages one can see combativeness and lifelong generalized anxiety and resentment bursting into expression without any control except that of Pegler's sense of rhythm in speech. And one realizes how he tormented himself as he continued to strain for that terrible and never satisfactory word, the last word. It is much better to hear it than to say it. There are astounding excesses, such as a reference to the "rich Hibernian gore" that stained Mrs. Kennedy's dress, or the statement that Mrs. Roosevelt's lower jaw was deformed, and contained a second set of teeth. Those of whom Pegler disapproved had become monstrous; when he gave Mrs. Roosevelt extra teeth, or raved about the Kennedy killings, he had lost touch with what he was saying: the matter had escaped him and only the manner remained. Was Pegler inconsistent, did he often reverse himself, did he start out liberal and end in the reactionary camp? No doubt he did. But let us note that W. H. Auden said "writers live by their wits, and every 'original' genius, be he an artist or a scientist, has something shady about him, like a gambler or a medium."

To understand Pegler we should recall his original impulse to draw pictures and his hopes of becoming a cartoonist. If he had been able to enter such a career, Moosejaw and La Boca might have been acceptable as satirical comic drawing under the caricaturist's privilege to seize on physical or psychological features for humorous exaggeration. That style of permitted savage caricature went back to Hogarth and his artistic descendants Thomas Rowlandson, the Cruikshanks, and James Gillray. Pegler has noticeable affinity with Gillray, who satirized George III and his court in merciless vitriolic style. George and his consort Queen Charlotte were tight with money, and Gillray liked to depict them living in shabby rooms surrounded with bulging money-bags, to indicate their meanness and greed. There had been attempts on the king's life, and a cartoon of 1793 showed George whirling through the air with his breeches on fire: "G-d d-n the dogs, I knew they'd blow me up at last!" This was all quite permissible; and Gillray made the royal persons hideously ugly, George obese and thicklipped, Queen Charlotte with a grotesquely deformed chin and spike teeth. The Prince of Wales married Mrs. Fitzherbert in 1785, and Gillray ridiculed the couple with a print called *The Morning After the Marriage—or—a scene on the Continent,* showing them in bed and obviously bored with each other. Gillray continued to lampoon the prince after his legal marriage to Caroline of Brunswick, giving special attention to his enormous debts. He showed William Pitt squeezing John Bull into a mill from which gold coins poured out into an inverted coronet held by the prince. Another attack on political authority was called *Sin, Death, and the Devil.* It showed the queen as a loathsome hag interposing between Pitt and the Lord Chancellor Edward Thurlow. This was Peglerism before Pegler. Gillray combined an instinct for the ludicrous with technical virtuosity, and for thirty years the public couldn't get enough of him, and people fought for places in line at printsellers' shops to buy the latest Gillray drawing. Gillray was a large muscular man of resolute appearance, who kept up a lifelong interest in sports. He went mad four years before his death in 1815; the *Dictionary of National Biography* says, "There are discernible traces of coming trouble in his last works."

Pegler had formed a vision of a free and noble America in the days of his youth when people still thought such a thing could be. He managed to keep his sympathy for George Spelvin and for "men with wives and kids and operations and mortgages." Rage began to build inside him when he saw what the rulers had done to his vision of individual liberty, every man for himself. At his best he touched life and wrote of it in concrete terms. He saw through the panoply and court costumes, and used the language of everyday life to attack holders of power who cloaked their greed with high-flown official language. He would pull down their vanity. In this vein, he pursued the great clown Wallace, harried crooks in unions, ridiculed Presidents, and lampooned Congress and the courts. There is always need for writers like Pegler, who warn us away from the swamps of national self-praise, the worship of authority, and superstitions about the Presidency and the Flag. All this leaves something more of Pegler than just yesterday's newspaper. Pull down their vanity . . . I say pull down. . . .

In 1966 word came that three important New York papers—the *Herald Tribune,* the *World-Telegram,* and the *Journal-American*—had been put to death by their unions and their managements. Westbrook wrote to Murry Kempton of the *World-Telegram,* "If you have a spare half-hour please write what happened to our world. Peg." He also wrote to friends that the doctors had removed part of his stomach because of cancer. Pegler was thinking that it might soon be time to reach for the old overcoat like the sports writer in the story he had written forty years before. He had been around a long time. He had seen them come and he had seen them go. He wouldn't want to live on and on like Arthur; but as long as he had any strength at all, Westbrook would keep fighting, even though he wasn't able to define what he was fighting for. On his birthday in that year of 1966 came a note from George Pattullo, who had once recommended him to the *Saturday Evening Post.* Pattullo was one of those cheerful, loyal people whose friendship shines like gold when age comes on. He wrote, "Good luck to you old timer. It staggered me a little to learn that you are now seventy-two. I keep thinking of you as a boy of seventy." And John Madigan at WBBN-TV wrote to thank Pegler for kindness when he was a cub on the old *Chicago American.* A stranger wrote, "You have been more of an influence on my life and spirit than I ever cared to express . . . you have always been a fighter . . . much as I disagreed with you, I admired your splendid spirit. . . ."

Pegler took up a legal fight when he recovered from the operation, and the fight was connected with the Reynolds case. In 1966 a Broadway play producer had put on *A Case of Libel,* based on the Reynolds suit, and the Ed Sullivan television program had broadcast a scene from it over the Columbia Broadcasting System. In 1968 the American Broadcasting Company presented the entire play and the Arizona Civic Theater put it on in Tucson. Pegler retained counsel and started suits against all these producers for invasion of privacy. It was announced that Pegler had not written any articles since he became ill but he was feeling all right now, and "ready for a fight." The defendants claimed that Pegler was in the public domain, but the points of law were not to be settled in or out of court.

In the late spring of 1969, Pegler suffered ominous symptoms and pain. They took him to St. Mary's Hospital where he underwent another serious operation. This hospital is a large, adobe-colored building in the outskirts of Tucson, and you can see mountains from any of its windows. Pegler died there on June 24 at 3:14 in the morning, a little too early for sun on the peaks. There were flowers at the funeral and at the Gate of Heaven Cemetery, where they buried Pegler beside Julie's unmarked grave.

INDEX

Index

As Pegler Sees It:

How Green Is Our Valley in Texas!

By WESTBROOK PEGLER

HARLINGEN, TEX.—Harlingen is the capital of a relatively small patch of the United States so rich that Nazi Germany and the Soviet empire would have gambled millions of lives to capture it had the Rio Grande Valley lain within reach of their ... it is actually a terra incognita to us, as the Lower Rio Grande Chamber of Commerce awkwardly admitted in its publicity folders thus: ... ley is undiscovered as a area, but everything's ..."

... r country hasn't even a squad ... diers on guard along the border ... the few unhappy patrolmen of ... Immigration Service are looked ... pon with mild hostility even by ... Americans because it is their job to keep out wetbacks—Mexicans who want to work for American employers ... hire them.

... y is so efficient, diligent and prosperous, so important to our country, that I feel ... d after all my travels never to have dis- ... ne place before. Harlingen is the com- ... capital of the valley, in a county that went ... en for Nixon in 1960 and the center of a ... civilized in the most favorable Ameri- ... that word. It has an astonishing ... and grain crops and a large ... fruit which neither Florida ...

As Pegler Sees It

Tax Man and Your Bank Account

By WESTBROOK PEGLER

PEOPLE and corporations have been so ... ly cowed by the threat of crim- ... tions of Treasury regula ... olations, that we flinch an ... on of the men employed ... this purpose. Banks ... demands from Treas ... in violation of the ba ... to their depositors.

I asked the man ... nk whether he ha ... bank's lawyers ab ... sibility and liabil ... ners. He was abs ... t important phas ... e's duty. Comp ... orders of Intern ... yielded so lon ... d that this w ... that a cust ... bank had no ...

A Ruse Tha...

After the D... 1919, a promoter ... himself to take a ... the movies a few ...

Pegler Sees It:

Making Prayer A Federal Case

By WESTBROOK PEGLER

...TY YEARS AGO it would have been outrageous to suggest that the Supreme Court would ever ... down as the law of the land that it would be ... to open or close classes in a public school with ... er to God.

...en I was a child in the only public school in Excelsior, Minn., Mrs. Benton, our teacher in fourth grade, always bowed at the start of the day and ... led us in The Lord's Pra... was a Methodist and mo... population were Protest... their version was a little ... from the Catholic ver... the Catholic children acco... themselves to this slight sc... our parents just let it go. ... no need to kick up a row. T... thought of appealing to the Court. We were praying to ... e Methodists, Baptists, Congregation... and the intent was the same.

... the Court has decreed that Mrs. ... duct would be a violation of the Firs... day in the part which forbids Co... y law respecting the establishment ... prohibiting the free exercise thereo... a criminal act and if a latter-... hould insist on leading a class in th... he might be sent to prison. Would ... of the Supreme Court or of som... ourt? It could not be a violation ... in the case on appeal because th... r was gotten up by the New York ... a body of the State gover... 's imprimatur.

... look to that por... cerning reli... Court wa...

As Pegler Sees It:

Boxing ... Gone ...

By WESTB...

PRIZEFIGHTING HAS ... years since teevy co... temptations toward insi... finest traditions at he... but not protest if publi... coup de grace with a ...

PEGLER

Taylor was a scr... youth from the B... of Frankie Jerome ... he had been an ... thought he was h...

It Just Hap...

He had had a ... main event in ... bantamweig... Flyweigh... bantamwei... rweight ... were ba...

As Pegler Sees It:

Garner Still Makes For Good Reading

By WESTBROOK PEGLER

I FEEL a temptation to sentimental extravagance in thinking of John N. Garner. His honesty and his patriotism, not merely to our geographical country but to our beautiful old ideals, are a treasure which few of us comprehend.

Few of us have been able to visit the Kremlin, but I think of it as a mausoleum where the soul of Russia awaits resurrection, a shrine of something impalpable, spiritual and unspeakably potent. We have nothing that may be compared with it. I have felt a similar emotion in St. Peter's and in St. Paul's in London.

It seems ludicrous to hint that I would sense a spiritual vibration in thinking of this frail, very untidy, lonely old man in the little town of Uvalde, Tex., but he personifies virtues we recklessly repudiated with the advent of Roosevelt.

PEGLER

Bascom Timmons performed a public service with a book published in 1948 called "Garner of Texas; A Personal History." It did not sell very well. But I find comfort in Timmons' life of John Garner, like an old woman fingering her Bible. Garner's son, Tully, walked into his father's office the day after Garner voted for Woodrow Wilson's War and said, "I aim to go, Dad." The Old Man said, "Hell, you are going! I would not vote to send other boys to war if I hadn't known I was sending my own. And one more thing. Your mother and I will want to hear from you, but promise me you'll never ask me a favor. I might be in a position to get it and I don't want to be exposed to temptation."

A Letter from the Veep

Garner almost fought Roosevelt on recognition of Russia. The country was against recognition, Roosevelt and his cult wanted recognition.

Garner said: "If this outfit has kept its word to anyone or done anything in good faith, I have not heard about it. My considered judgment is that th...

...d is shielded by a sand dune 125 ... ding way over to Galveston. Most of ... re Island because a Spanish Catholic ... s stranded on it a couple of hundred ... o the eastward its continuity is broken ... breaches and the segments have other ... as Mustang, St. Joseph and Matagorda. ... way of speaking, it is a graceful crescent ... shore and impounding a private Texas pre- ... relatively calm water which is jammed with ... yond imagination and our capacity to eat or ... This barrier reef is supposed to be beautiful ... ou have to give your imagination an assist ... illusion.

...reeby:

Little Man With a Big Idea

... is another autobiographical chapter in the ... Spelvin, American,' as recorded by Westbrook ...

By WESTBROOK PEGLER

HERE IS a new family in Dudgeon He... name is Freeby, he is an internati... olicy executive, you probably heard of ... Freeby Worldwide National Manager ... They manage countries, they furnish ... ager, a board of directors, print th... stamps and collect ... a broad-vision A... basis. No electi... democracy but ... plus manager ... ioned Americ...

So if A... Baluchista... Afghanist...

As Pegler Sees It:

HUAC Didn't Trust Dept. of Justice

By WESTBROOK PEGLER

AFTER EIGHT YEARS as Vice Preside... ...er service in the House and Senate, ...ld that the House Comm... ...ot trust the...